Pursuit

by Lianne Cruz

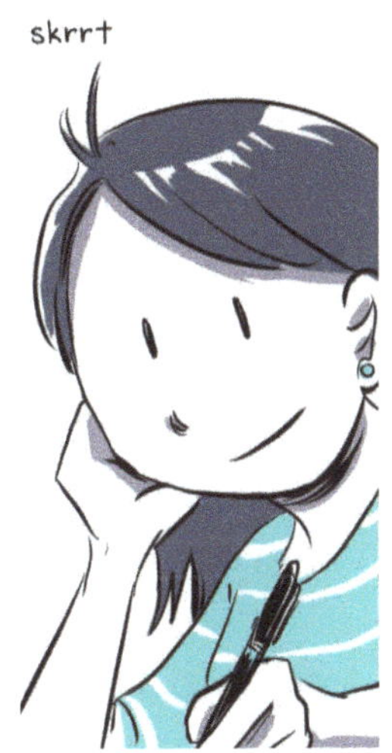

Published by

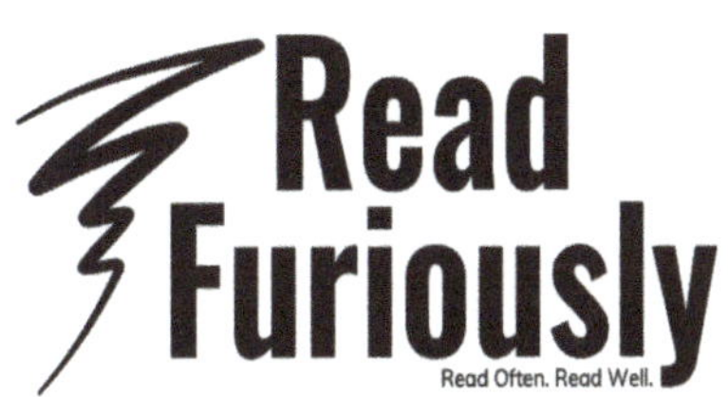

Published by Read Furiously. First Edition.

ISBN: 978-0-9965227-8-6

Comics & Graphic Novels
Art Books
Sketchbooks
Asian-American Artists

For more information on Pursuit or Read Furiously, please visit readfuriously.com. For inquiries, please contact samantha@readfuriously.com.

Edited by Samantha Atzeni

Read (v): The act of interpreting and understanding the written word.

Furiously (adv): To engage in an activity with passion and excitement.

Read Often. Read Well.
Read Furiously!

INTRODUCTION

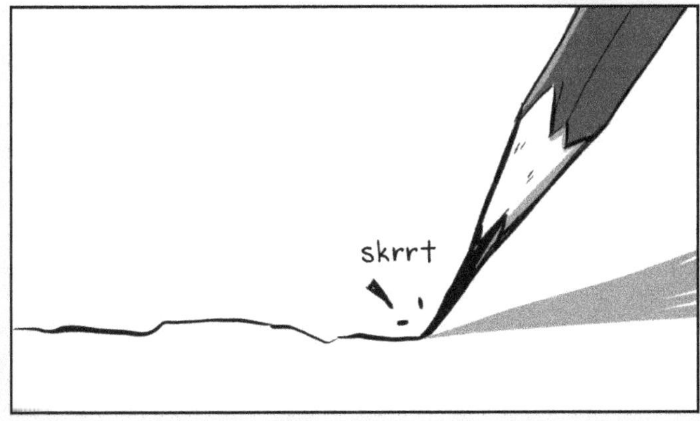

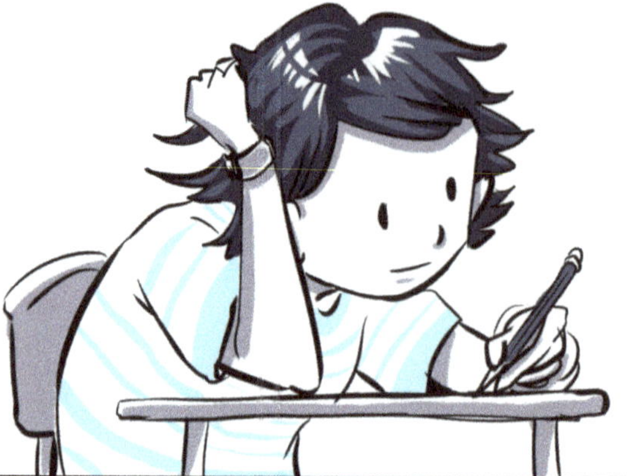

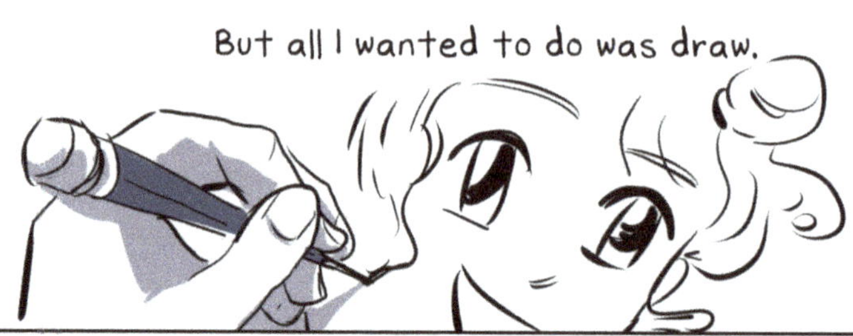

My parents weren't surprised when I told them I wanted to be an animator.

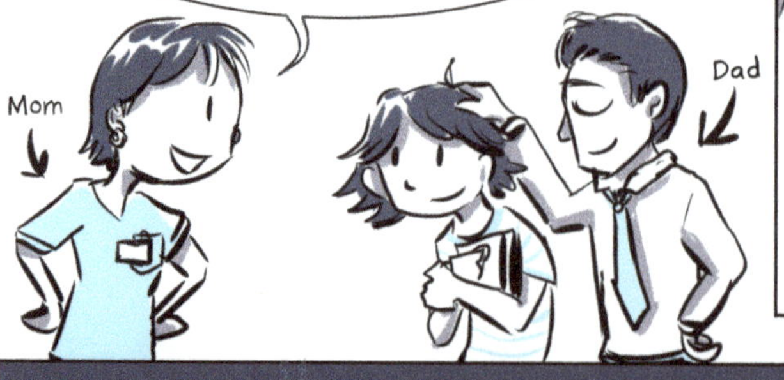

Though supportive, my parents didn't have an understanding of animation or how to go about becoming one...

...And I honestly wasn't quite sure how to become one either

I remember going to National Portfolio Day in New York City where high school seniors presented their artwork to admissions staff.

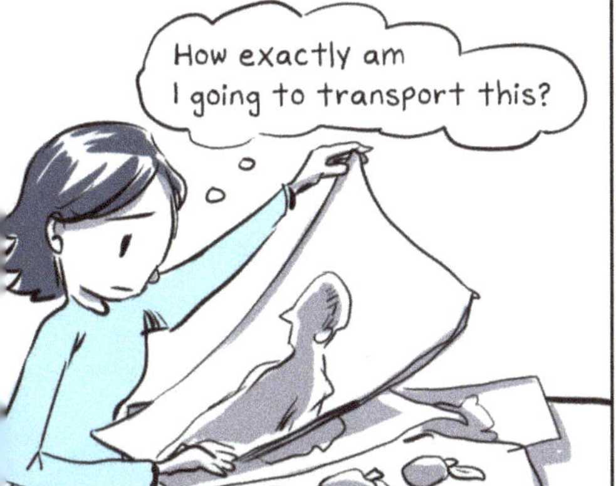

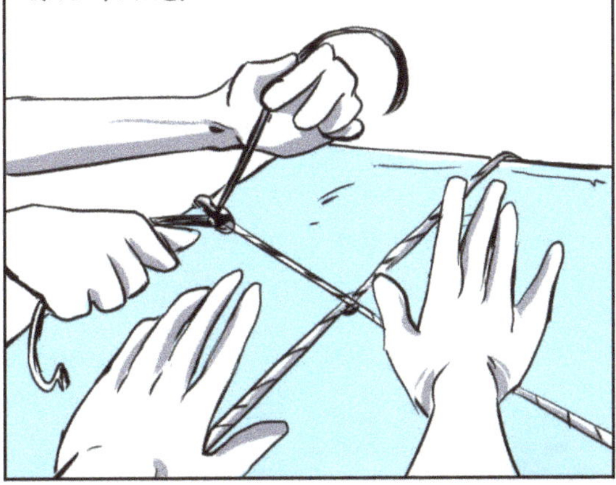

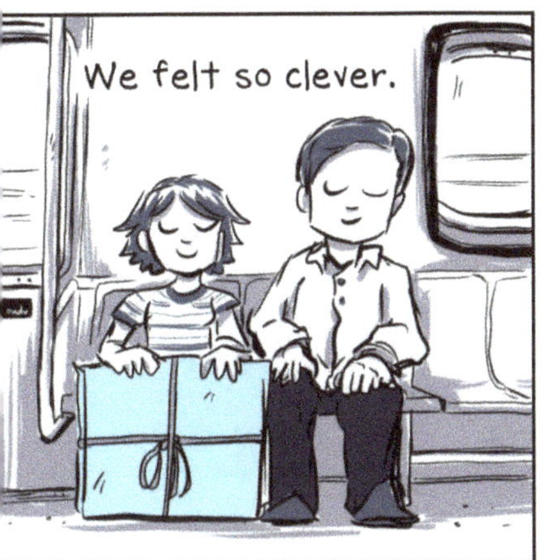

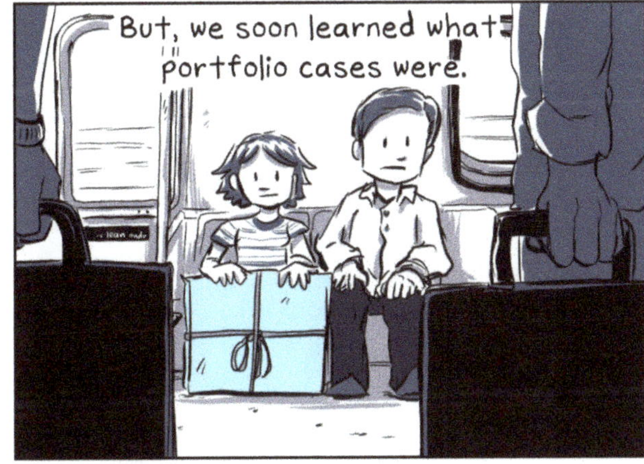

While other students were zipping and unzipping their work with ease, I was fumbling with the twine that tied up the brown paper bag. Every admissions table had a bemused expression on their face.

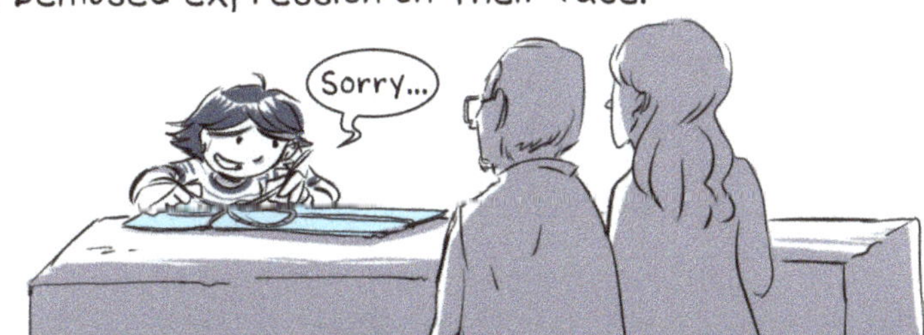

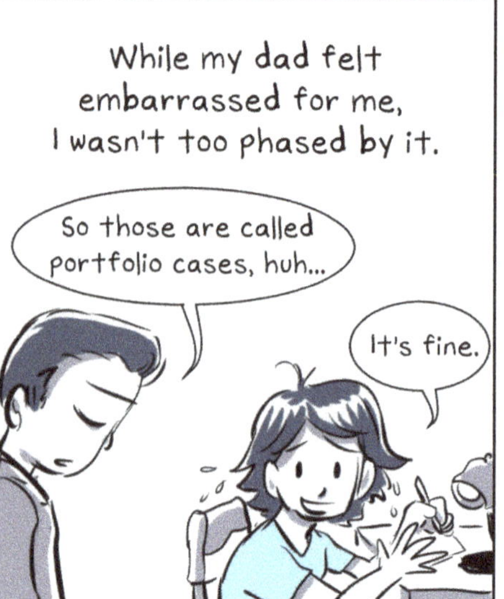

While my dad felt embarrassed for me, I wasn't too phased by it.
So those are called portfolio cases, huh...
It's fine.

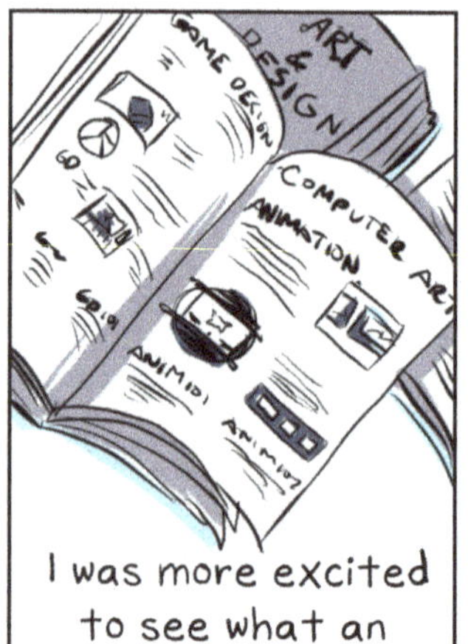

ART & DESIGN
GAME DESIGN
COMPUTER ART
ANIMATION
ANIM 101
ANIM 107
I was more excited to see what an art school education could offer me.

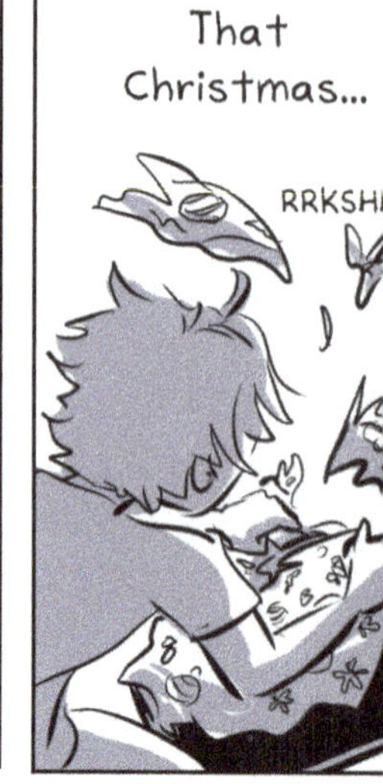

That Christmas...
RRKSH

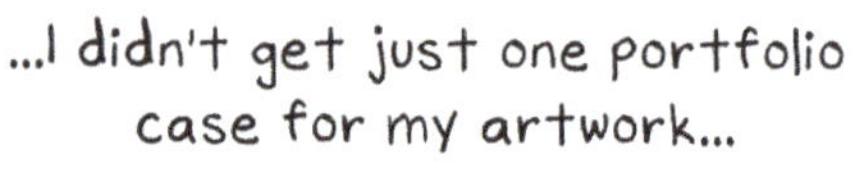

...I didn't get just one portfolio case for my artwork...

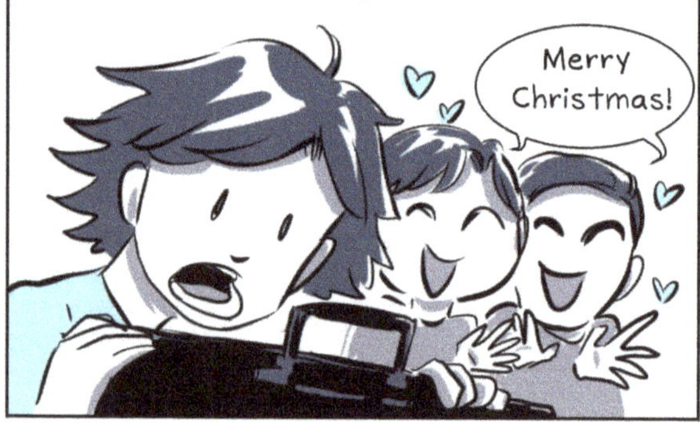

Merry Christmas!

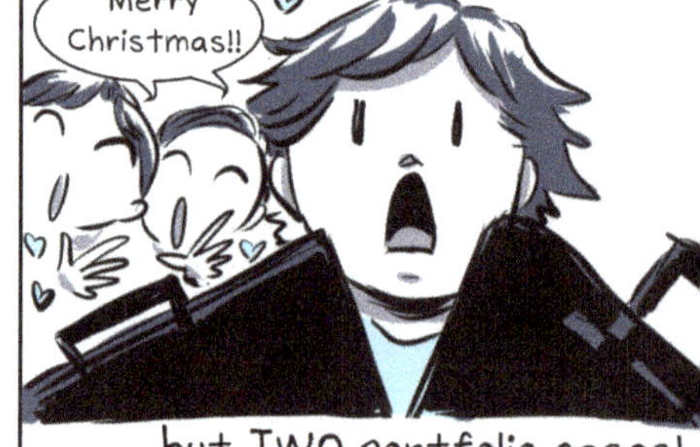

Merry Christmas!!
...but TWO portfolio cases! One from my parents, and one from my aunt's friend who heard the story of our NYC trip.

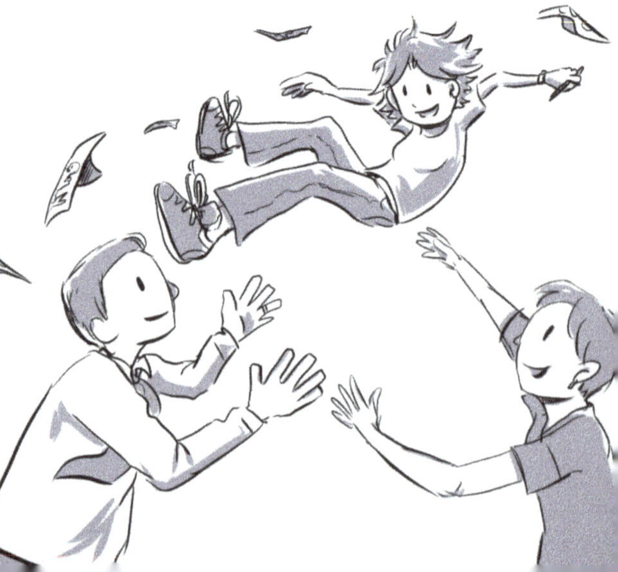

These portfolio cases served me well in art school. Whenever I looked down at my case, waiting for my next class, I was reminded of my family's unyielding support.
LIANNE

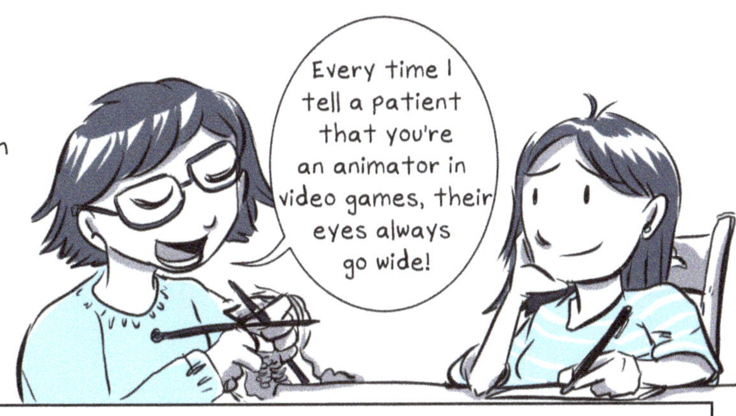
That is never lost on me, nor the fact my parents have never lectured me on my career choice.
Every time I tell a patient that you're an animator in video games, their eyes always go wide!

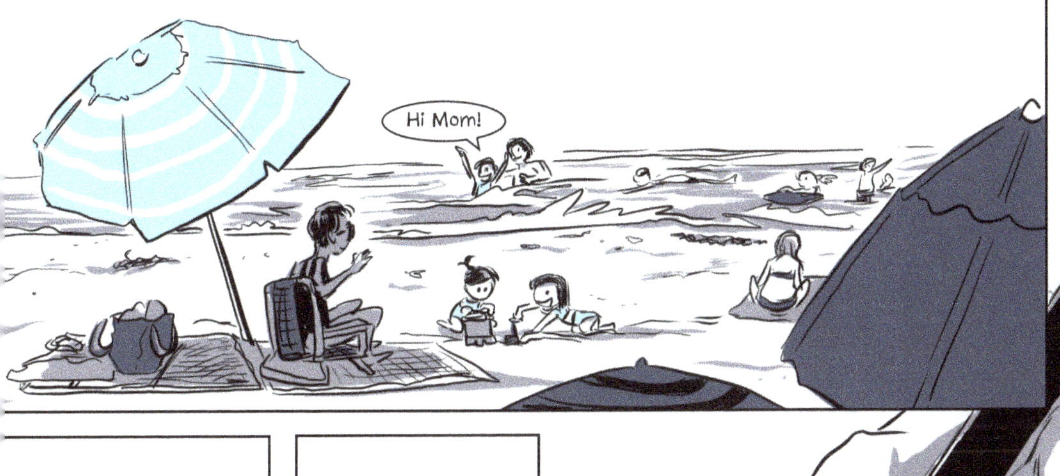
My parents moved here to the United States and started over, so my sisters and I may have a better life.
Hi Mom!

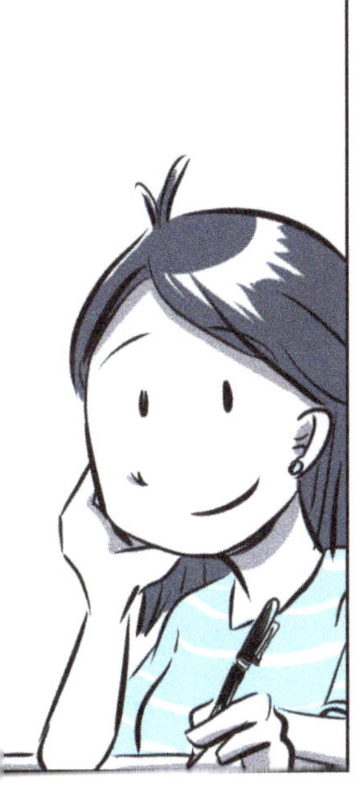

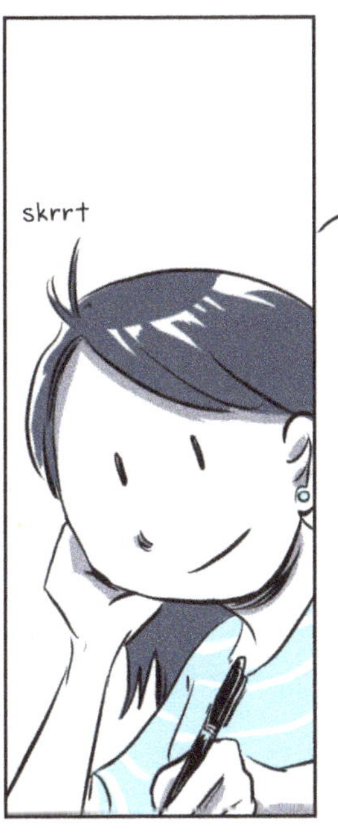
skrrt

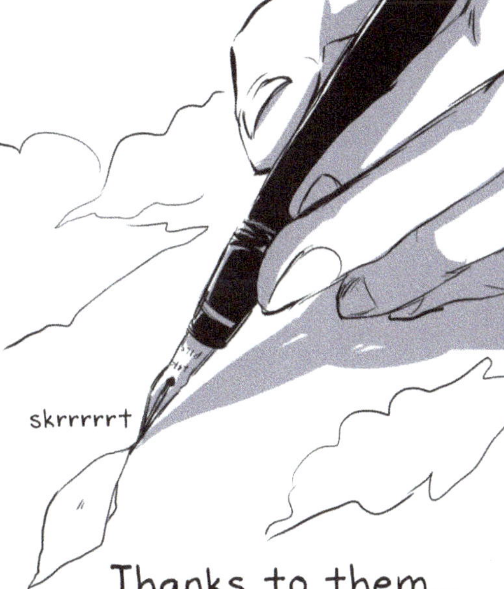
skrrrrrt
Thanks to them...

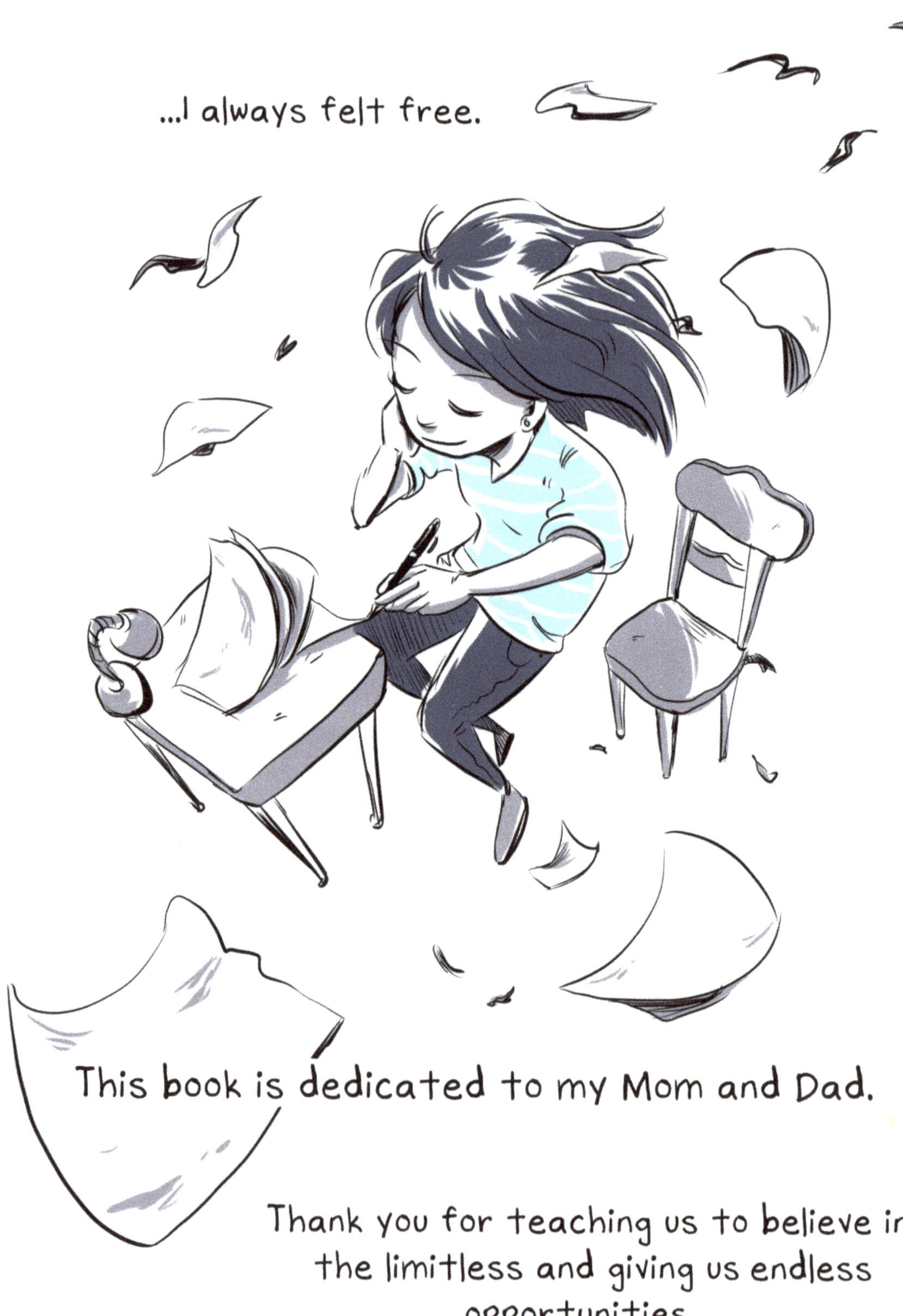

...I always felt free.

This book is dedicated to my Mom and Dad.

Thank you for teaching us to believe in the limitless and giving us endless opportunities.

PRACTICE

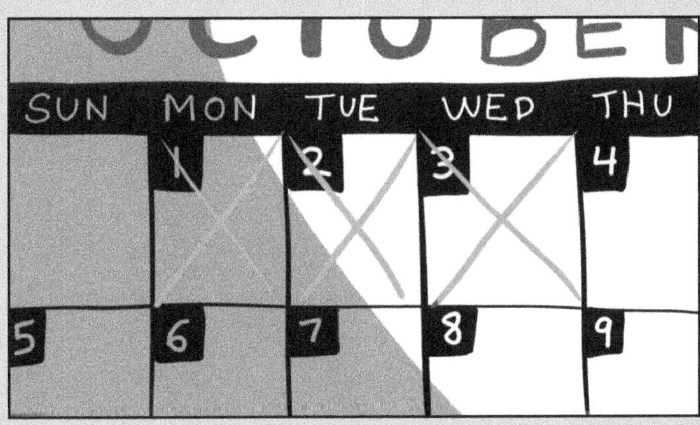

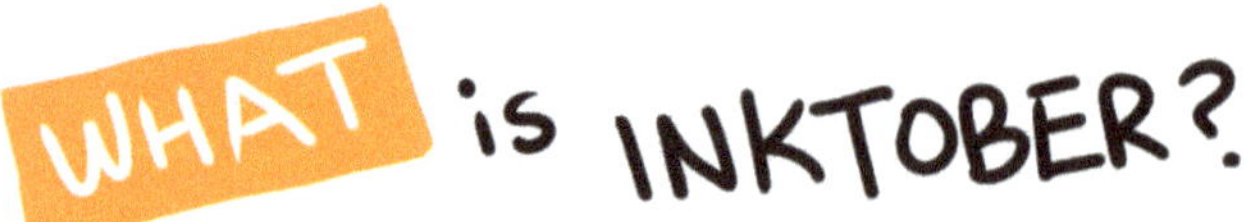

They say the best way to develop a good habit is to practice it daily for 1 month. Artist Jake Parker established Inktober as a wa for him to develop his handling of ink, a medium he struggled with.

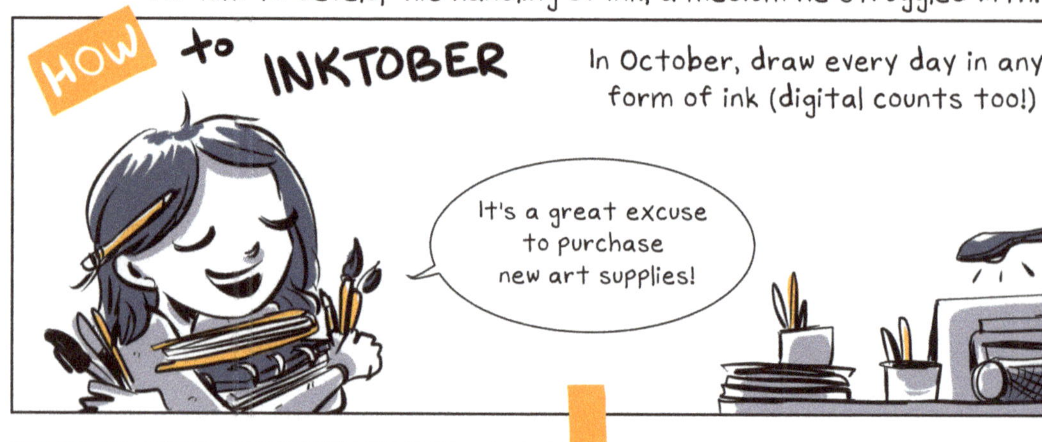

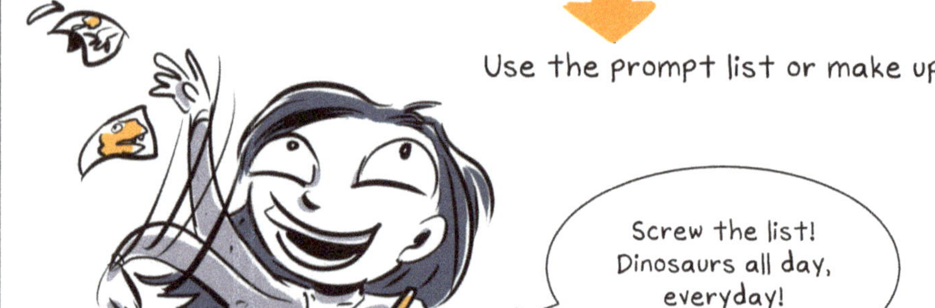

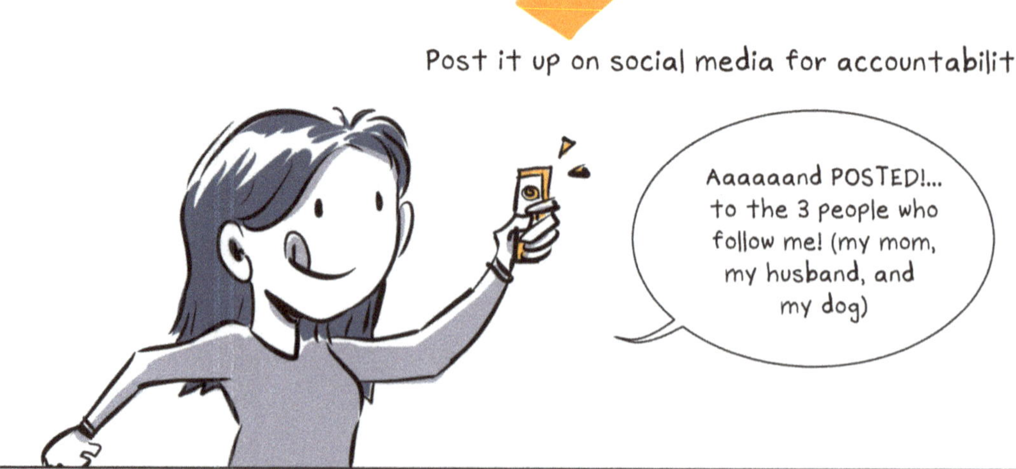

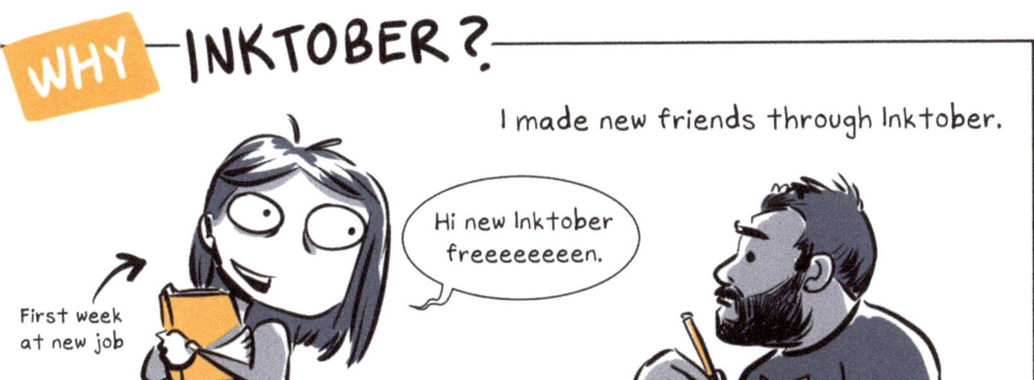

Practicing instills confidence and gives you permission to fail in a safe space.

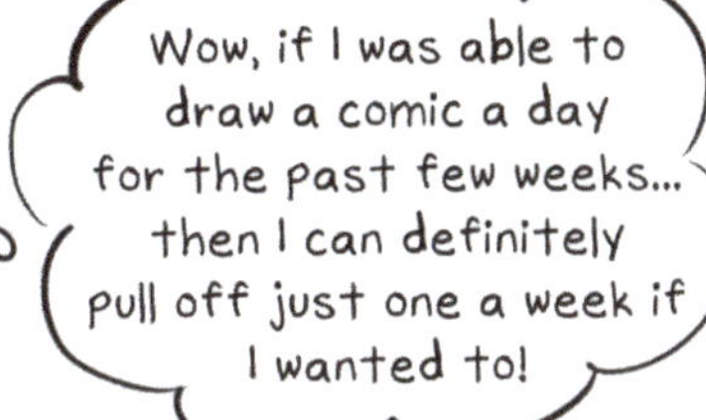

You draw for yourself, and pursue what interests you. You can experiment on a small scale with potential for it to grow bigger after Inktober.

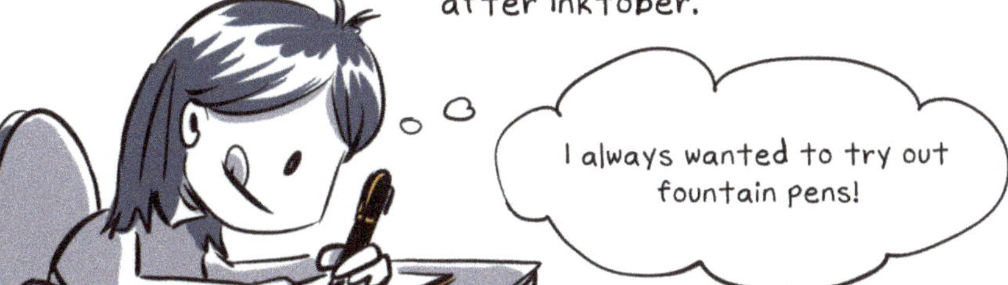

Exposure! This shouldn't be the primary goal, but it's an excellent bonus. Using social media informed me of what people related to or appreciated in my daily drawings.

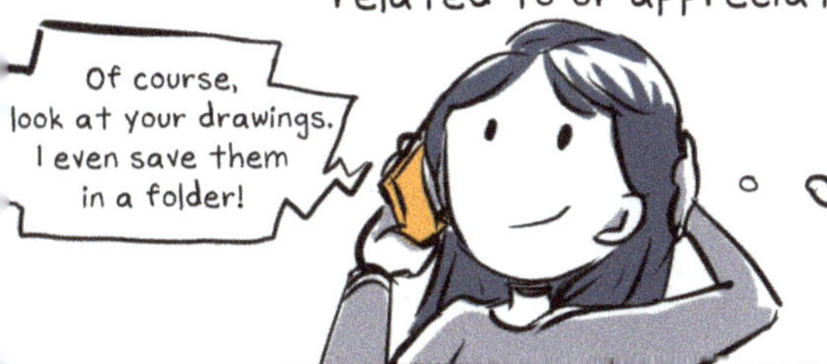

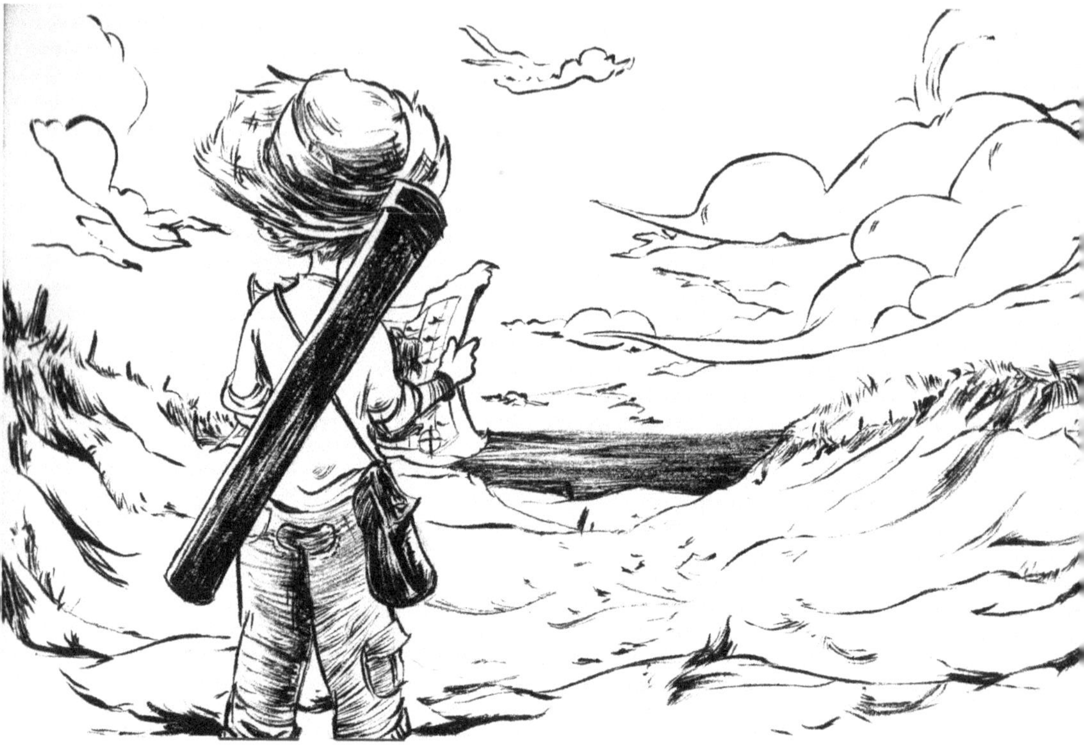

I started participating in Inktober in 2014. These 2 images were my first entries into the drawing event. The above image was inspired by a visit to the Jersey Shore.

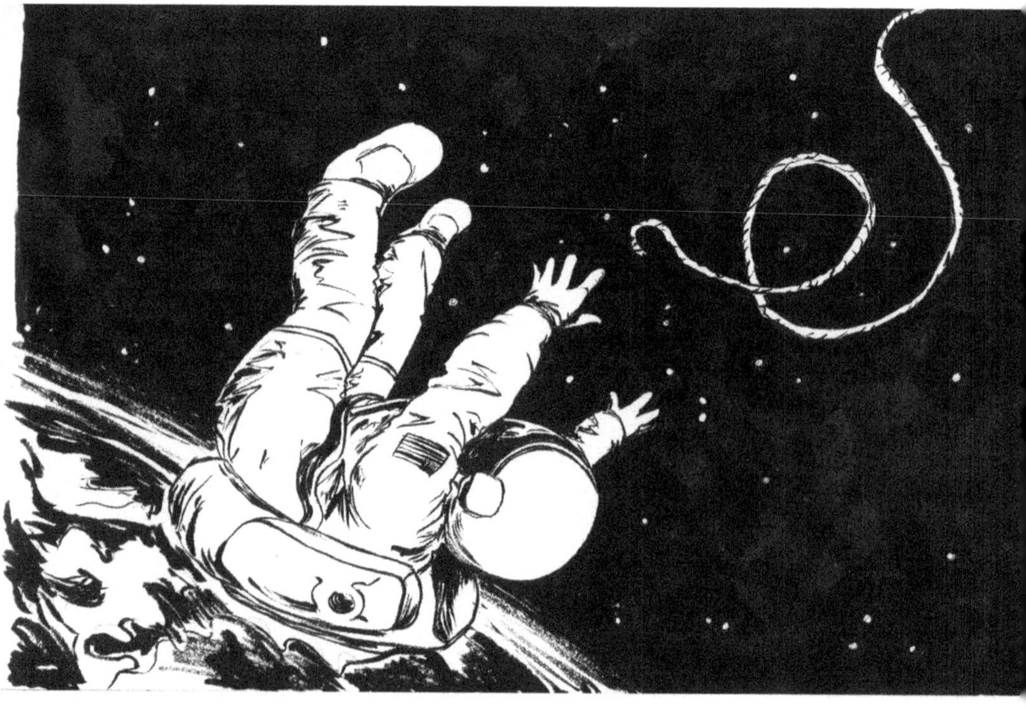

If I were to choose an alternate profession, it would be paleontology. As a kid, I was obsessed with dinosaurs. Art gives me a chance to play with my childhood loves again.

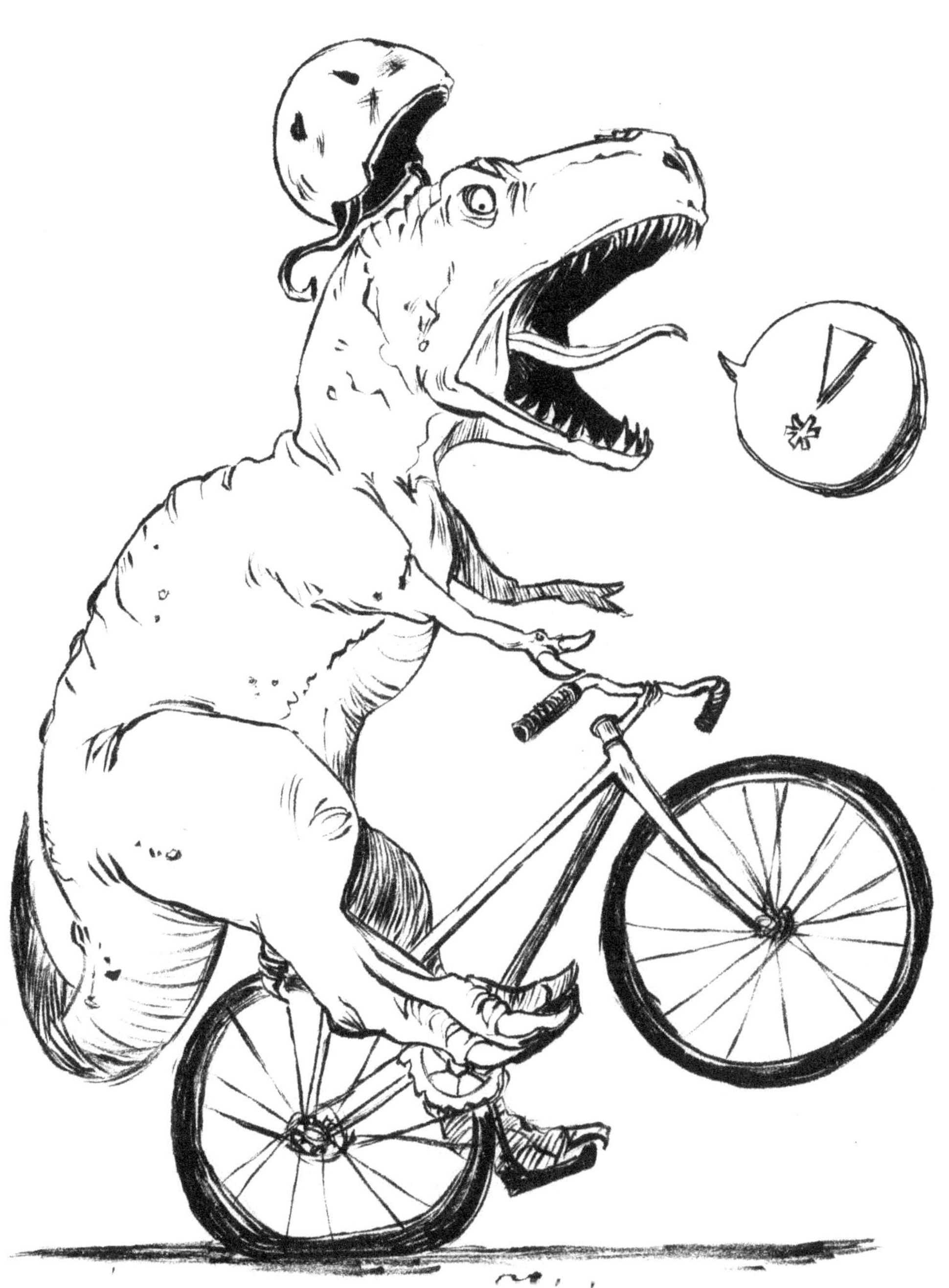

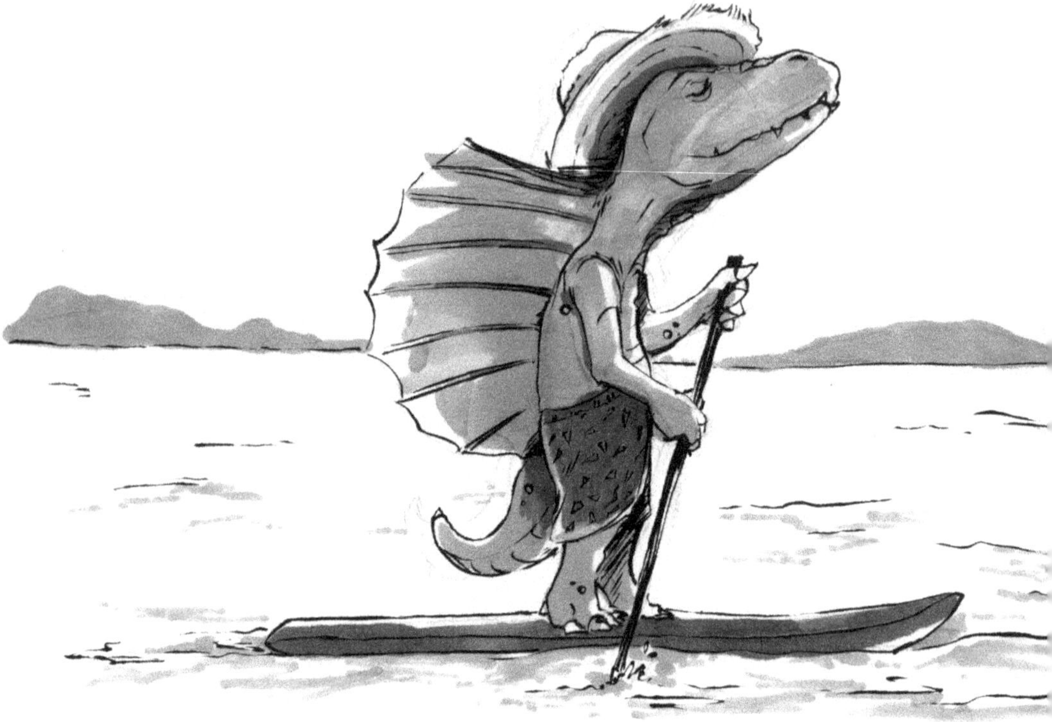

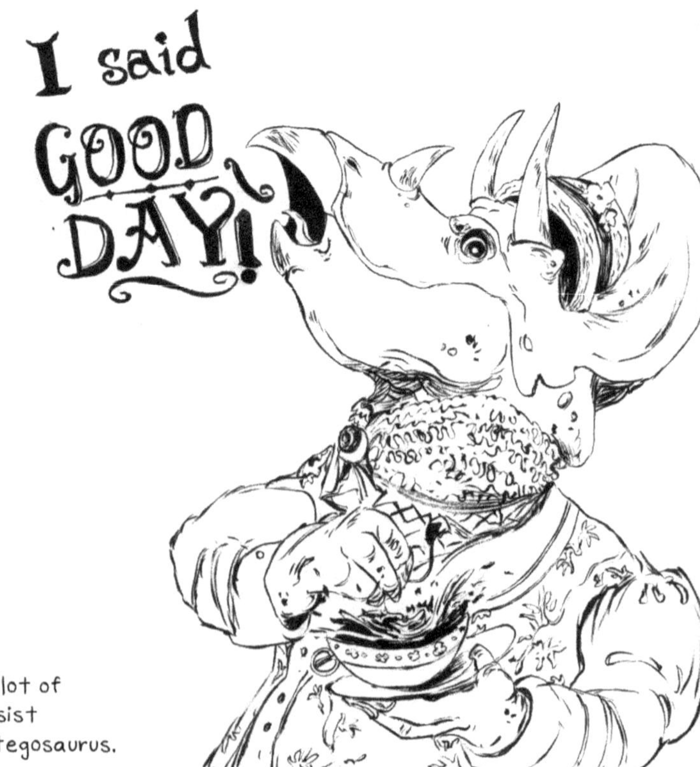

At the time, I was watching a lot of period dramas and couldn't resist drawing a Victorian inspired stegosaurus.

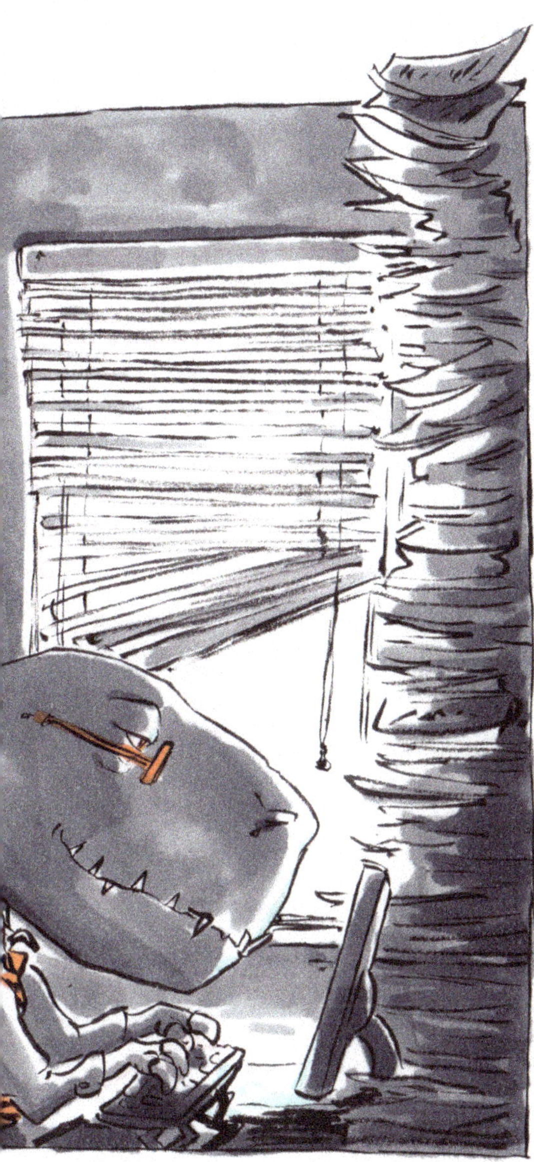

OFFICE DINOS

"Office dinos" was a series of drawings I did during one week of Inktober. The idea of dinos doing everyday, mundane tasks tickled me.

I think it's important to not just draw what interests you, but also what amuses you.

The image on the left was inspired by my dad who is the most patient, hardworking man I know.

Going back to being inspired by period dramas, I thought about 2 certain characters from "Downton Abbey" who especially love their smoke breaks.

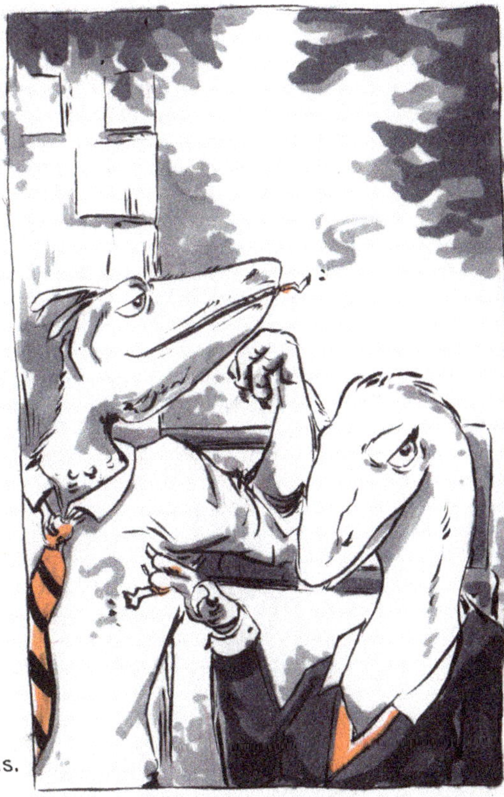

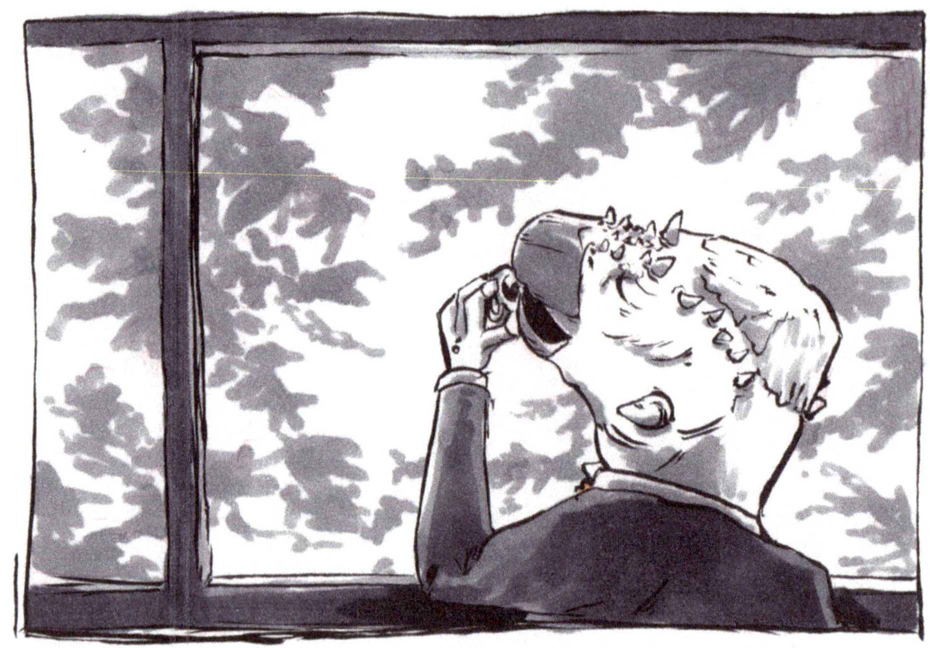

The window backdrop was inspired by my office's window. There used to be these gorgeous maples that would cast these beautiful silhouettes against the window.

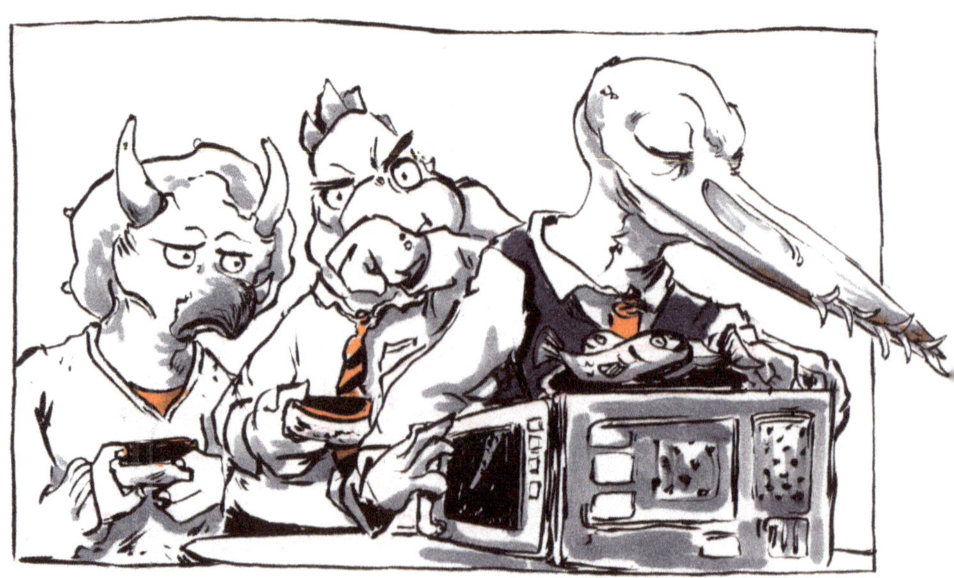

Don't be that guy at the office that microwaves fish. Please, just don't.

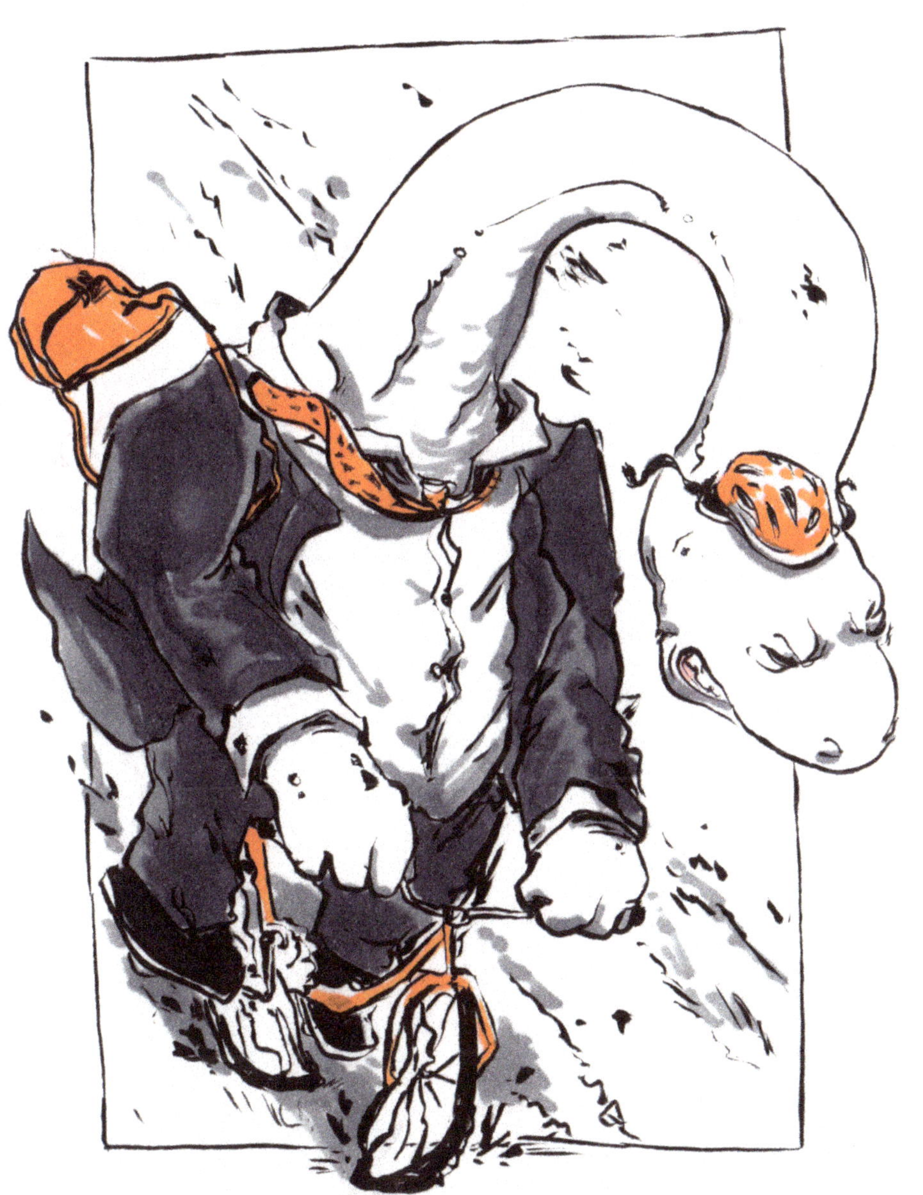

At one of my previous studio jobs, I had a good friend who would take walking breaks with me. I miss those times.

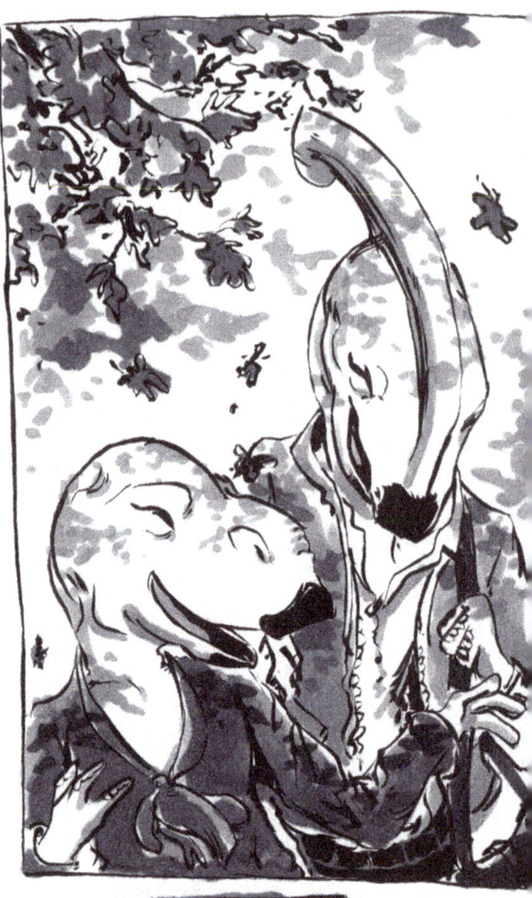

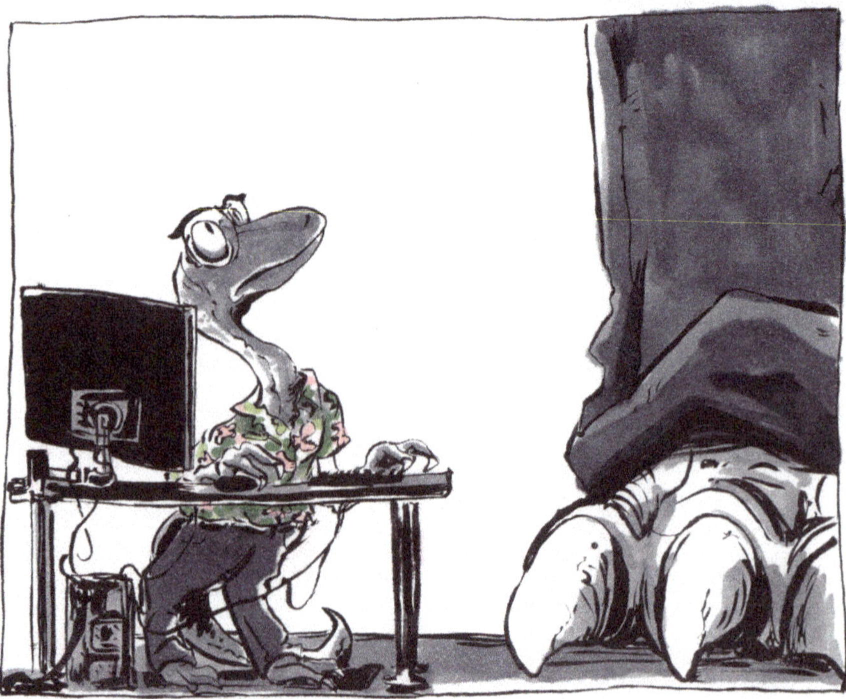

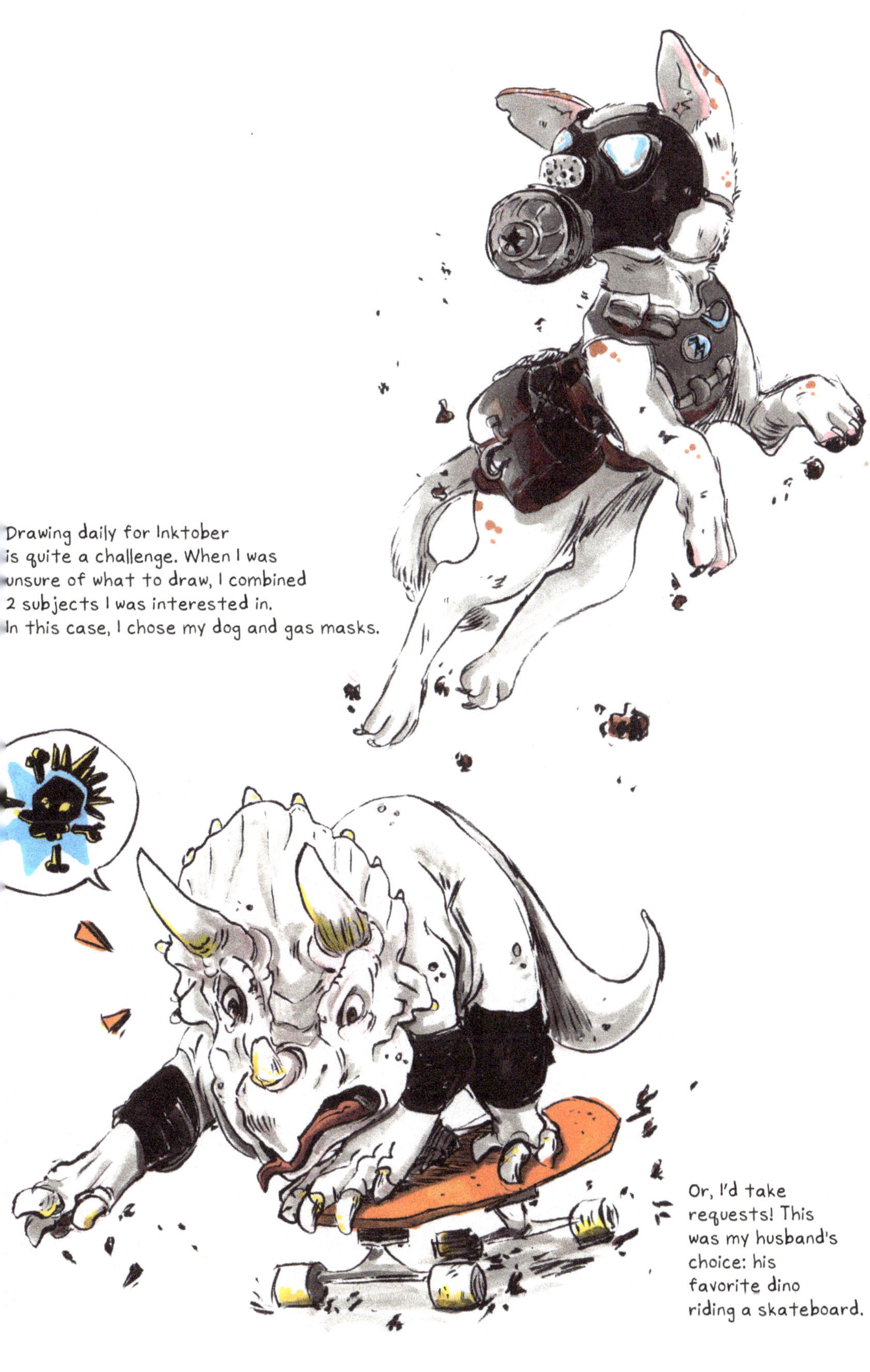

Drawing daily for Inktober
is quite a challenge. When I was
unsure of what to draw, I combined
2 subjects I was interested in.
In this case, I chose my dog and gas masks.

Or, I'd take
requests! This
was my husband's
choice: his
favorite dino
riding a skateboard.

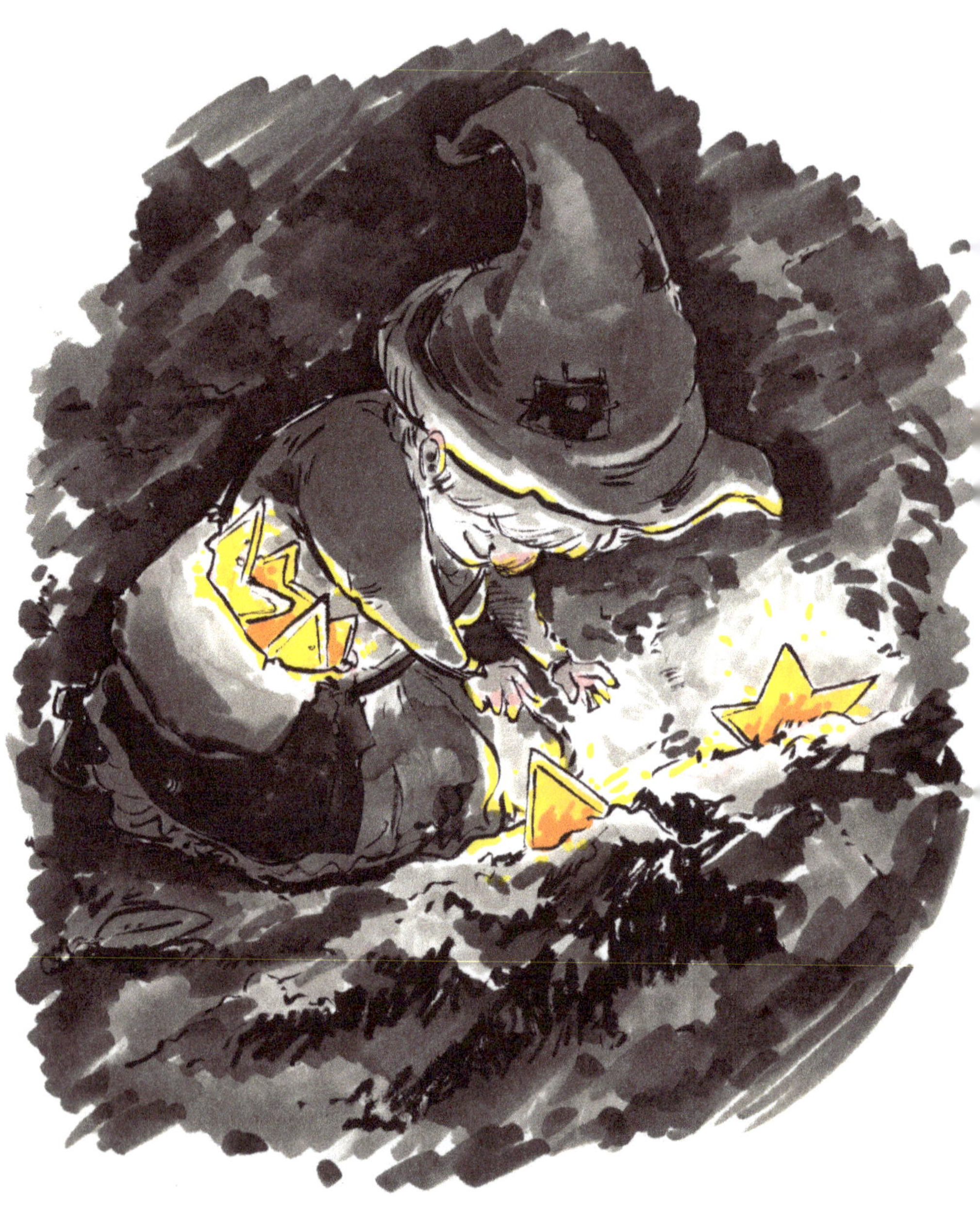

Inktober is also a fun way to experiment with story ideas.
This illustration centers around a witch who plants stars.

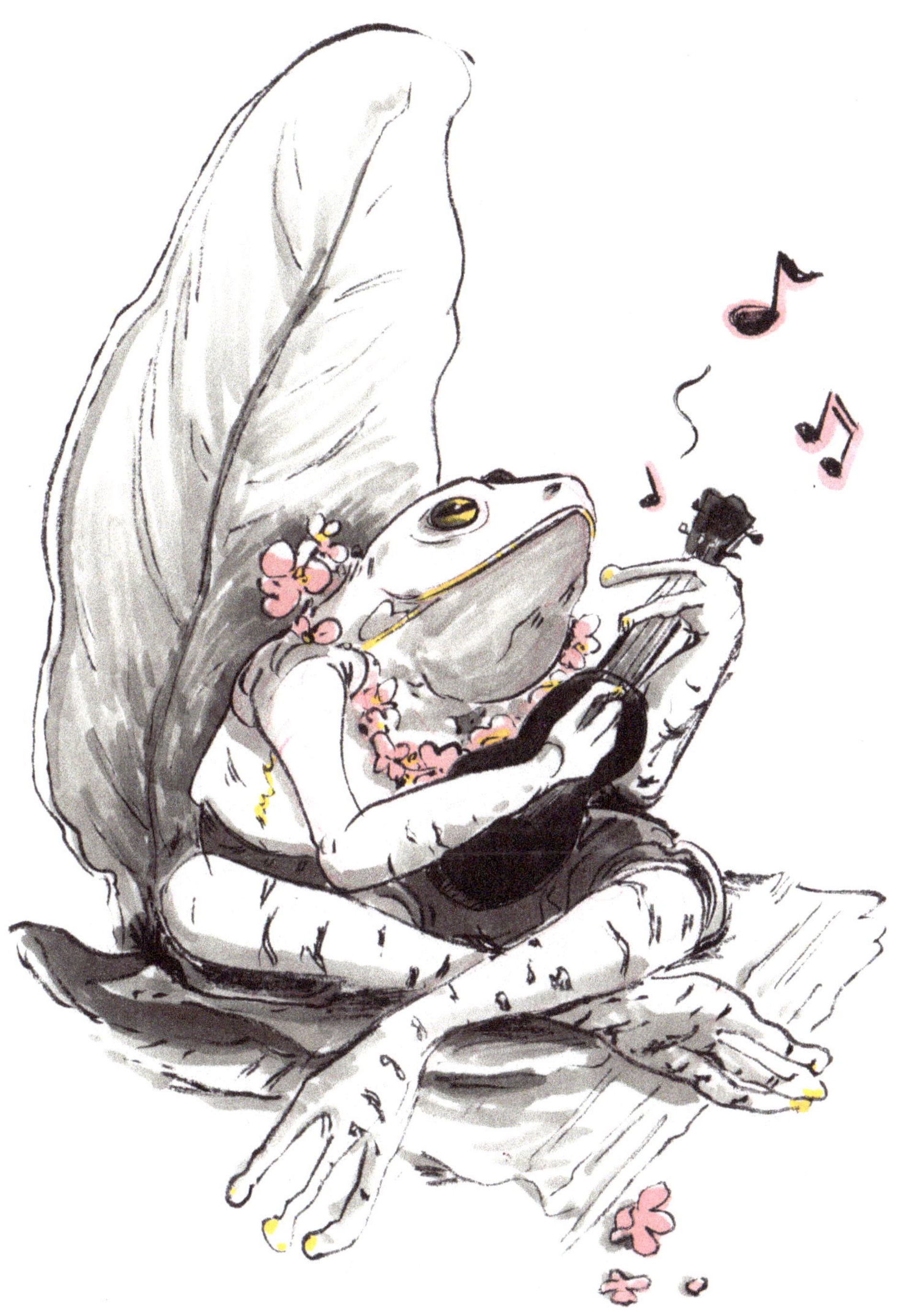

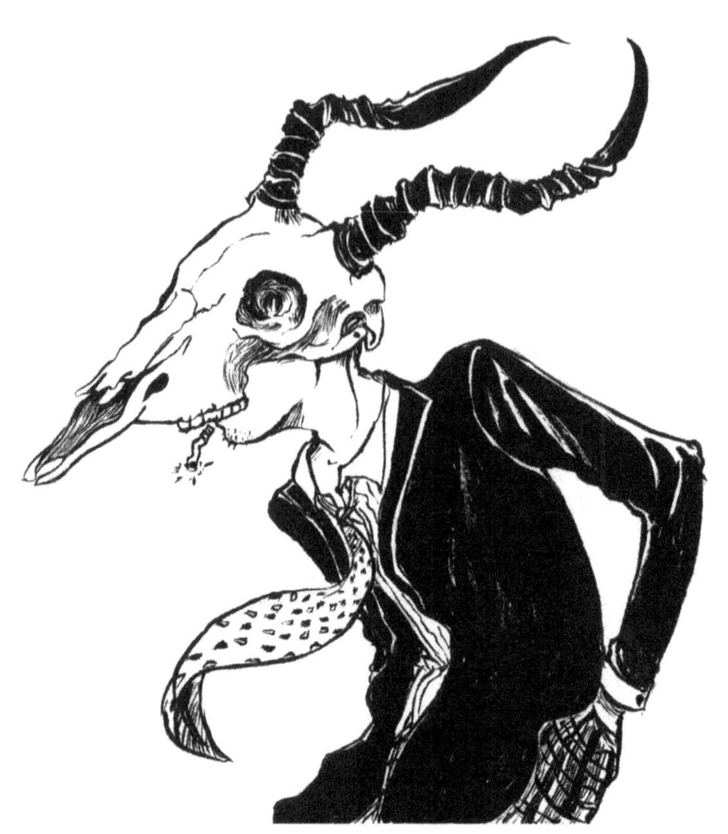

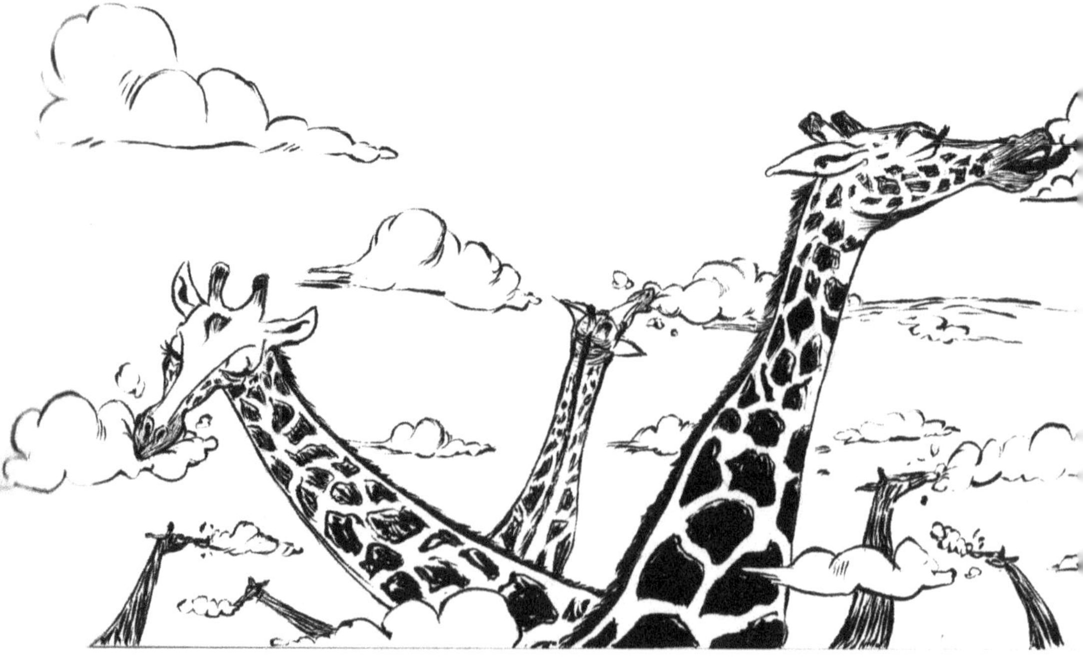

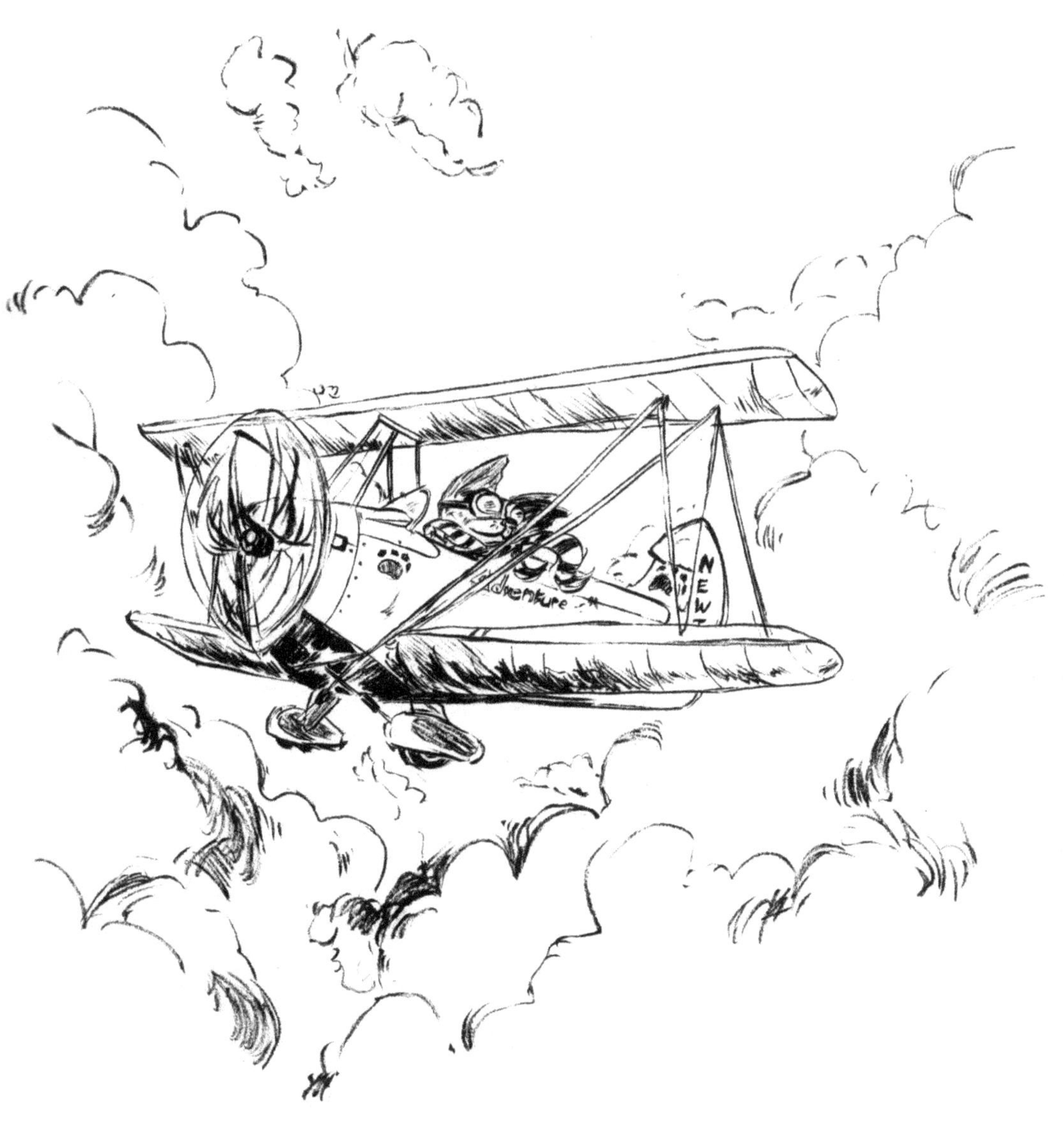

My dog often is the subject of my drawings. He gets so excited when you tell him he's going on an "adventure" (a.k.a car trip). So I decided to draw him going on an actual adventure.

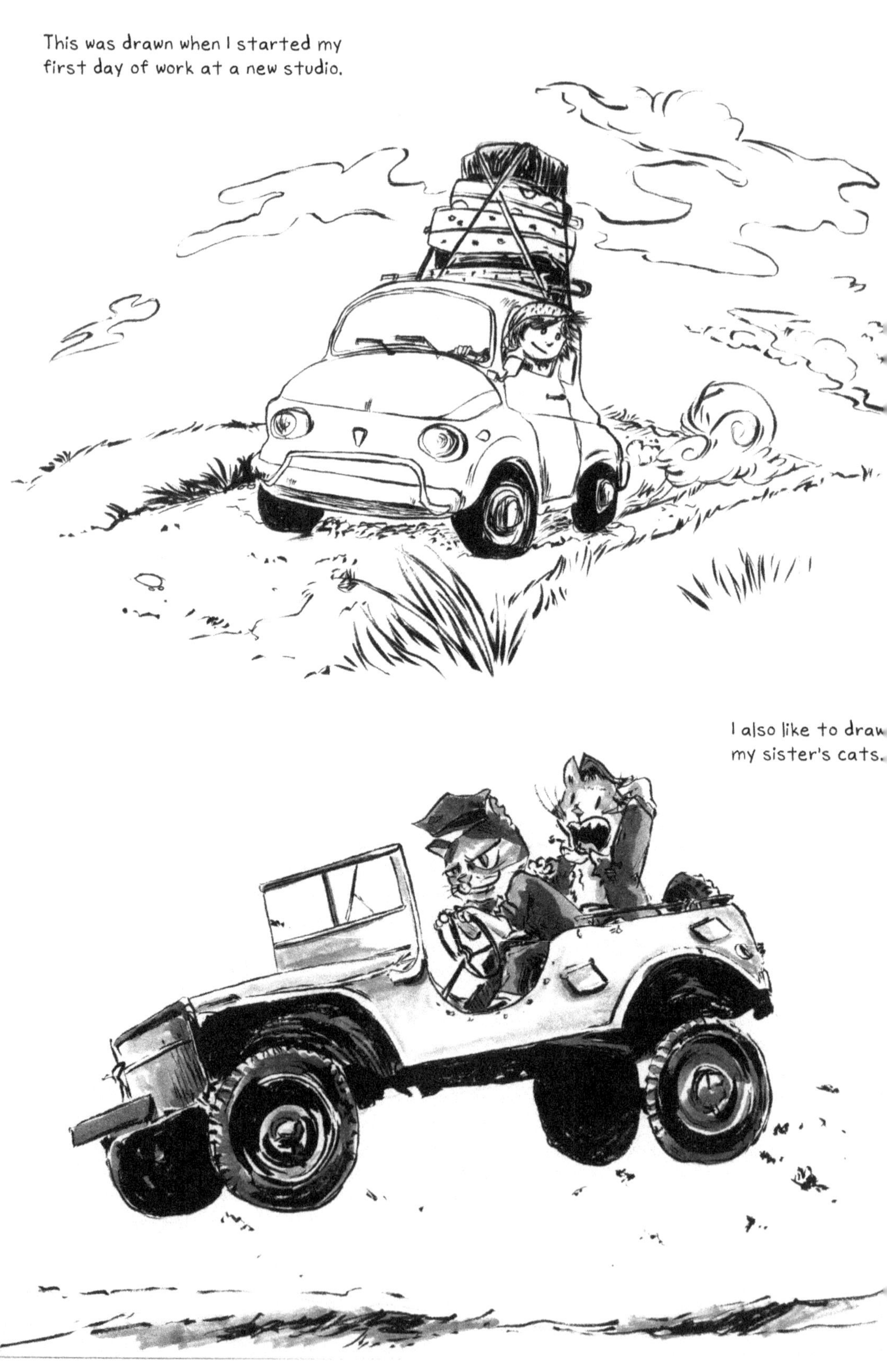

This was drawn when I started my
first day of work at a new studio.

I also like to draw
my sister's cats.

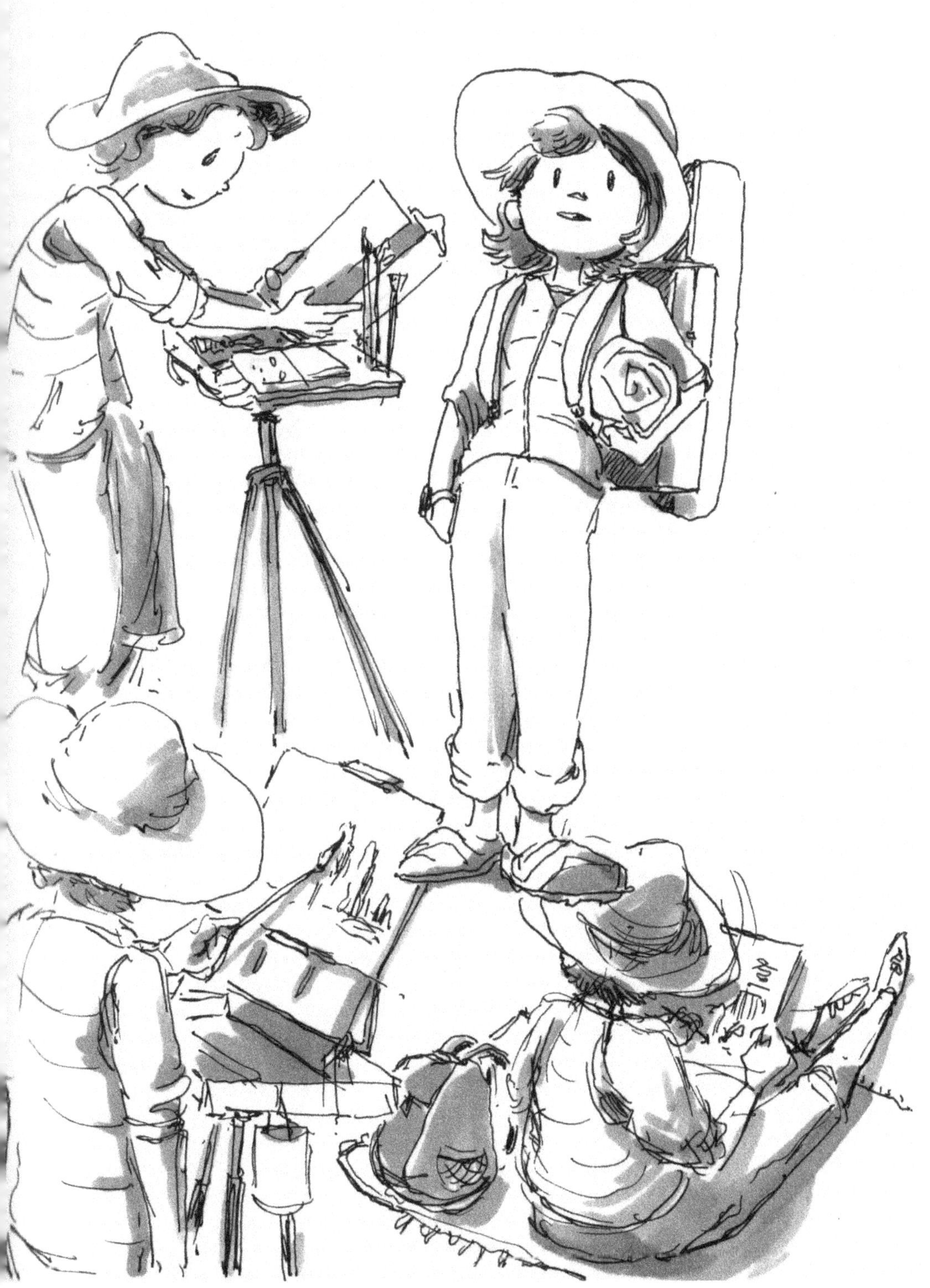

Awhile back, I met an elementary school teacher on a train to
Rome who spent her summers painting in Tuscany. (I was SO jealous.)
I always wanted to do a story centering around a traveling artist.

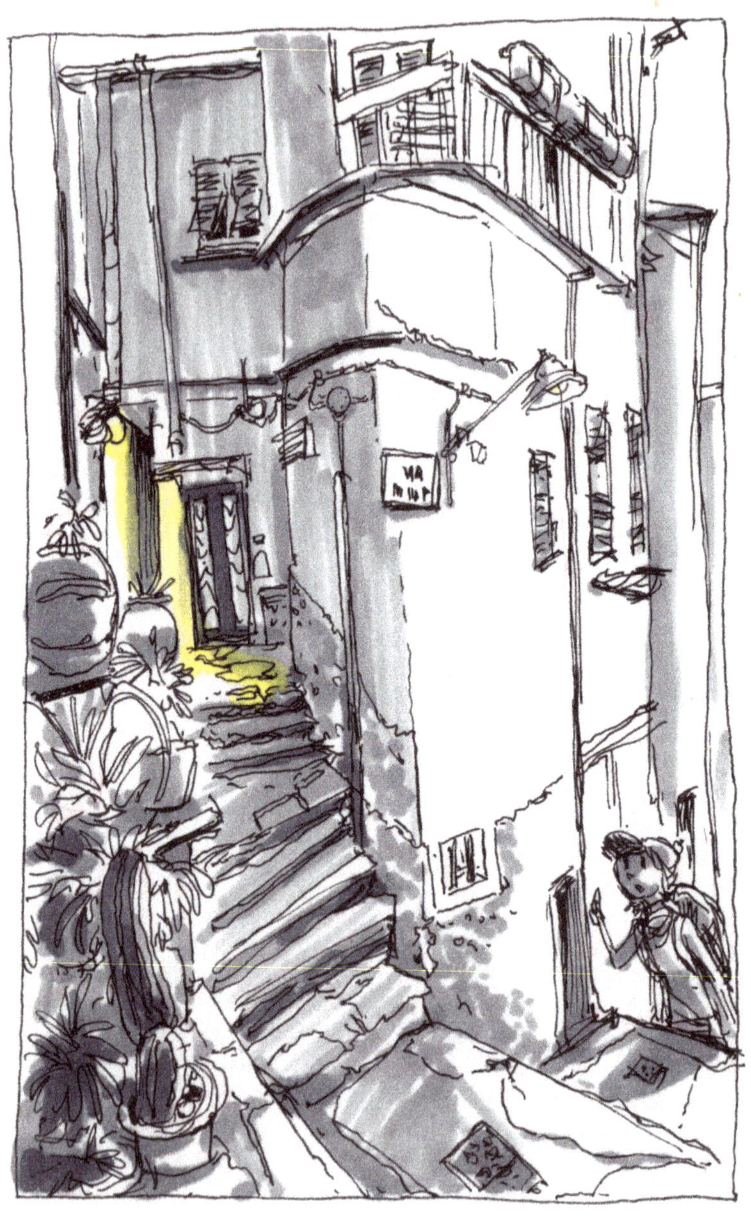

Seek inspiration everywhere! I used a photo I took of a stairway in Vernazza, Italy as reference.

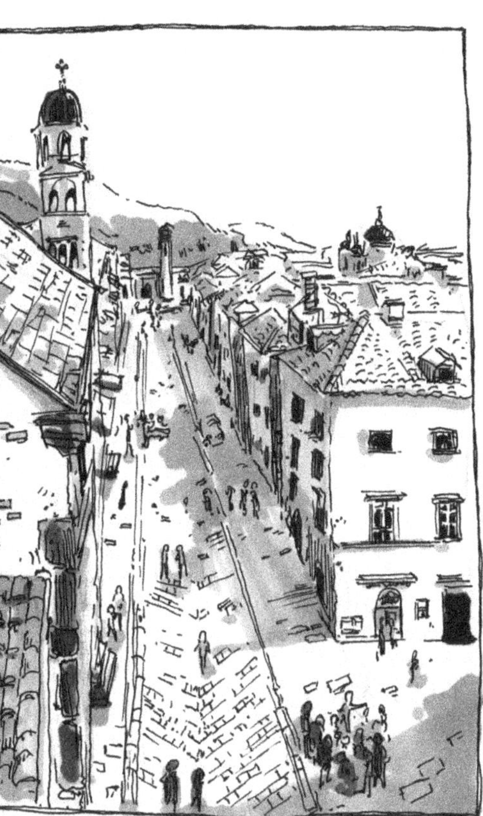

OLD TOWN - Dubrovnik, Croatia

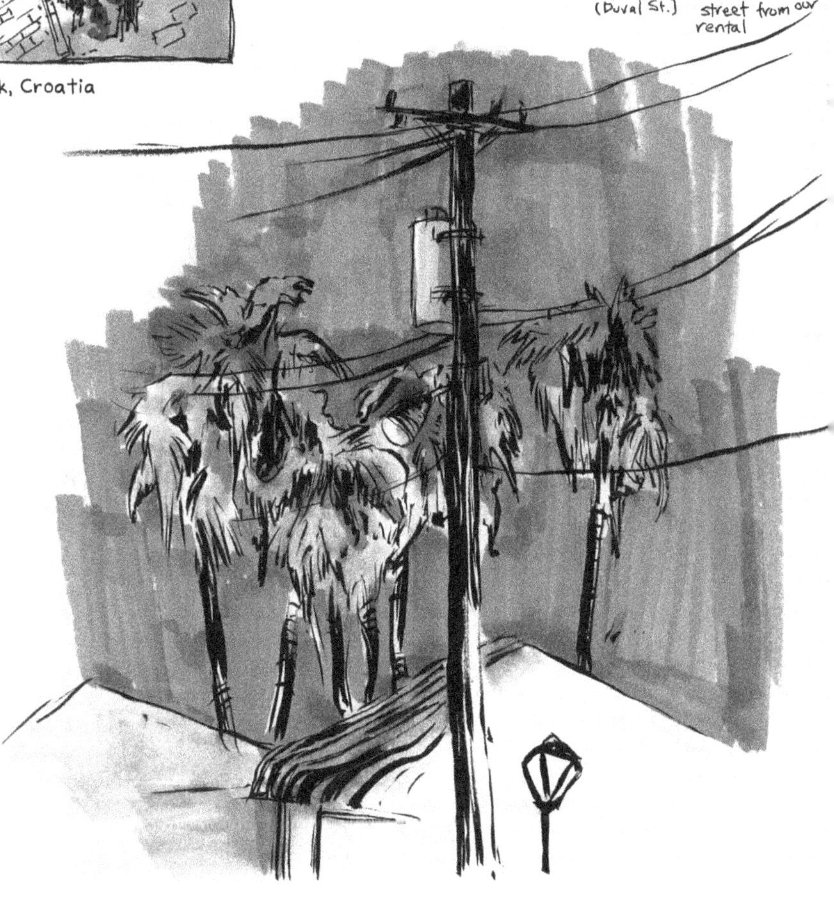

Drawing from life or from a place you visited is the best way to study and achieve authenticity in your work.

You are the sum of your experiences.

Key West - Across the
(Duval St.) street from our
rental

DUVAL STREET -
Key West, Florida

A drawing of our newly built deck
that took 2 summers to finish. My
husband and I did the bulk of the
work during one of the toughest
times together: when we were both
unemployed at the same time.

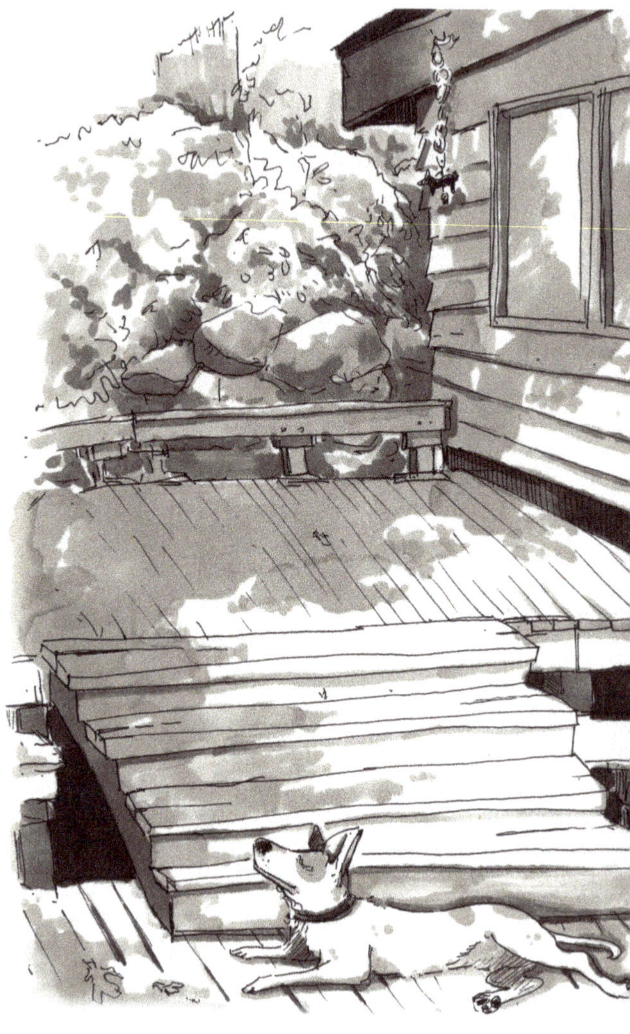

A drawing remembering
my recently decomissioned
car, a 1996 Toyota Corolla DX.
I had that car since I first
received my driver's license at 17.

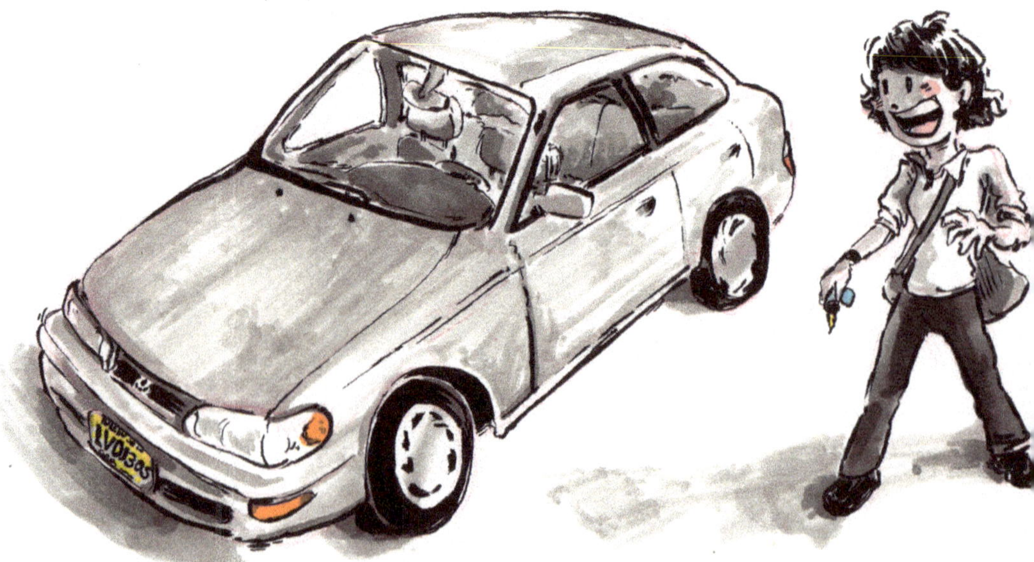

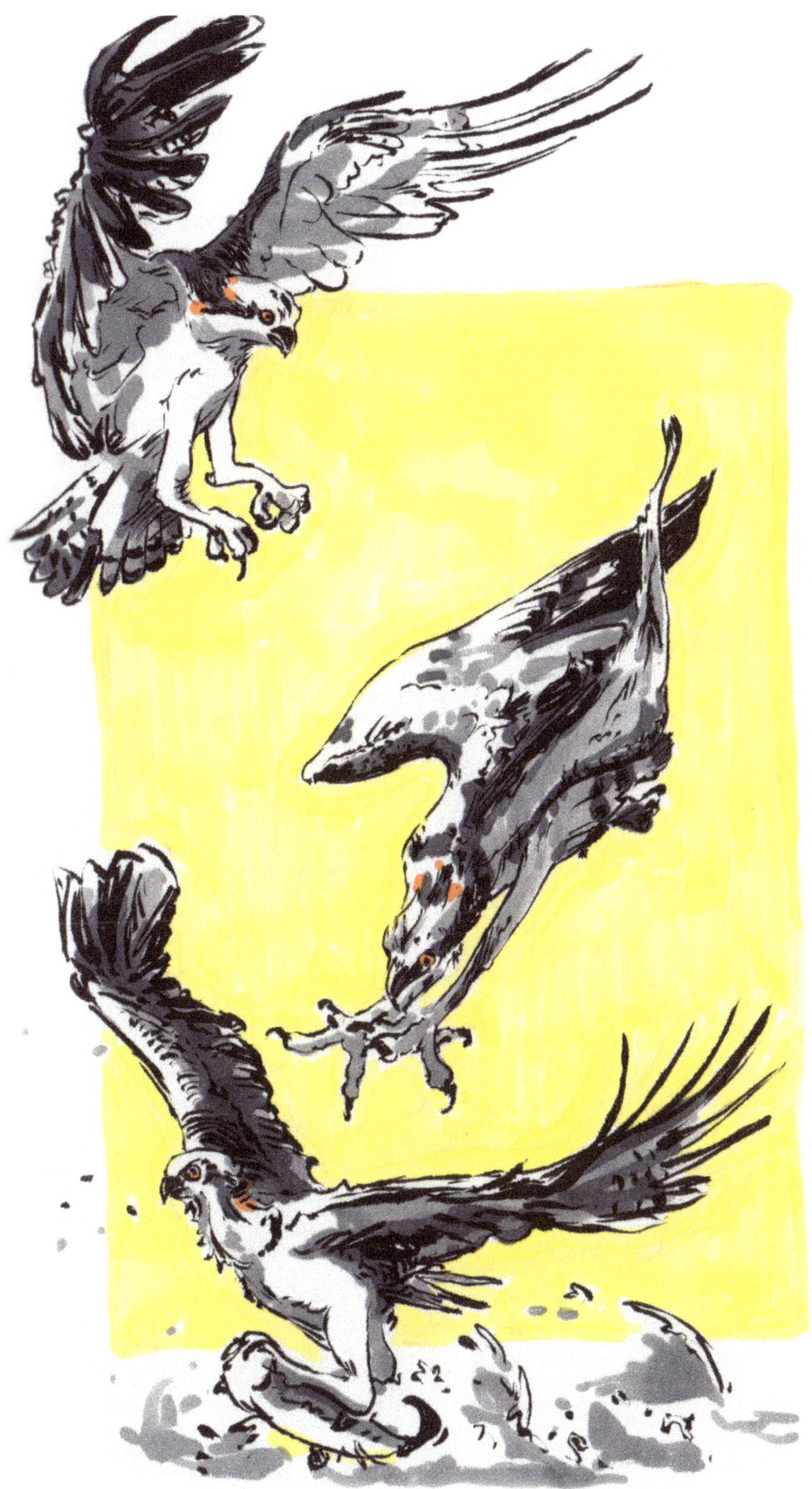

From time to time, my youngest sister, a wildlife biologist, will text me photos of her working with various animals: bald eagles, sea turtles, owls. Just thinking about these animals makes me want to draw them!

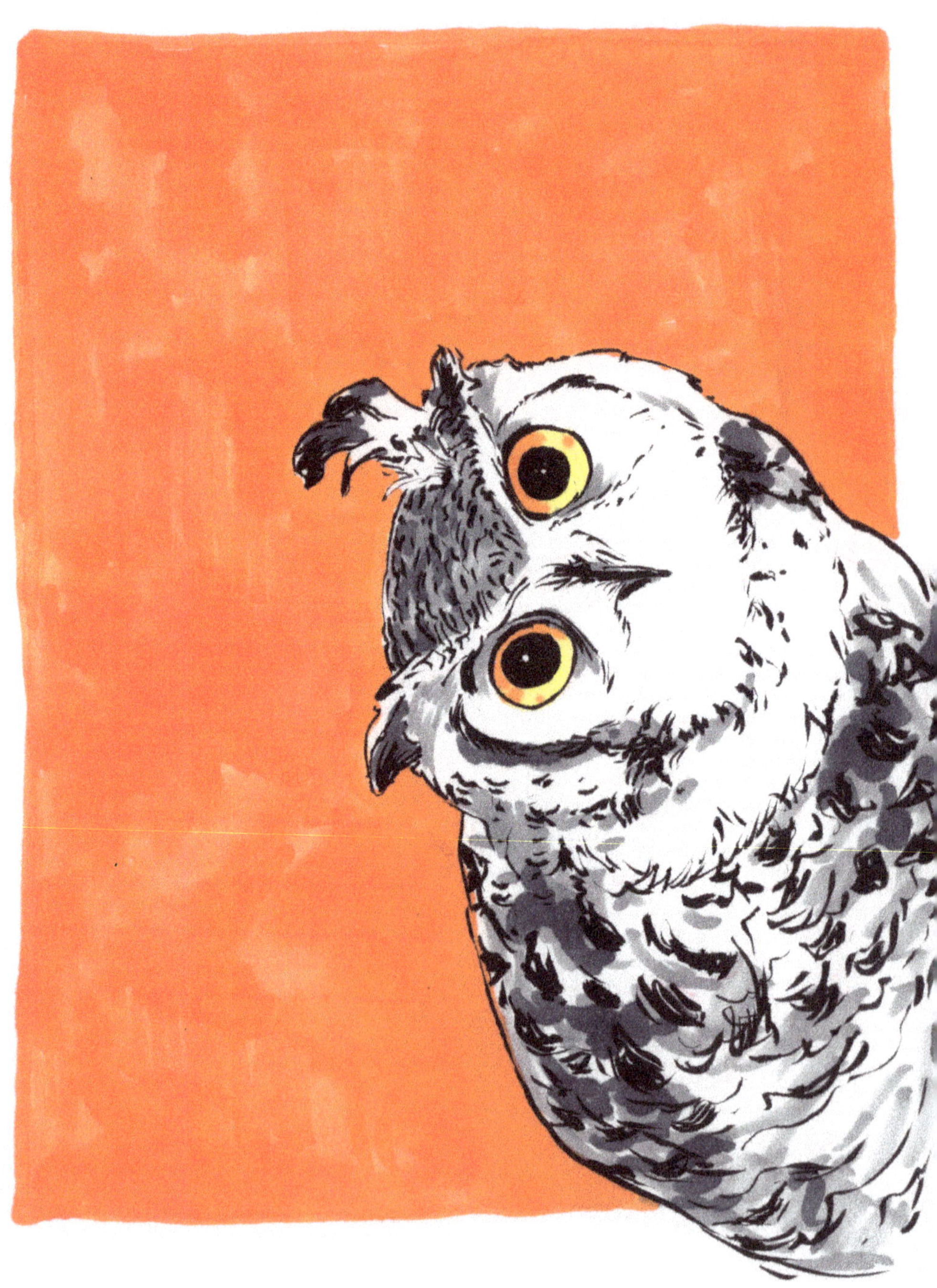

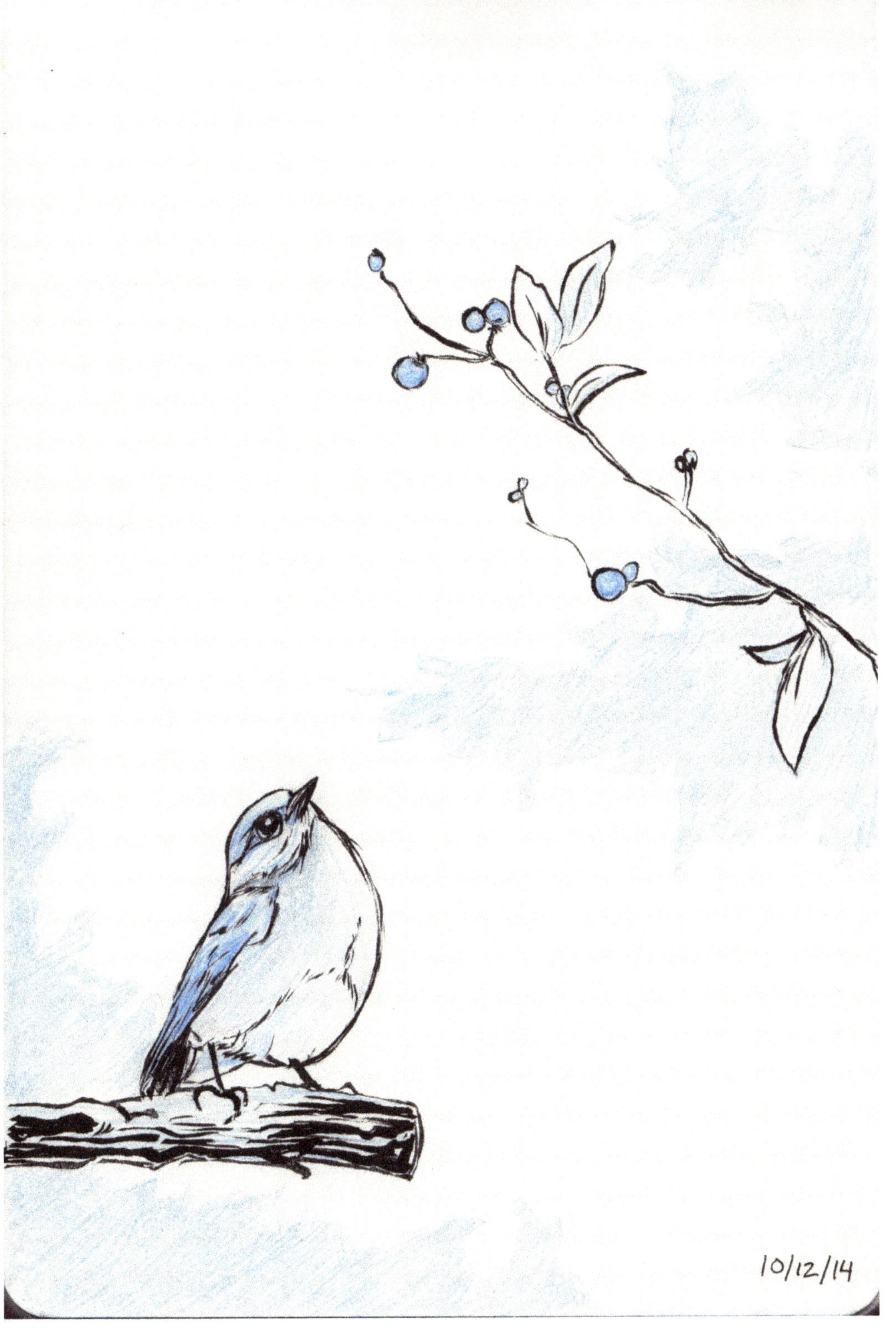

This was to commemorate the birth of my niece, who was affectionately referred to as "Blueberry" before she was born.

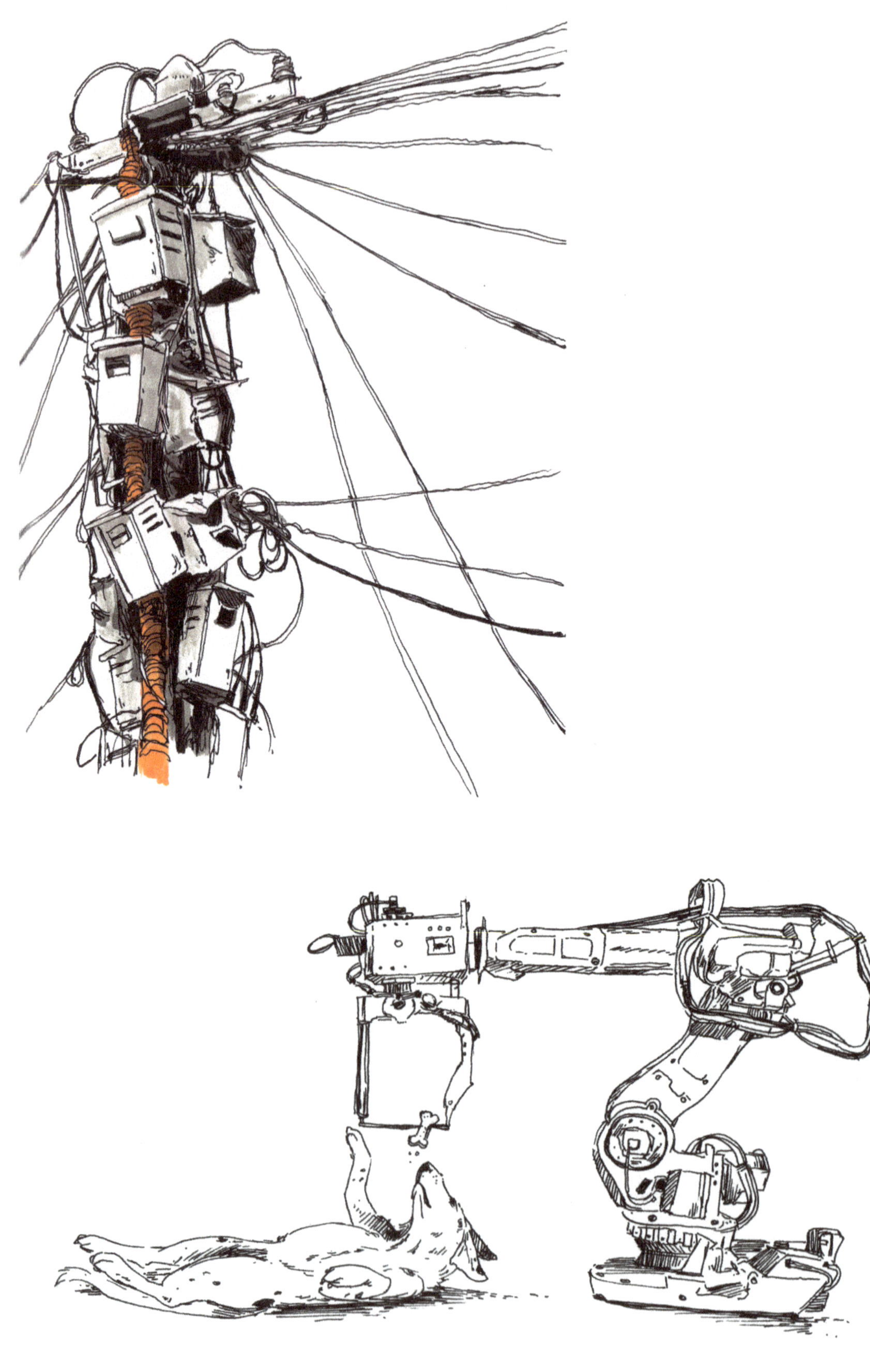

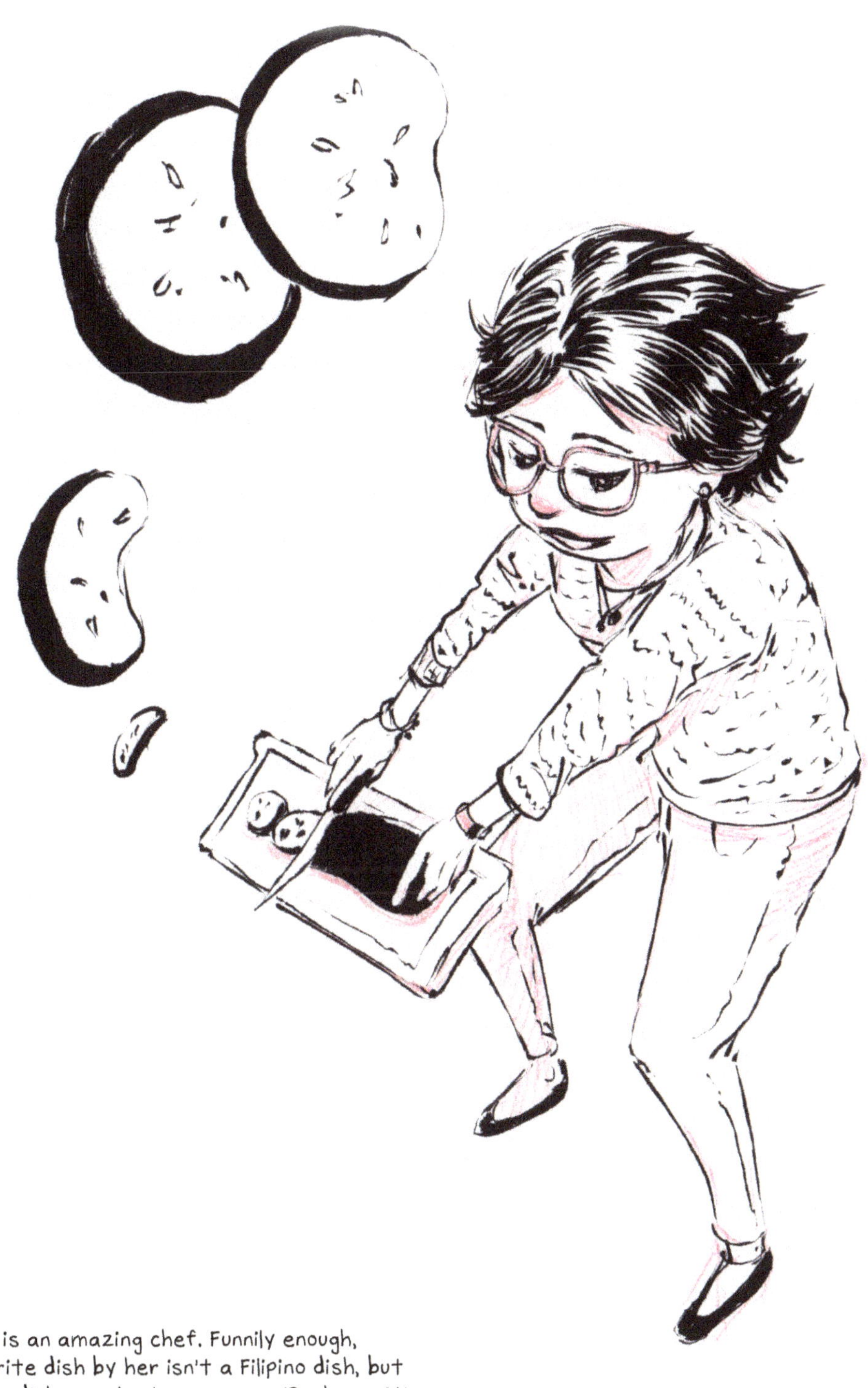

y mom is an amazing chef. Funnily enough,
y favorite dish by her isn't a Filipino dish, but
n Italian dish: eggplant parmesan. (Perhaps, it's
y New Jersey upbringing?) Whenever she visits,
he makes sure to cook me batches of eggplant parm
hich, given my appetite, doesn't last the week.

I tend to have pretty vivid dreams. One dream I had: my family was part of a neighborhod watch for zombies. I decided to draw it for Inktober.

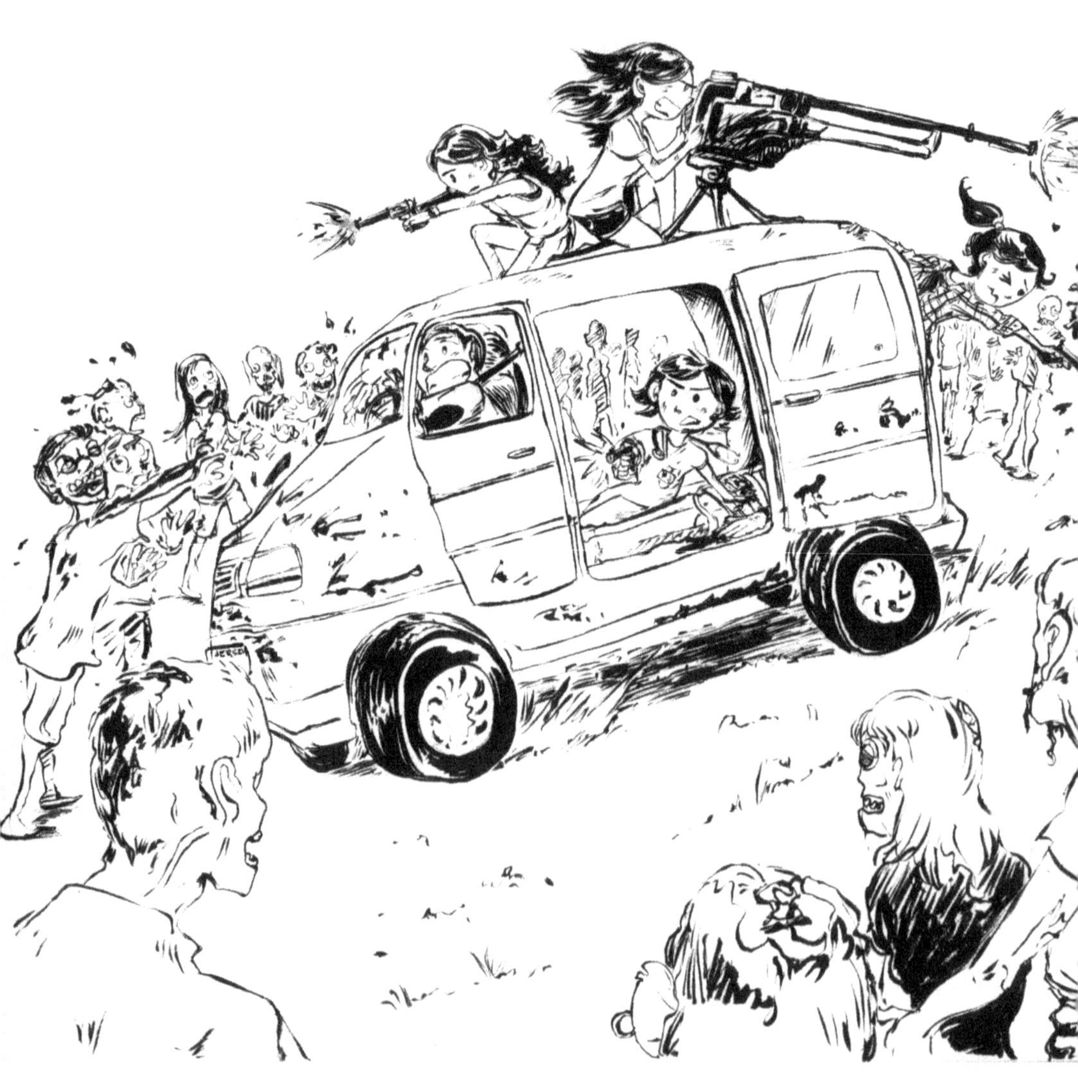

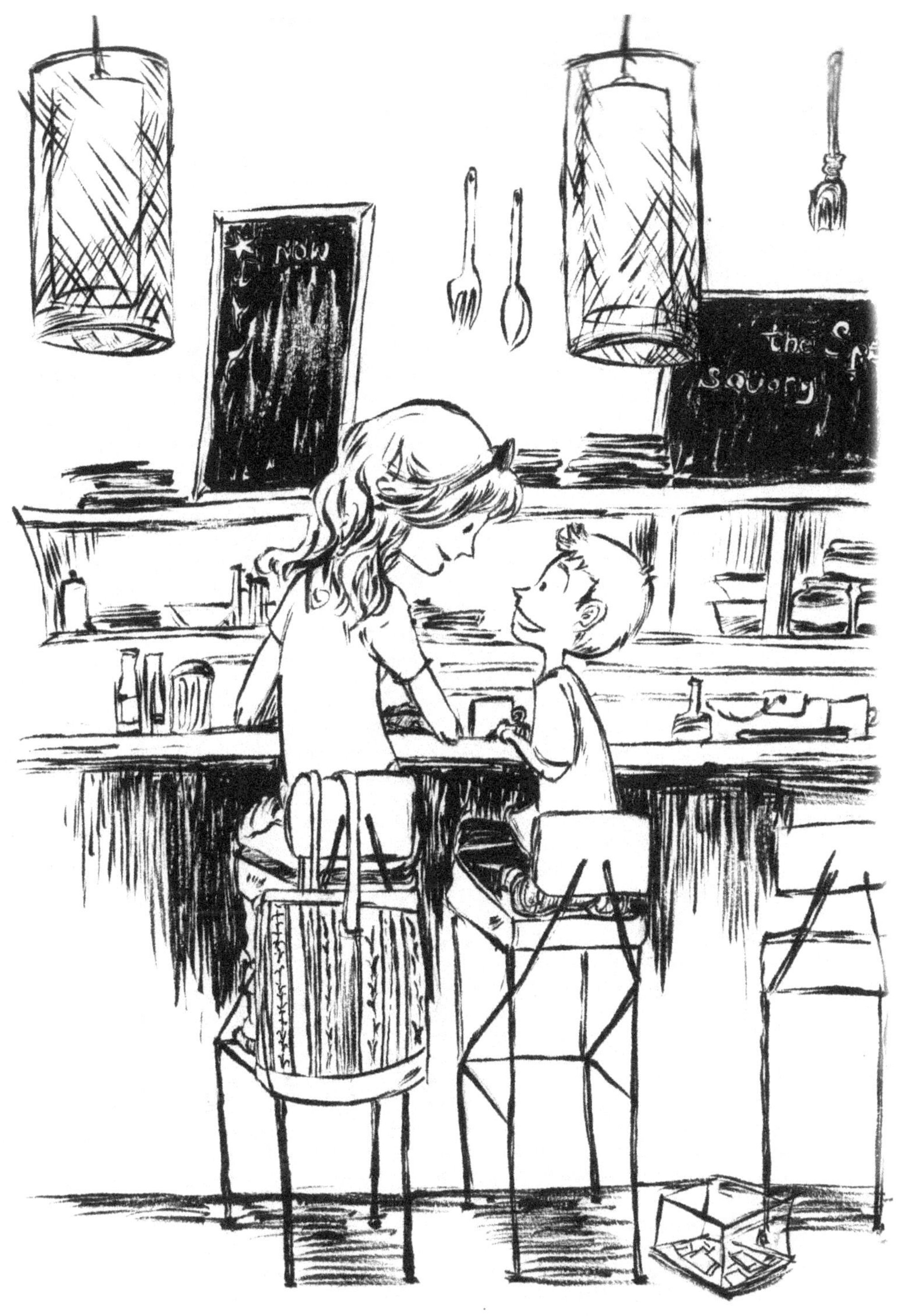

couldn't help but draw this mother and son (who was carrying a huge bin of Pokémon cards)
t a Seattle cafe. The mother listened so intently to what her son had to say. It reminded me
f how my mom listened to Every Single Thing I told her. I'm sure she didn't know what I was
lways talking about (M:TG? FFVII? Sailor Moon?), but I appreciated her effort.
hanks for always listening, Mom!

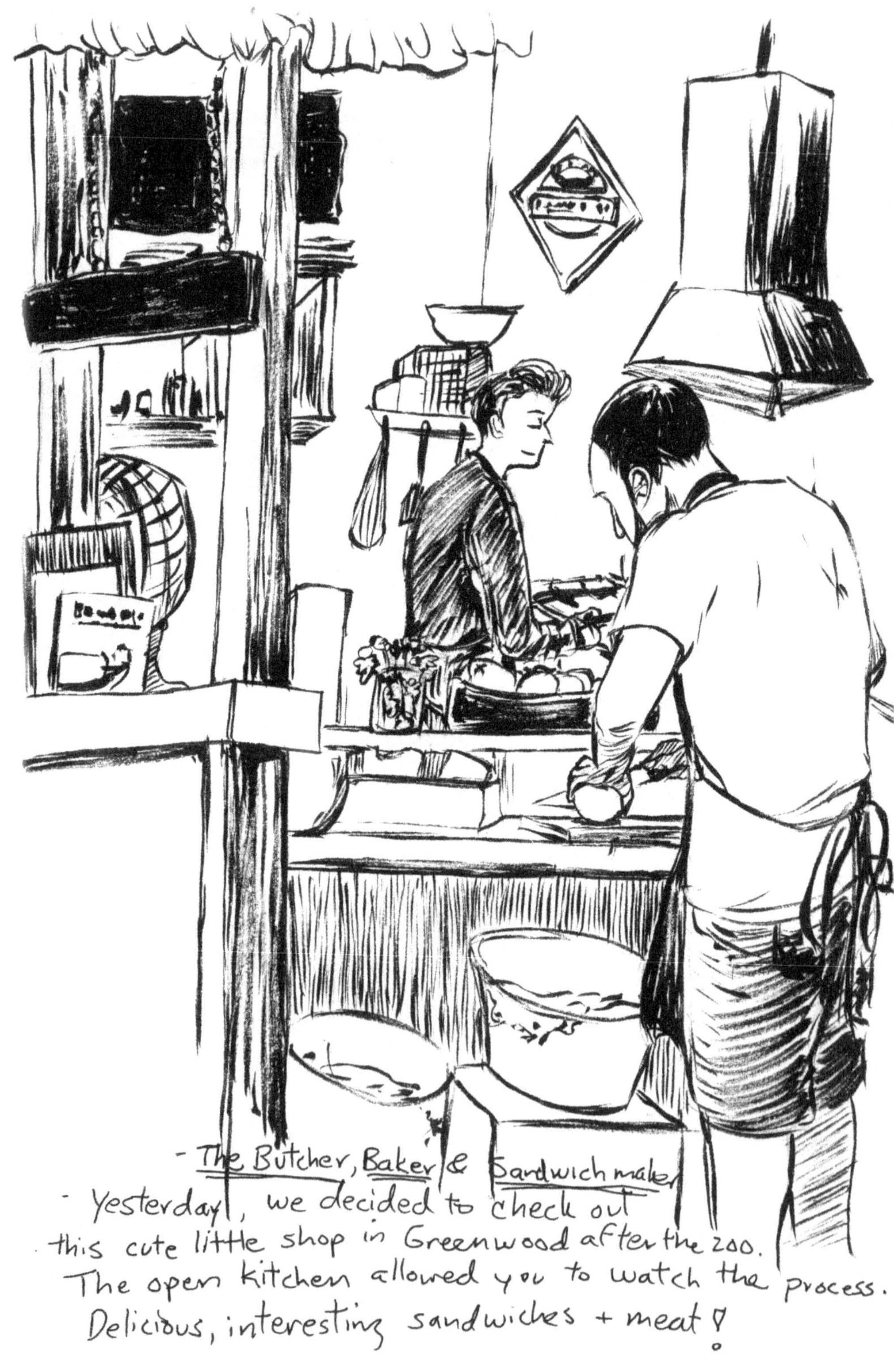

<u>The Butcher, Baker & Sandwich maker</u>
- Yesterday, we decided to check out
this cute little shop in Greenwood after the zoo.
The open kitchen allowed you to watch the process.
Delicious, interesting sandwiches + meat!

...ese were sketched during our trip to Key West. It was a great way to study the local flora ...d fauna. I always have a blast watching the pelicans dive into the water.

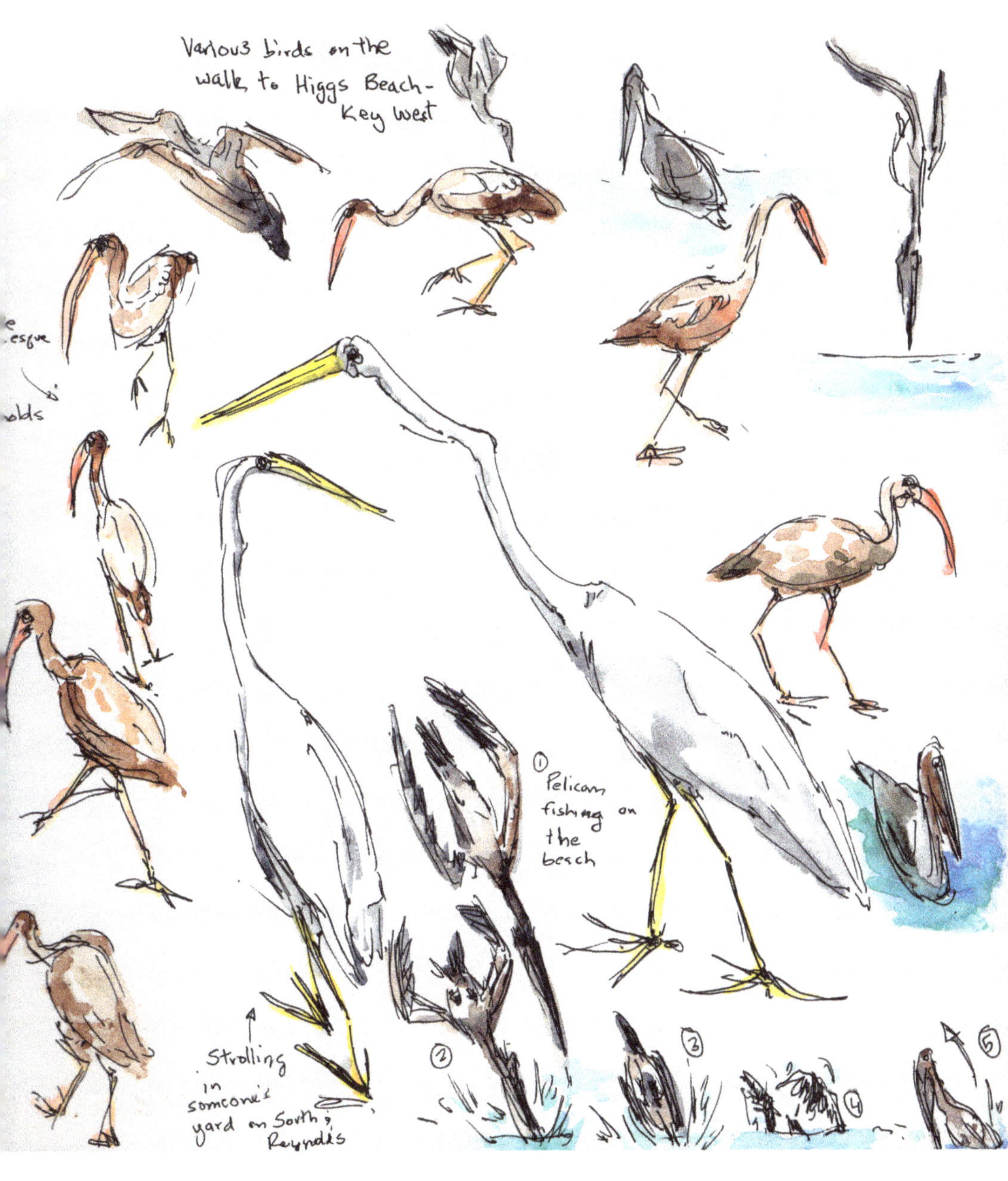

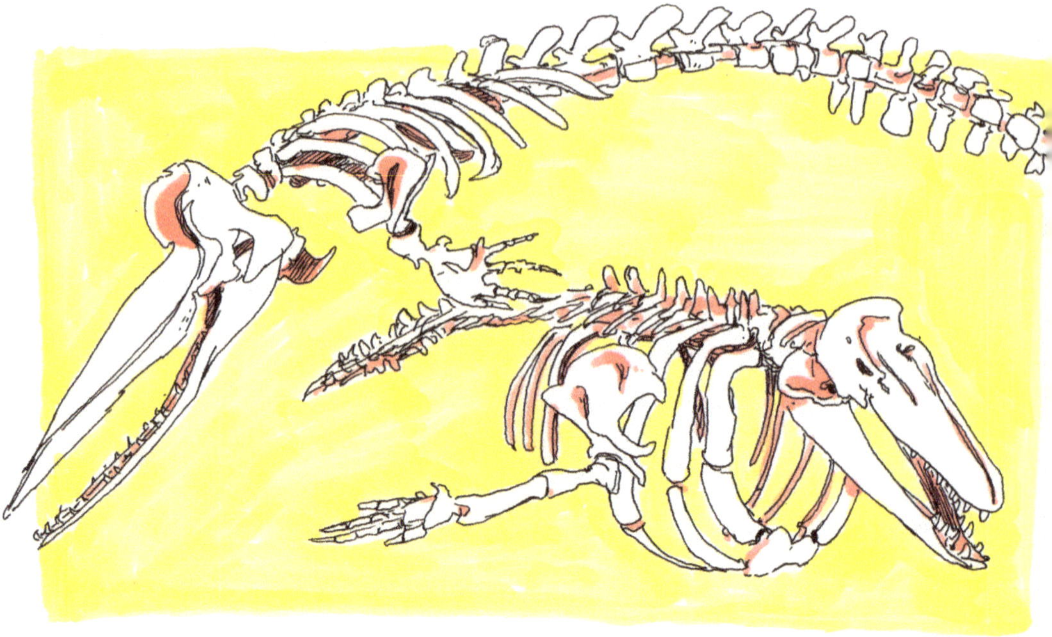

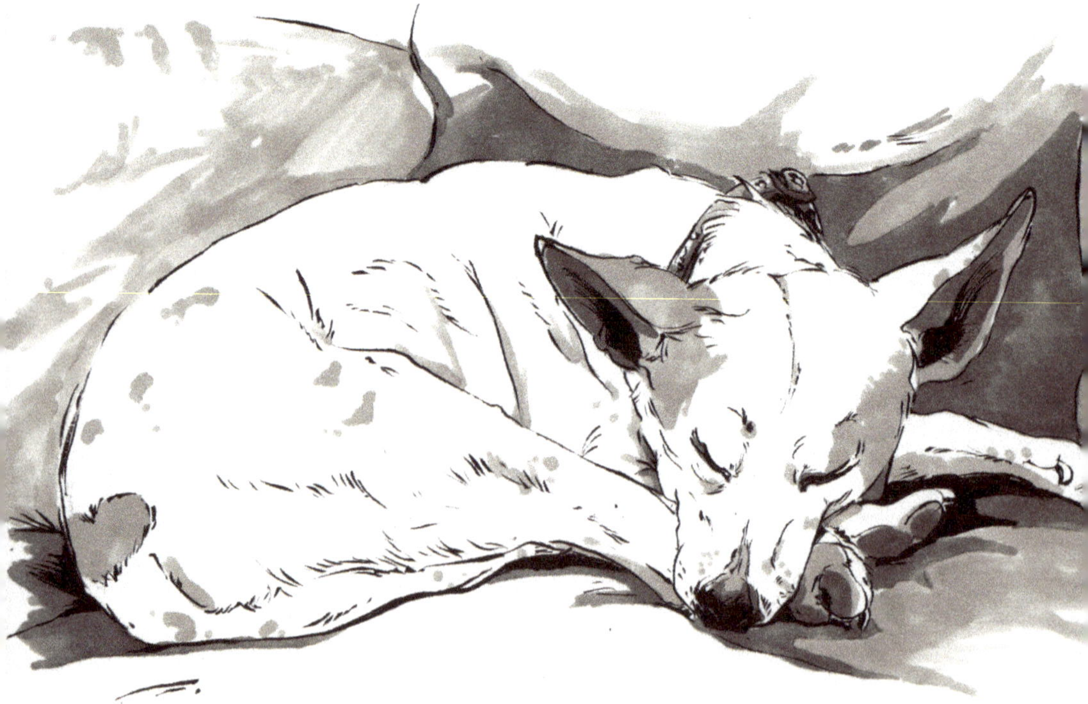

It's always nice to take a break and just draw what's in front of you. Usually, that happens to be my dog...and because he's a great napper, he's also a great model.

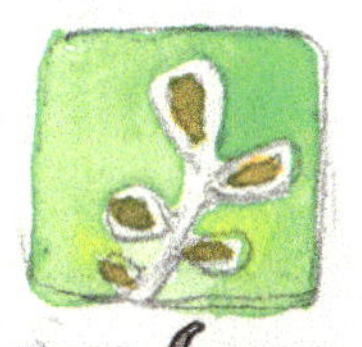

ma'ono

SEATTLE RESTAURANT WEEK EDITION
10/28/14

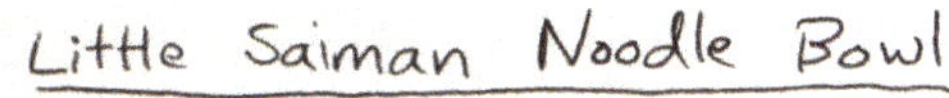

Little Saiman Noodle Bowl

- Egg noodles, smoked pork & chicken broth, shoyu egg, furikake, scallion.
- Loved the smoked pork, but there were more noodles than broth. Karl's Tako Poke won the Appetizer round.

5 Spiced Duck Leg Confit

- Roasted hen of the woods mushrooms, sauteed turnip greens, lo mai fun

- Amazing! The duck was salty + crispy in a good way. The mushroom was buttery + the turnips fresh. The sweet rice + Chinese sausage made me nostalgic.

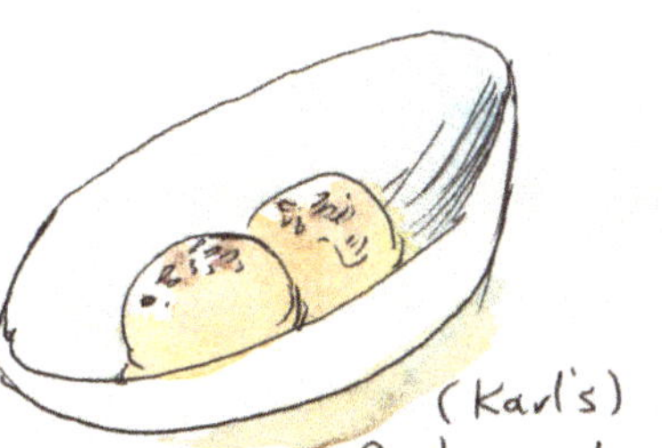

(Karl's)

5 Spiced Cashew Ice Cream

- Very filling + savory, creamy, can really taste cashews

cocoa nibs

Macadamia beer nuts layer

(Mine)

Sriracha-Peanut Butter Custard

- Alot more "solid" than I expected. Very peanuty and the sriracha added a kick noticeably.

SEATTLE
Restaurant Week
—2015—

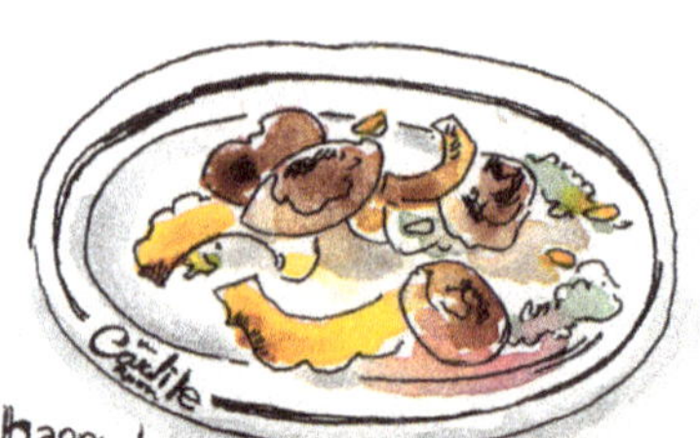

happy henryk's pan-fried ricotta dumplings
= delicata squash, myzithra, kale pesto, pumpkin seed =

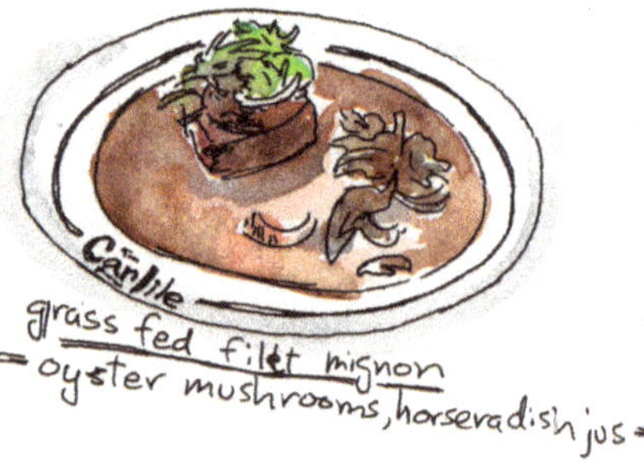

grass fed filet mignon
= oyster mushrooms, horseradish jus =

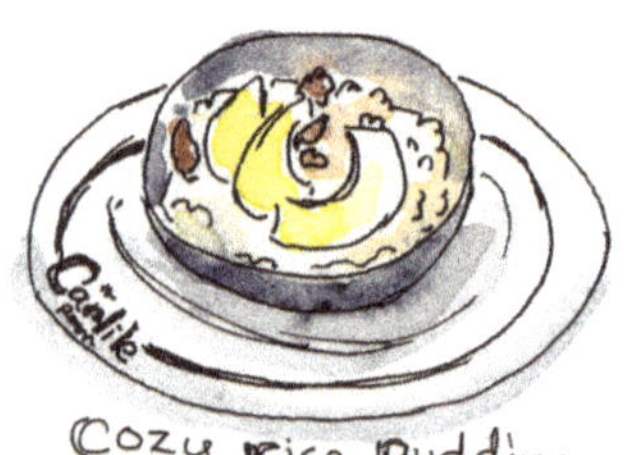

Cozy rice pudding
= almond poached pear, cinnamon streusel =

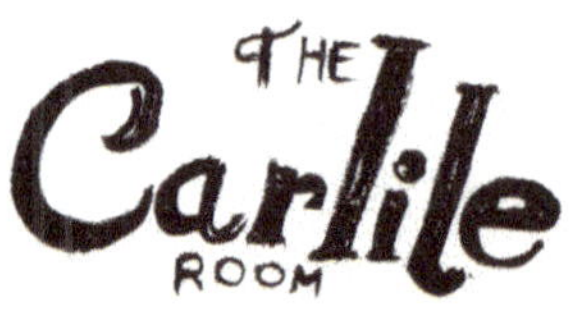

Tom Douglas's newest restaurant named after his favorite Seattle singer Brandi Carlile. The restaurant offers modern American dishes categorize into fun groups like "Plants" + "Carne Die Atmosphere carries a retro feel w/ mid-century modern furniture.

"Seattle Restaurant Week" usually falls during Inktober. It slowly evolved into a personal traditi to dedicate one Inktober drawing to the amazing food I get to sample in Seattle.

SEVENBEEF

- Seattle Restaurant Week 2016 -

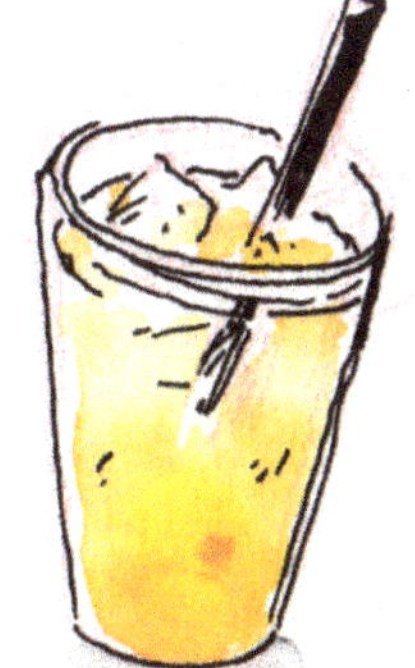

FLOWER POWER

Elder flower, Marigold

- **CAULIFLOWER SOUP**

Cougar gold cheese, grapes, champagne vinaigrette

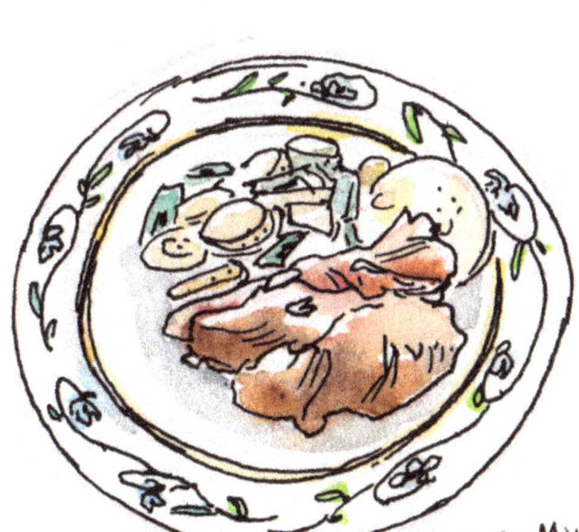

Smoked SHORT RIB

vegetables, mint, bearnaise sauce

LEMONGRASS CAKE

basil seed

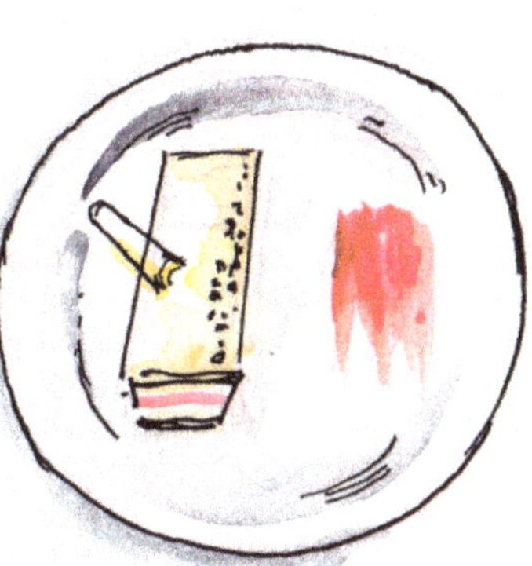

My husband noticed this restaurant awhile back, so we decided to go there for SRW. They're located in the southern end of Capitol Hill with a Vietnamese + steakhouse vibe.

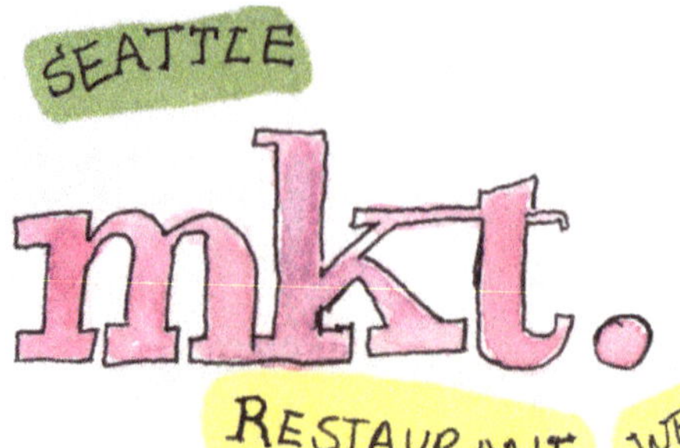

Ever since we've b[een]
to Staple + Fancy,
we always wanted [to]
check out its siblin[g]
mkt. We finally [were]
able to snag a
reservation for
SRW!

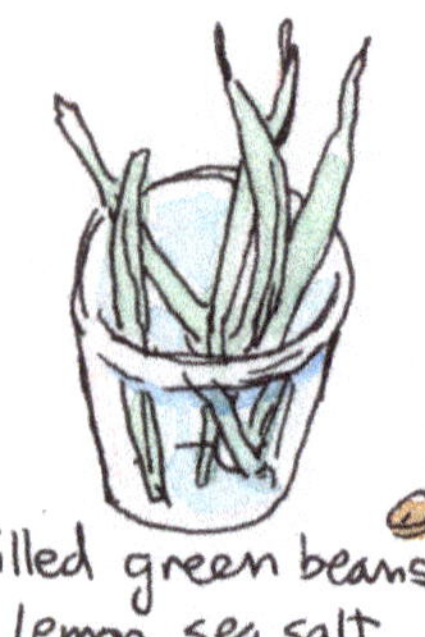

grilled green beans
lemon, sea salt

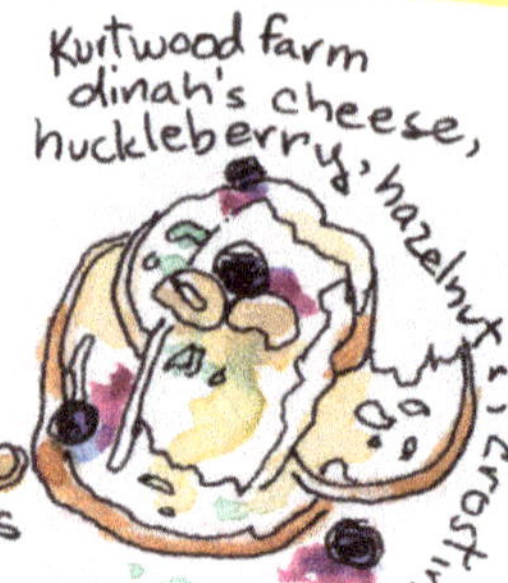

Kurtwood farm
dinah's cheese,
huckleberry, hazelnuts, crostini.

poached St. Jude's
albacore's

Pickled Asian
pear, endive

roasted delica[ta]
squash,
black currant

pepitas, mapl[e]
sherry vinagret[te]

grilled double R ranch beef,
fingerling potato,
crispy spring onions

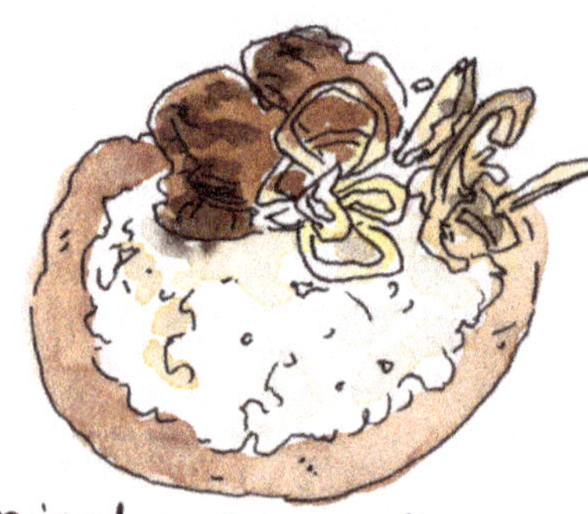

braised pork cheeks,
ansom mills grits,
wild mushrooms,
fried shallot

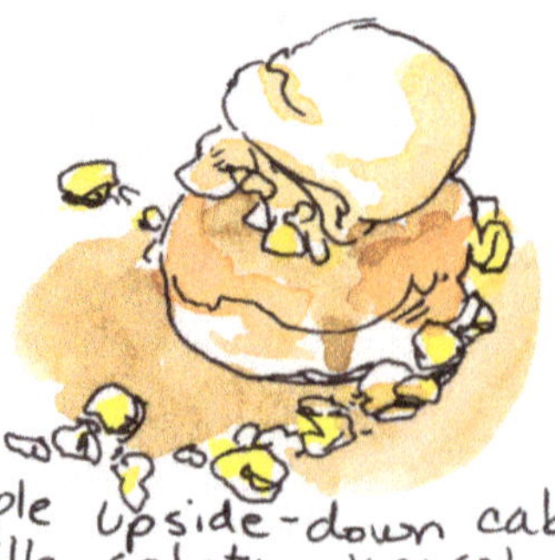

pineapple upside-down cake,
vanilla gelato, streusel +
cajeta sauce

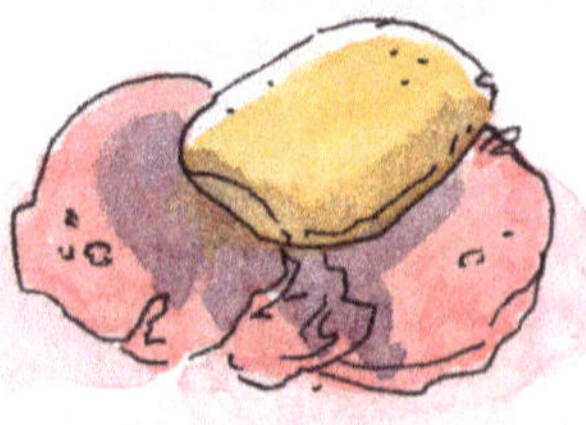

Plum sorbet (seasonal),
shortbread cookie

The day I realized that

raising the thermostat = $ $ $

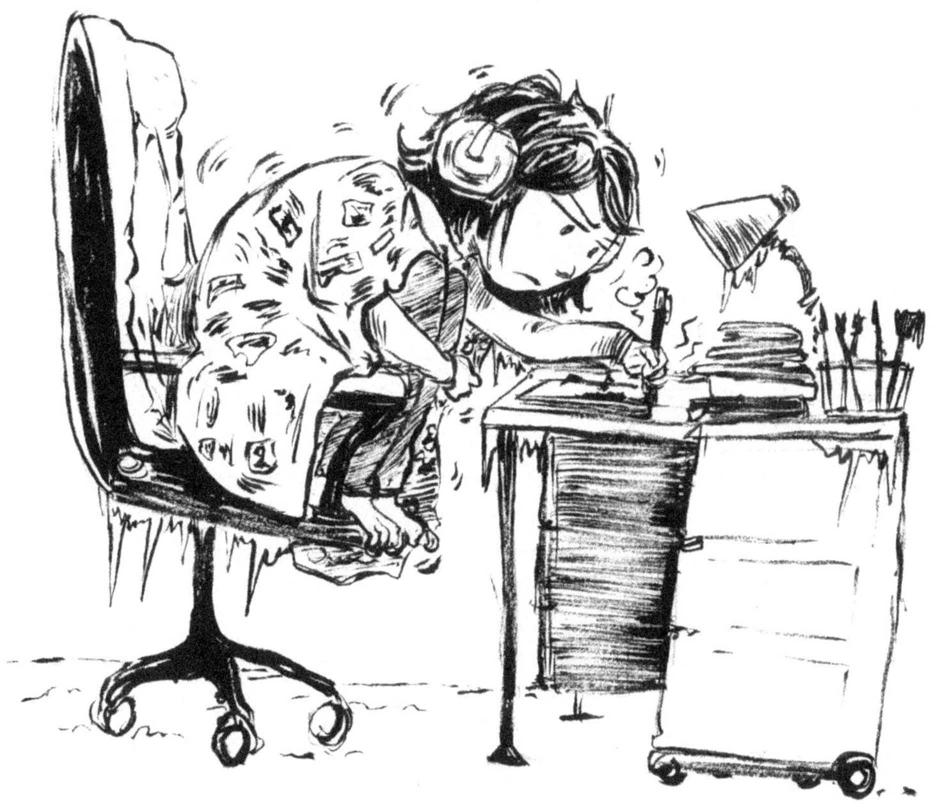

When I was kid, I would always complain to my dad how cold the house was because he kept the thermostat temperature low. Now that I am a homeowner myself, I fully understand his reasons.

Awhile back when I was down in the dumps about my artwork, my husband framed my worries with the question: "What would your 7 year old self think of everything you've accomplished?"

When in self-doubt, it always helps to get a reality check from the "you" that was inspired in the first place.

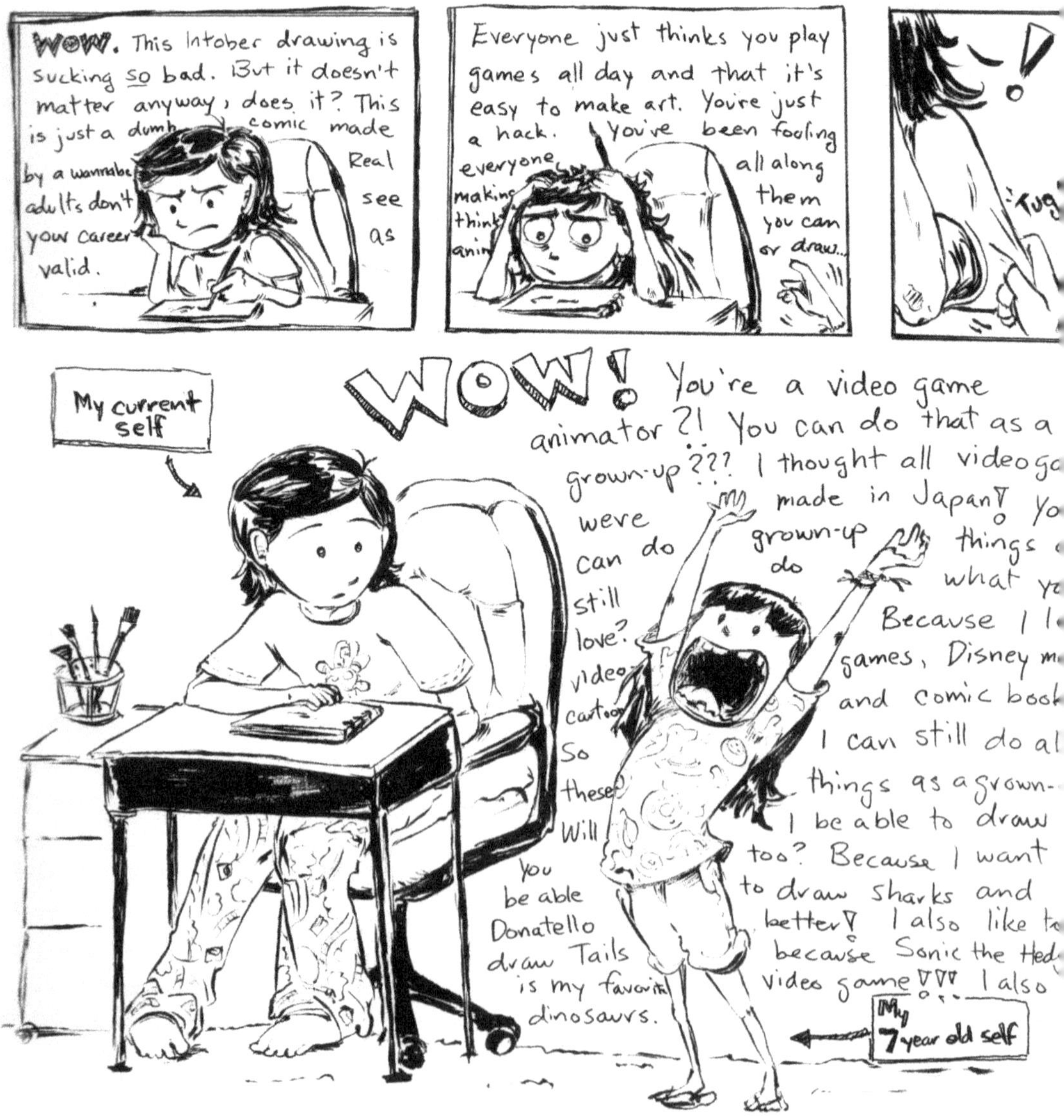

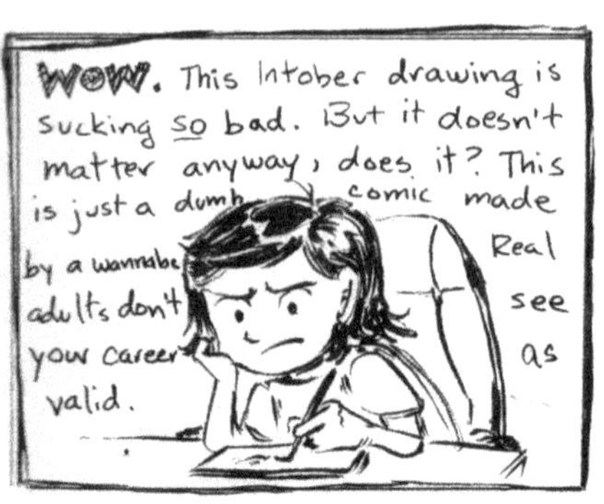

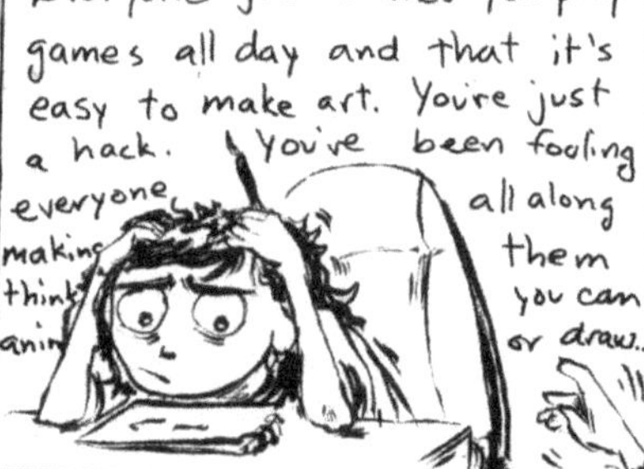

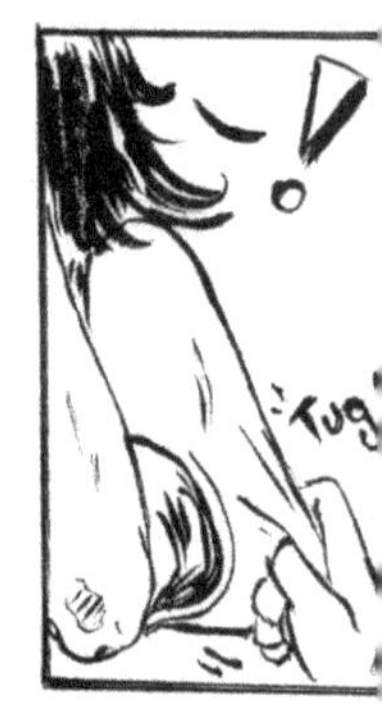

...learn a lot about my husband when hiking with him. In this case, I learned that he and I had very different childhoods.

WORDS IN THE WOODS

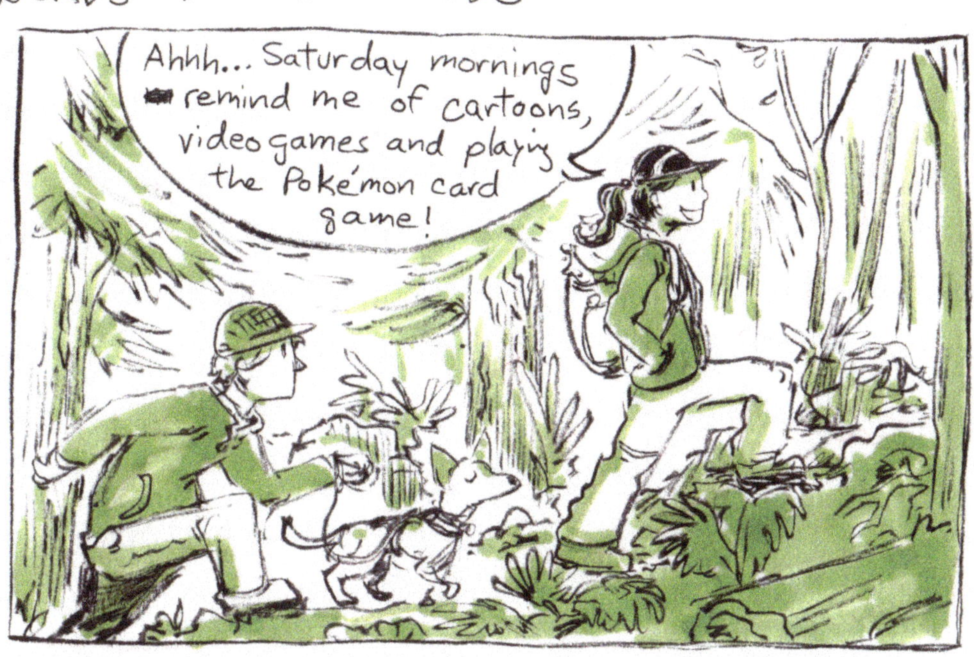

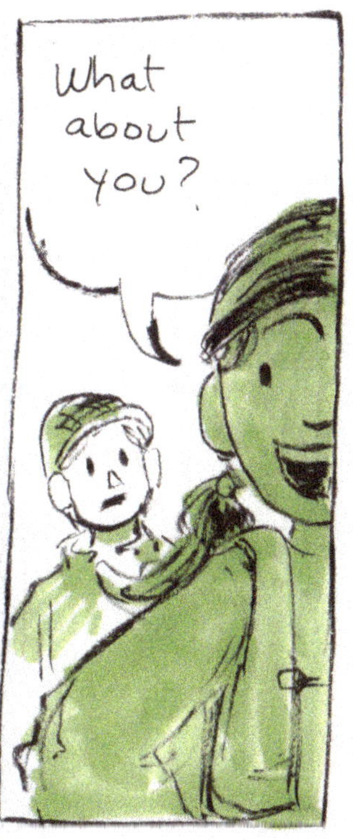

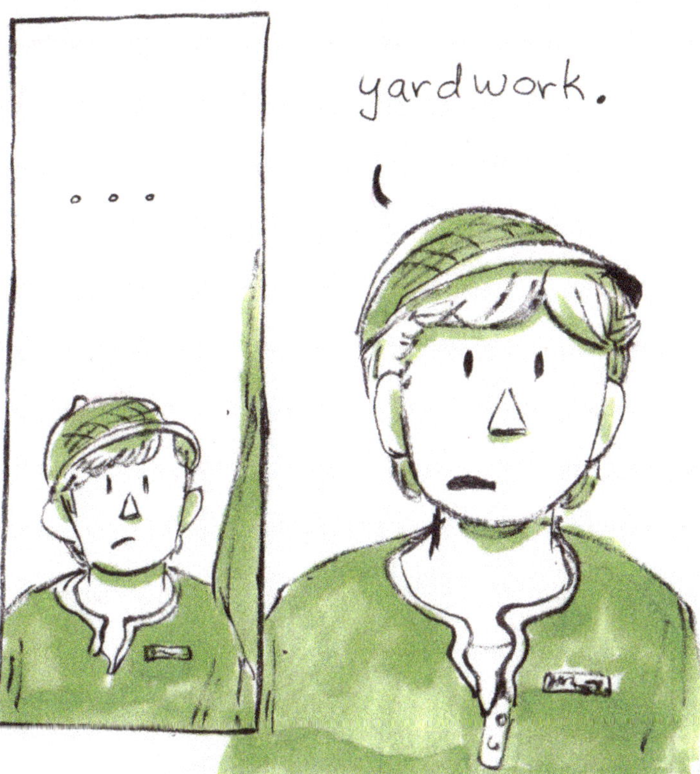

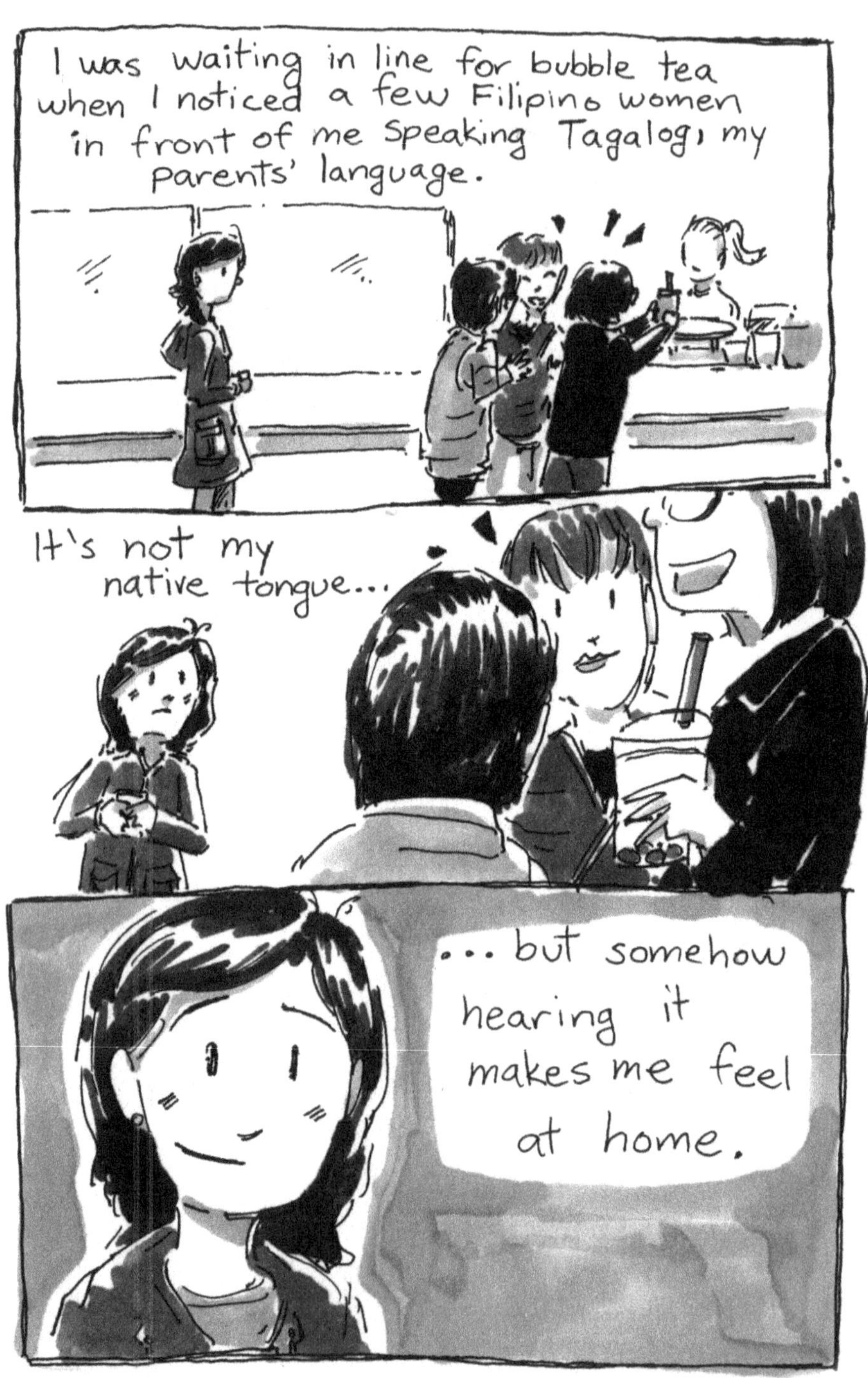

I'm always embarrased when I tell people (espeically other Filipinos) that I don't speak Tagalog. Even though I'm not fluent, the cadence and intonations are so comforting to me. There's alwa comfort in the familiar, especially when you live far from home.

My husband and I have been catching up on a lot of movies on our "To Watch" list, and I amused myself thinking of boring ways you could tell a story. No one likes to watch a protagonist make a straight path to their goal, getting what they want.

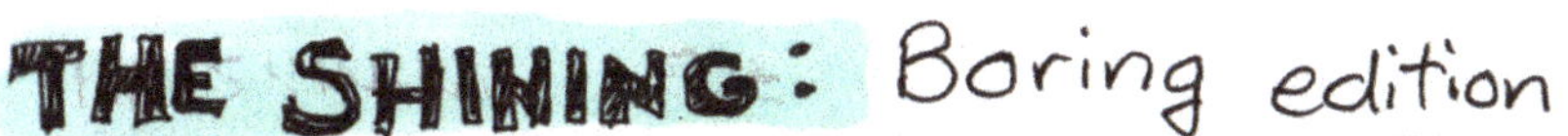

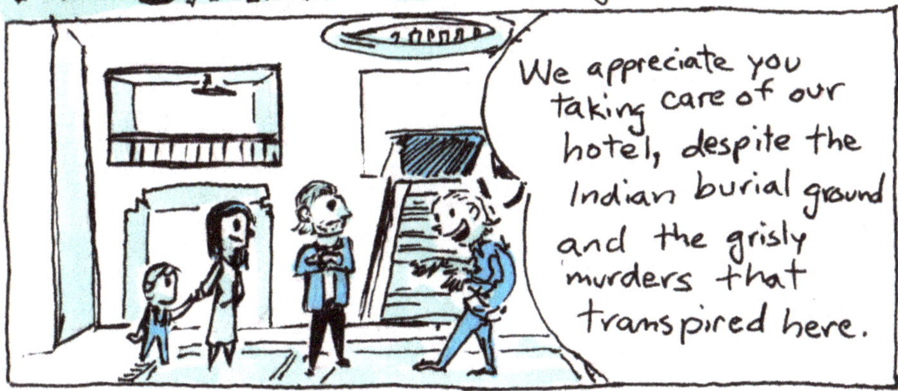

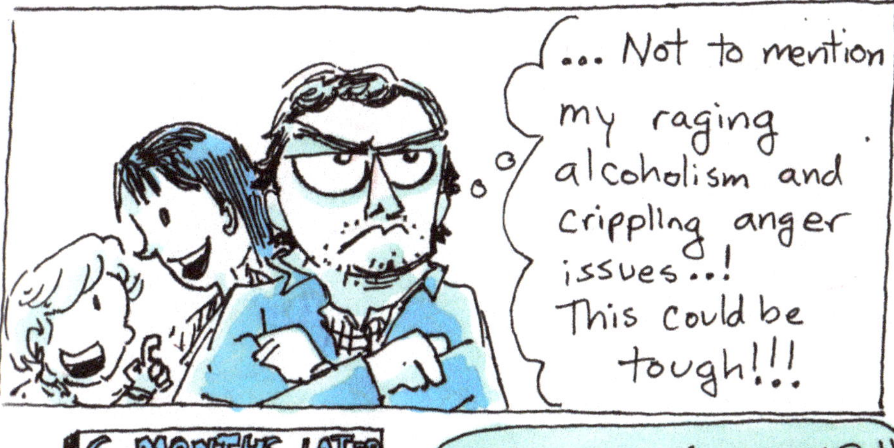

Experimentation is always a good excuse to buy
new art supplies. I bought bottles of colored ink
in Canada and thought it'd be fun to try washes
over my brush pen drawings.

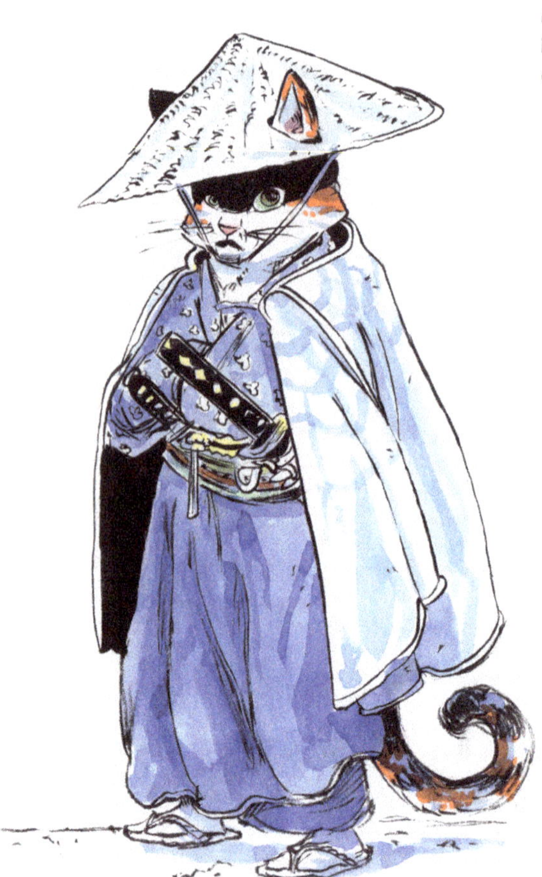

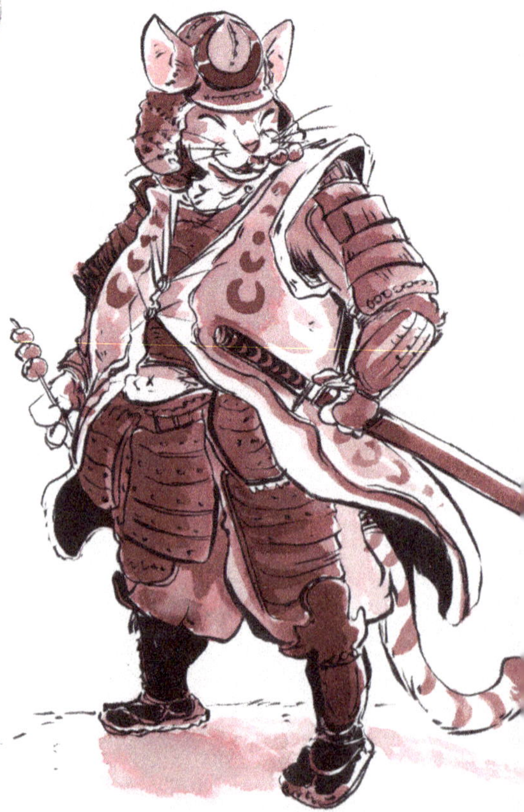

These characters are anthropomorphized
versions of my sister's 2 cats: a calico
and a tabby.

RPG ANIMALS

This was a series of drawings where I imagined some animal characters for a role-playing game. (RPG)

My best friend suggested a cat chef, so I drew one coming in with the morning's ingredients.

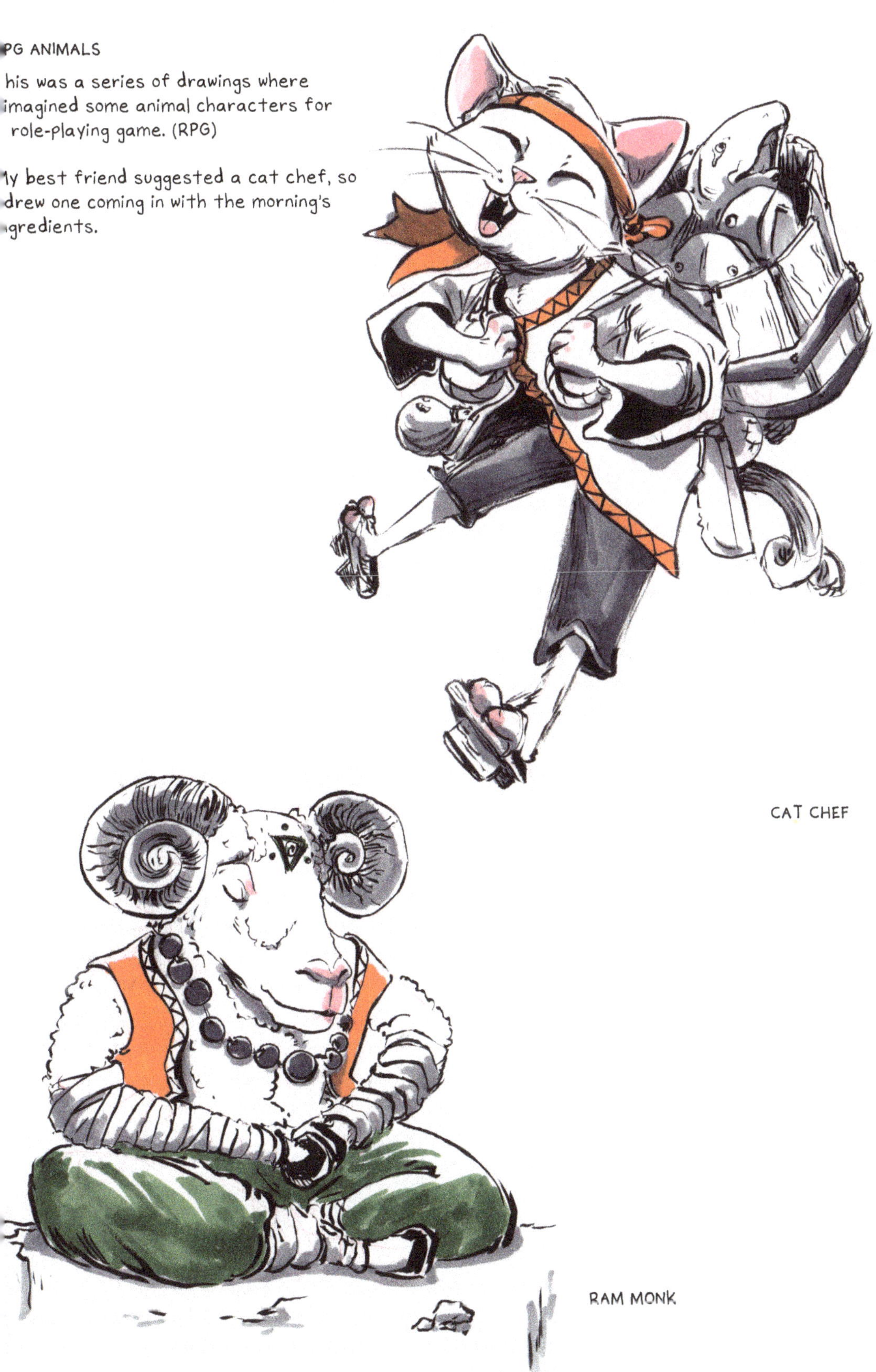

CAT CHEF

RAM MONK

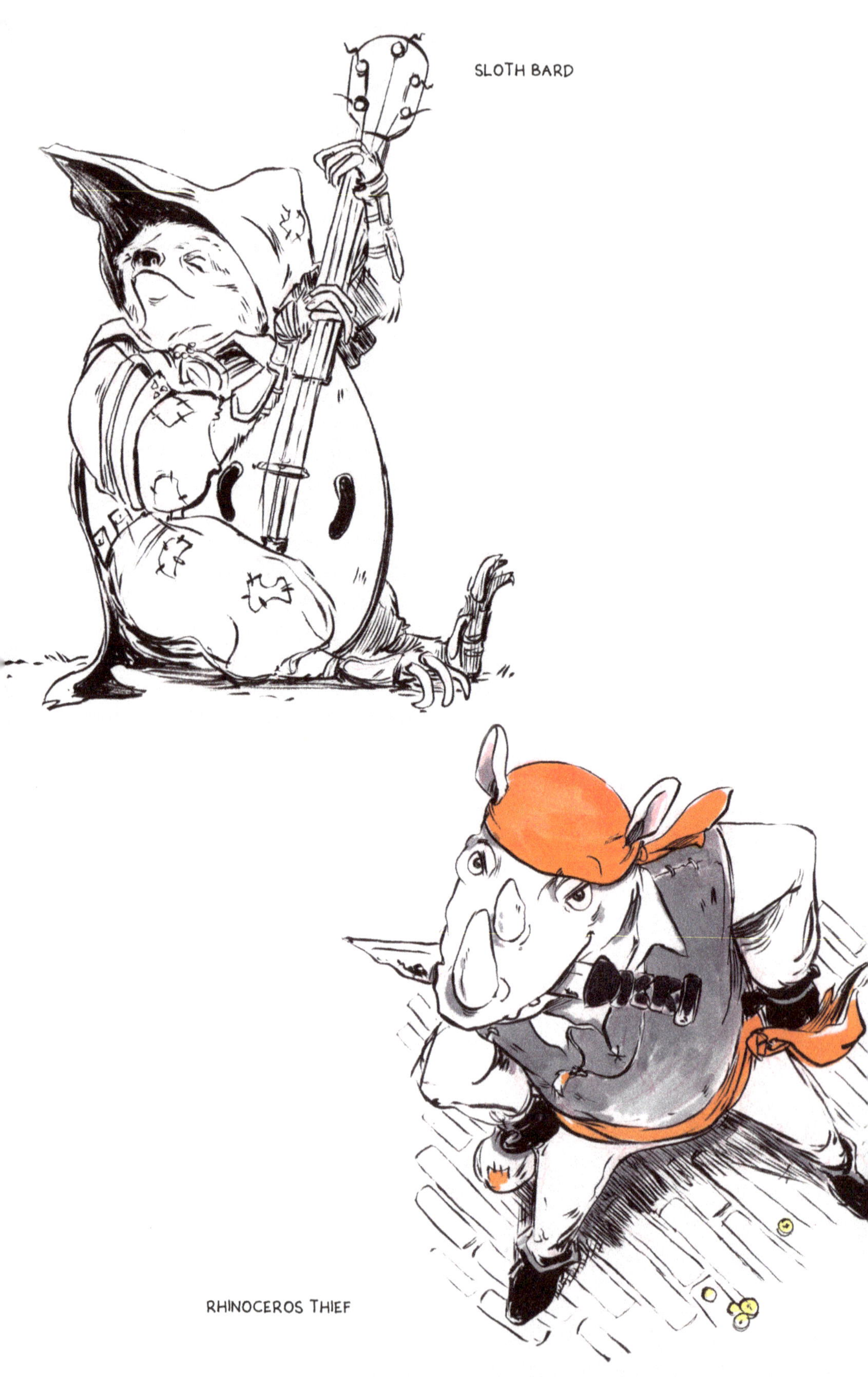
SLOTH BARD
RHINOCEROS THIEF

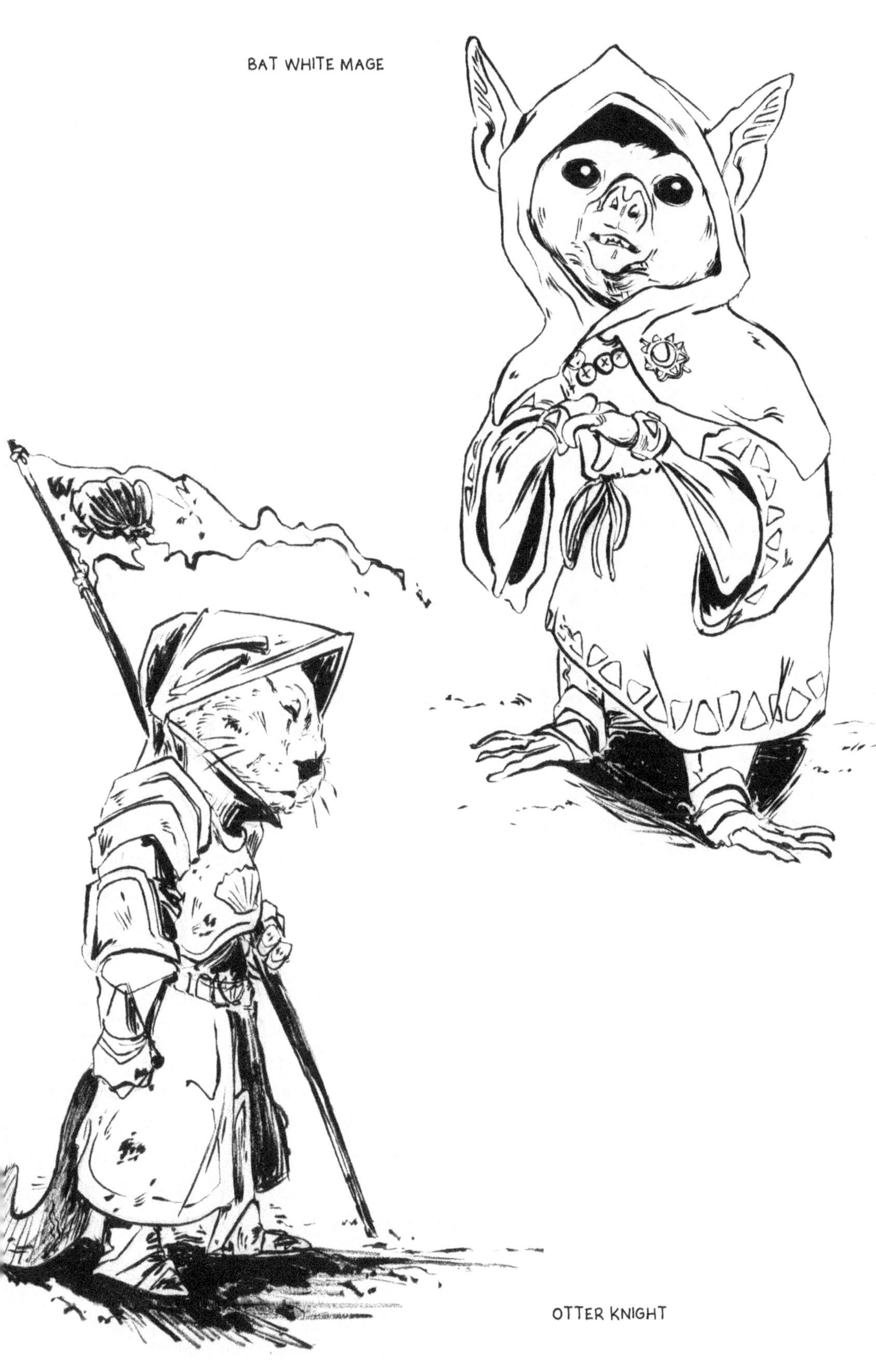
BAT WHITE MAGE
OTTER KNIGHT

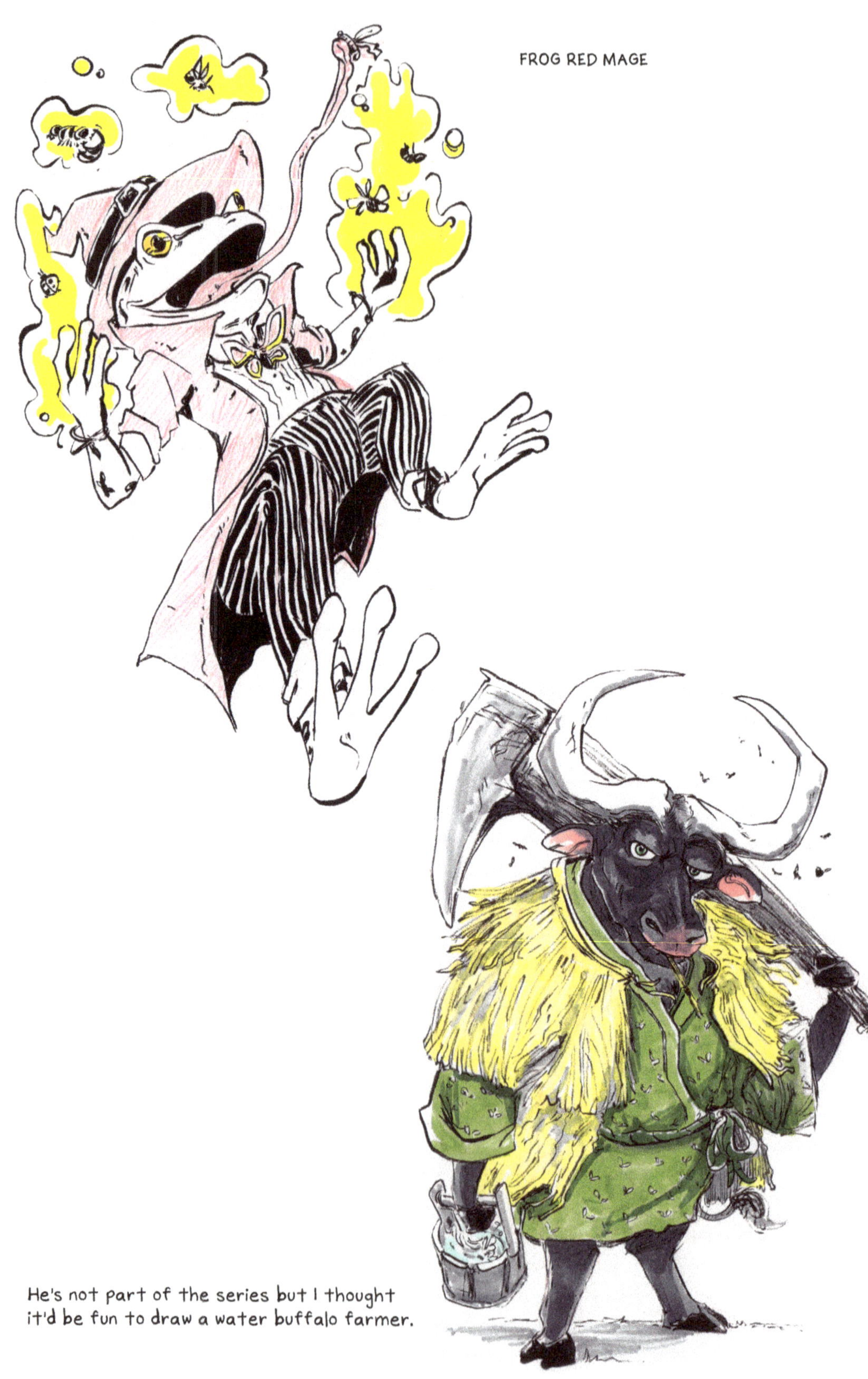

He's not part of the series but I thought it'd be fun to draw a water buffalo farmer.

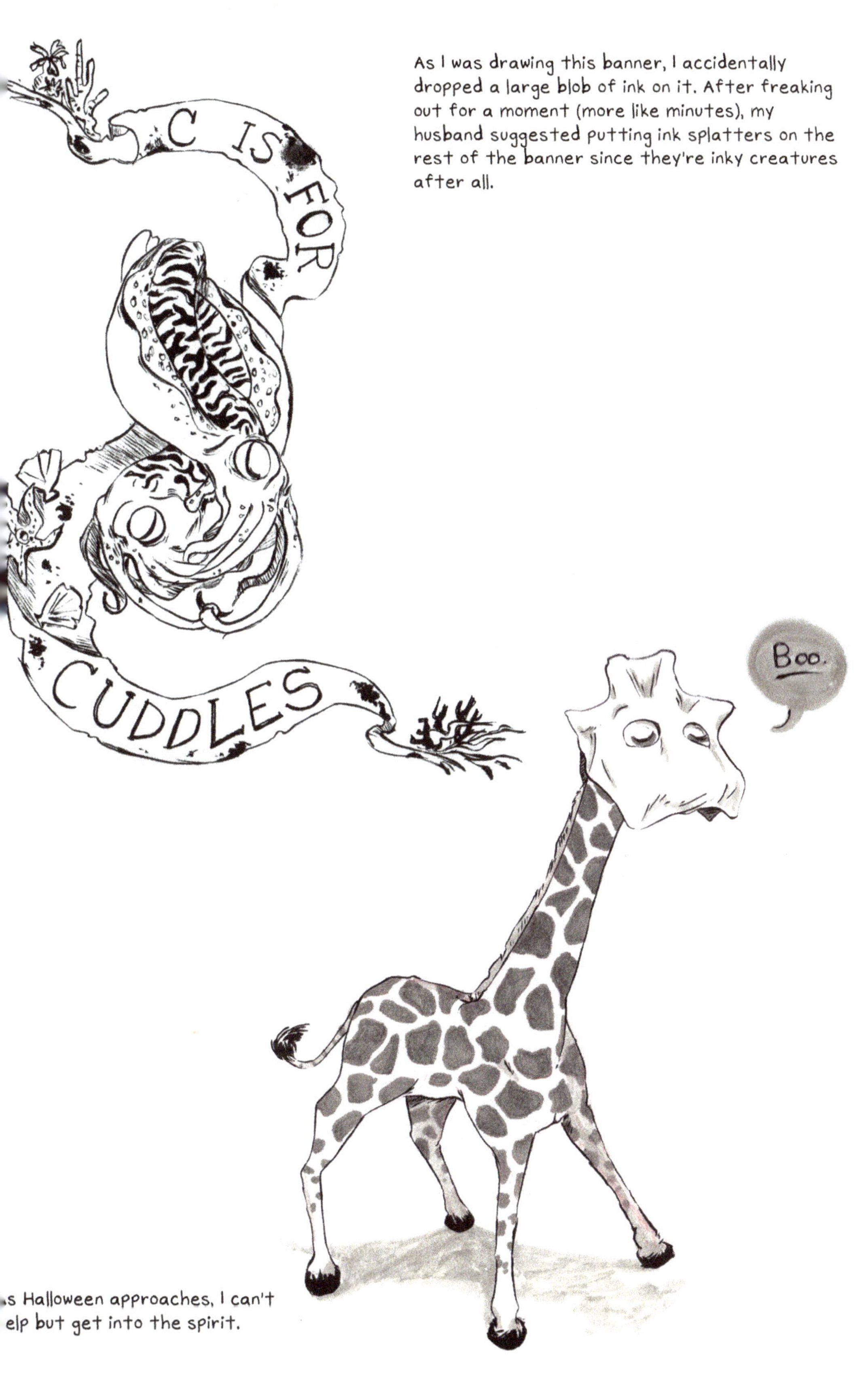

As I was drawing this banner, I accidentally dropped a large blob of ink on it. After freaking out for a moment (more like minutes), my husband suggested putting ink splatters on the rest of the banner since they're inky creatures after all.

s Halloween approaches, I can't elp but get into the spirit.

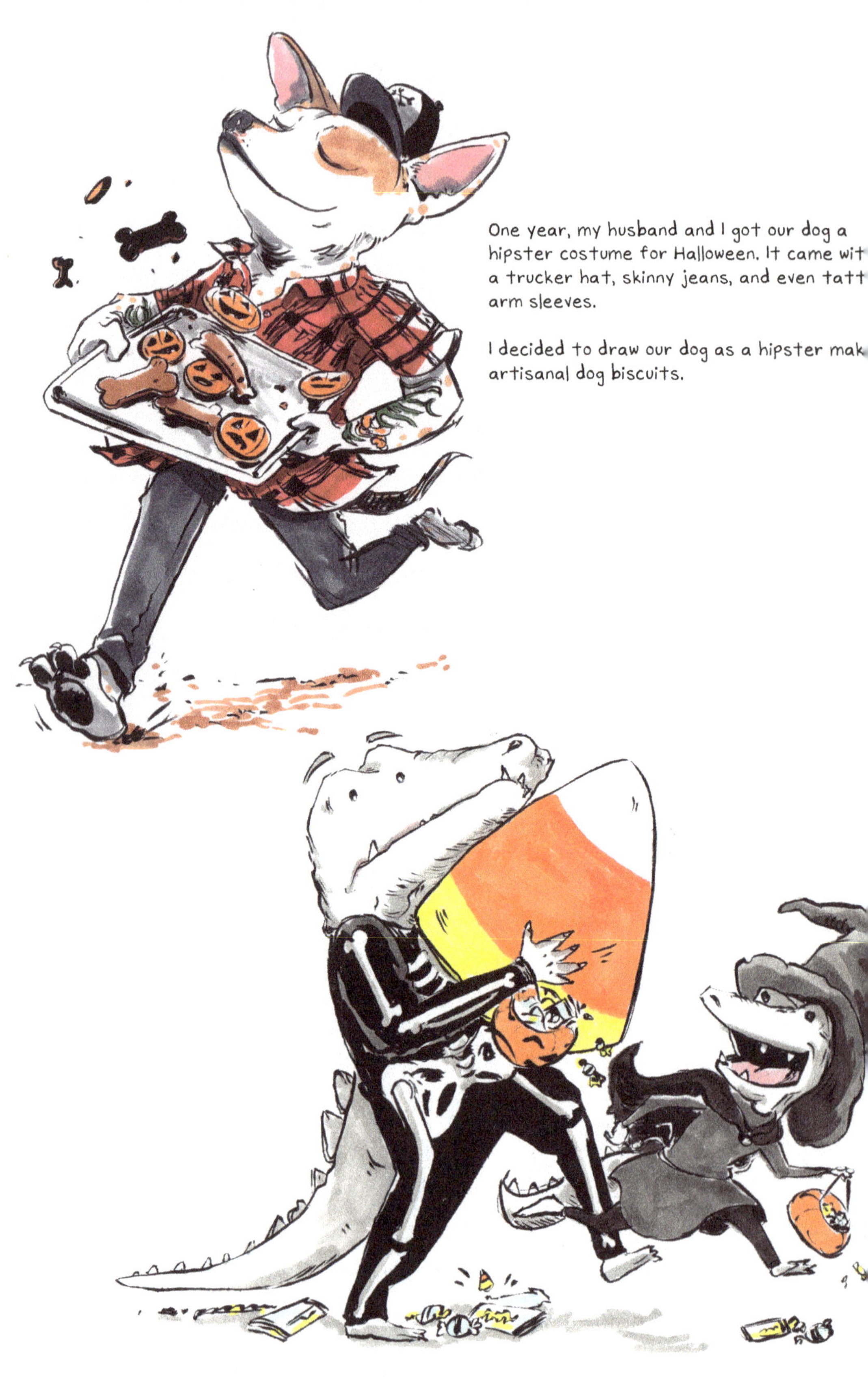

One year, my husband and I got our dog a hipster costume for Halloween. It came wit a trucker hat, skinny jeans, and even tatt arm sleeves.

I decided to draw our dog as a hipster mak artisanal dog biscuits.

PROGRESS

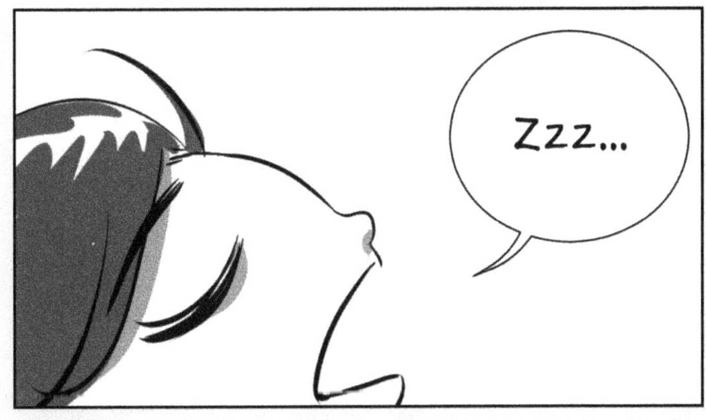

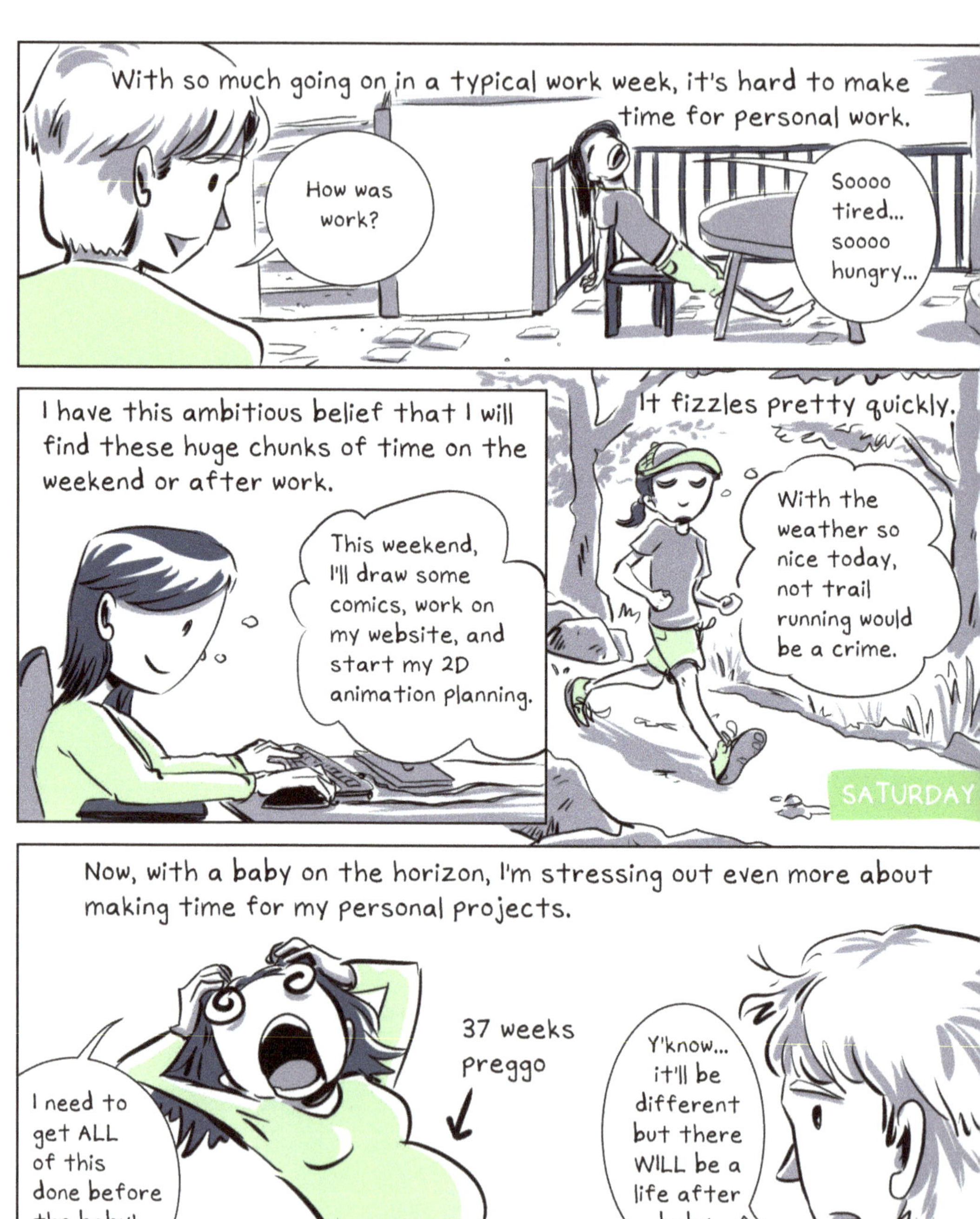

My husband has a point.

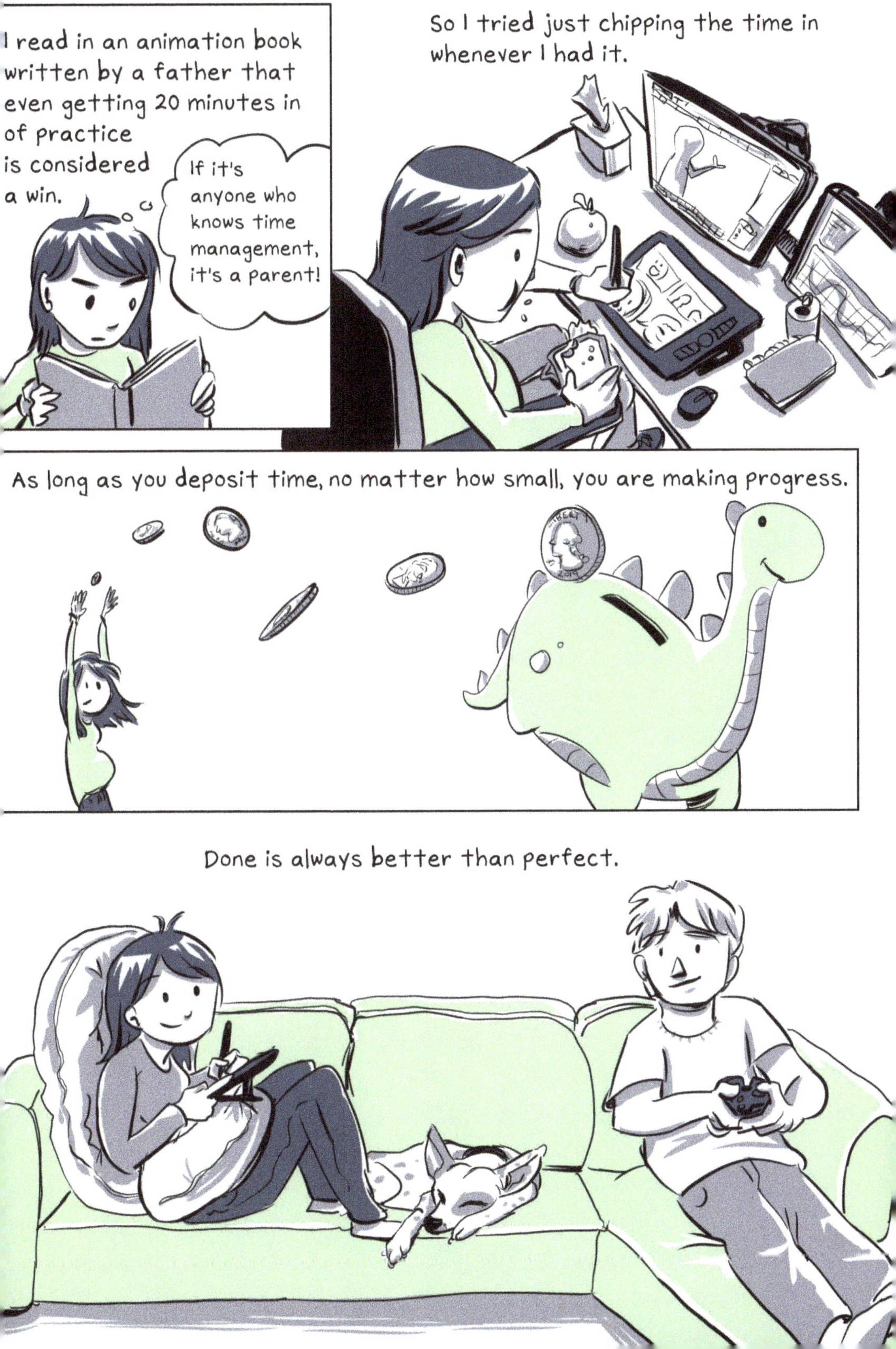

Done is always better than perfect.

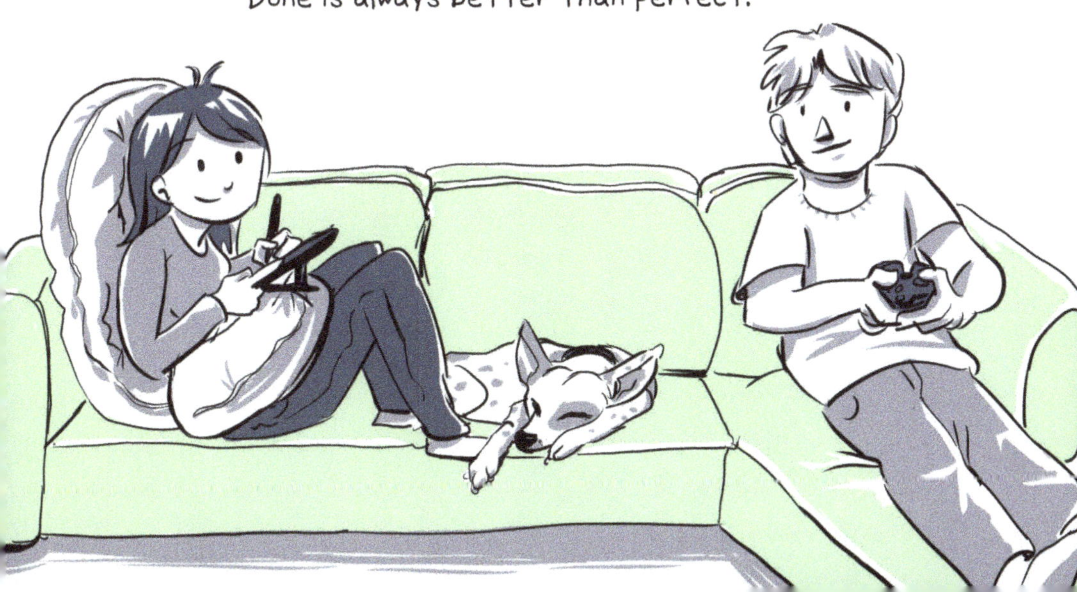

After drawing during lunch every day with my friends at work for Inktober, we decided to keep the cadence going and continue to draw during lunch after October. Lunch time ended up becoming my "go to" hour for working on personal art, whether it's sketches, comics, or even this art book.

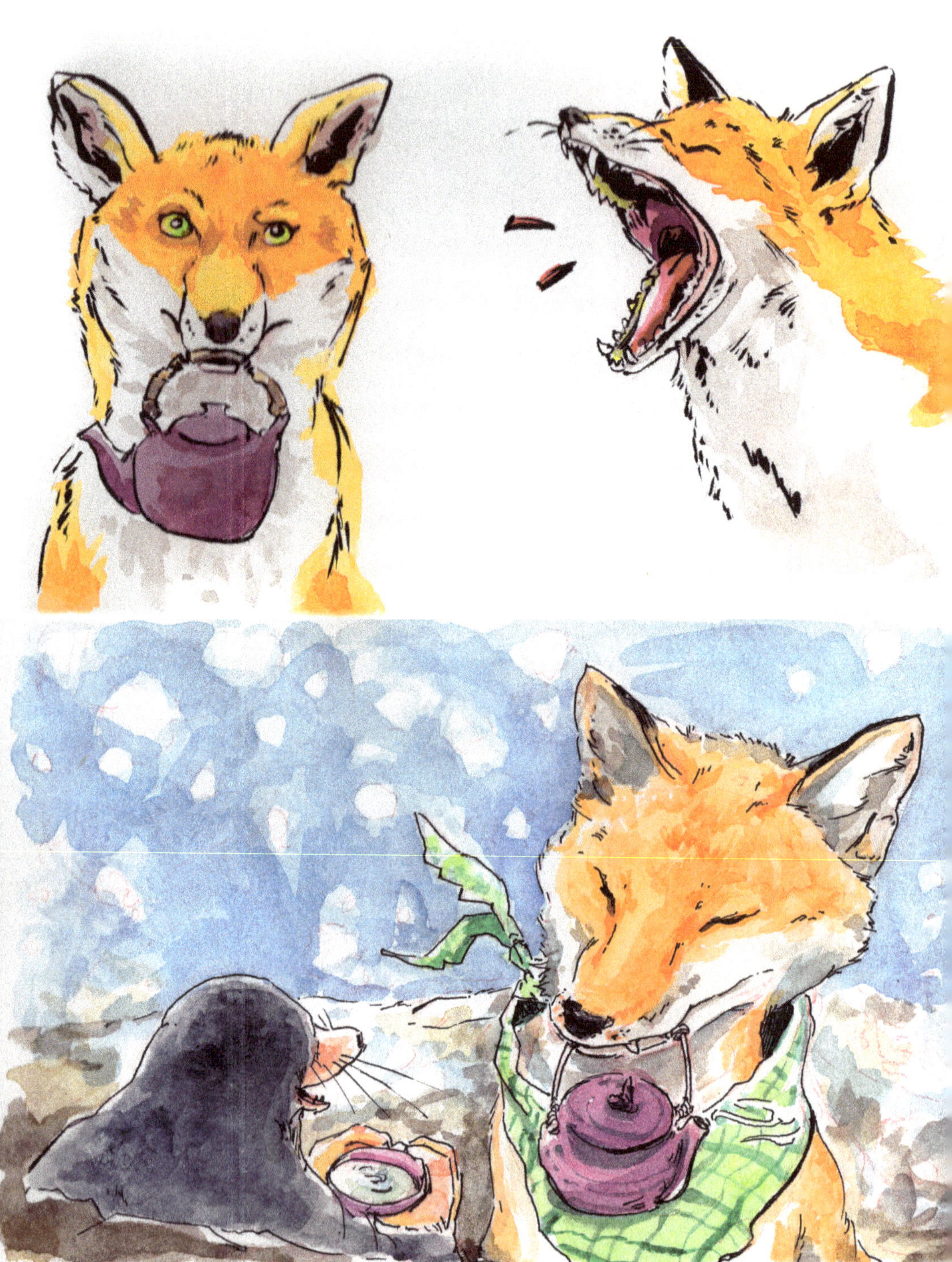

FOX FARMER

EEHOUSE STUDIES

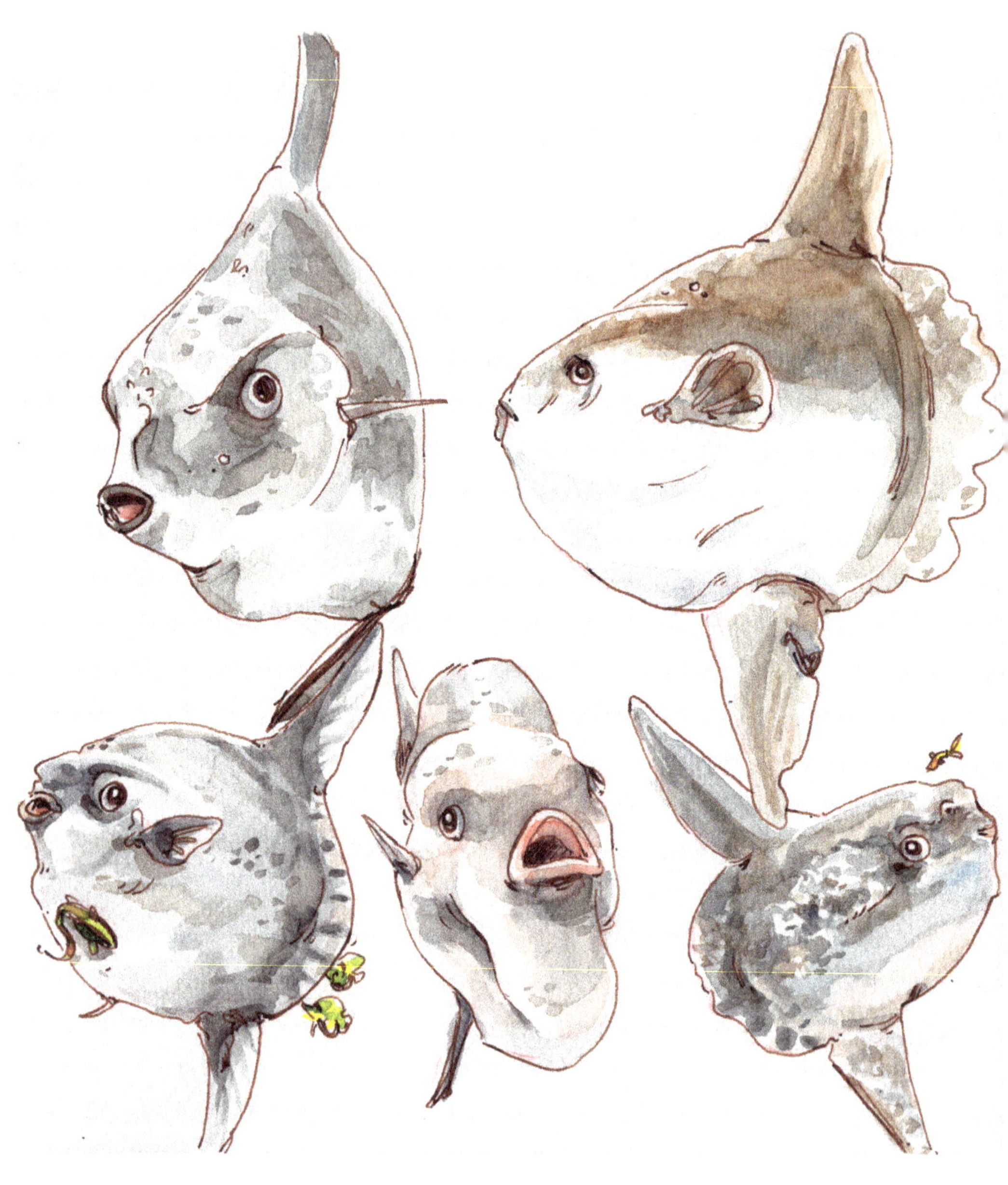

This was a fun experiment with a new ink and a new fountain pen, drawing my favorite fish, the ocean sunfish.

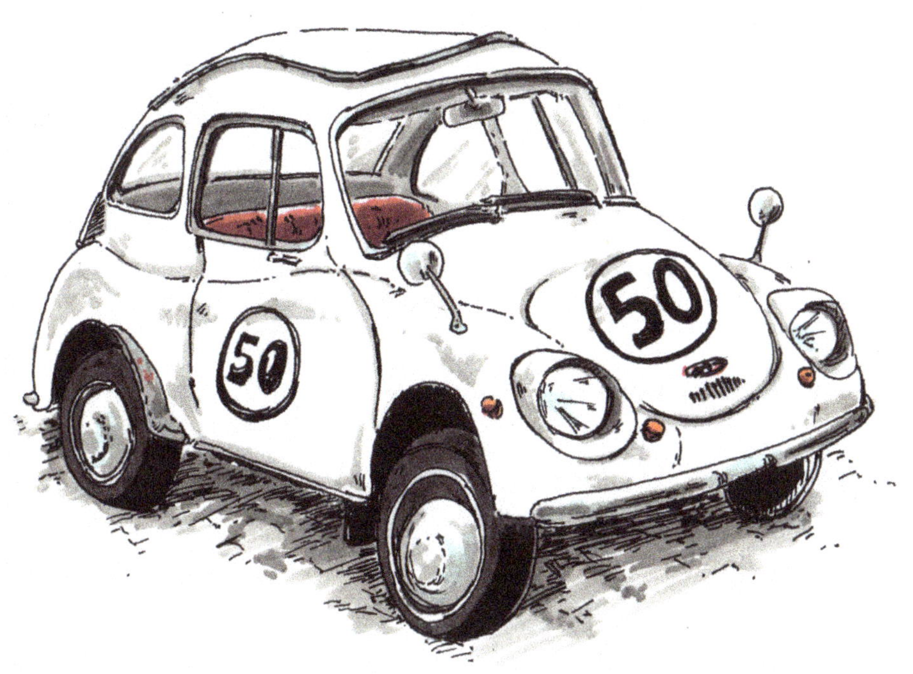

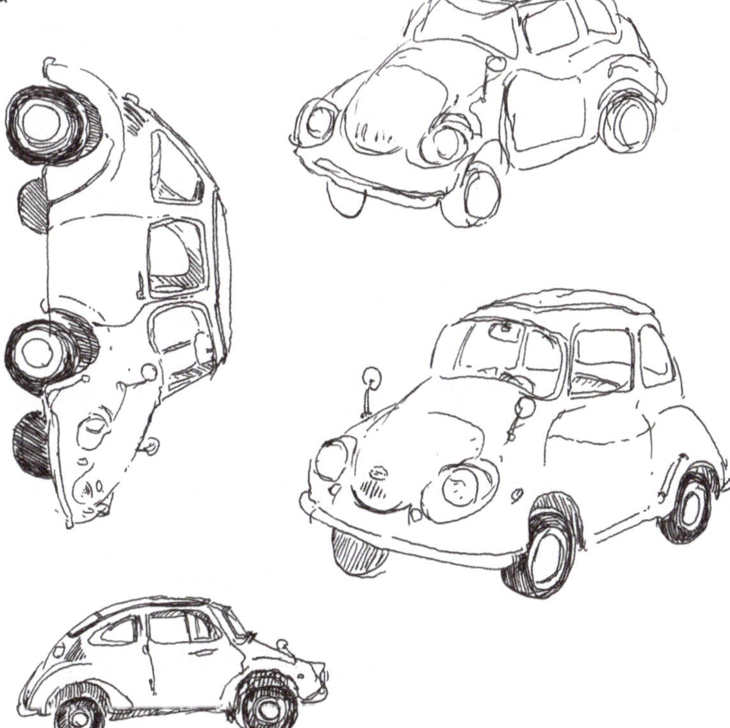

RIGHT:
Exploratory sketches for a commission before drawing the final (above).

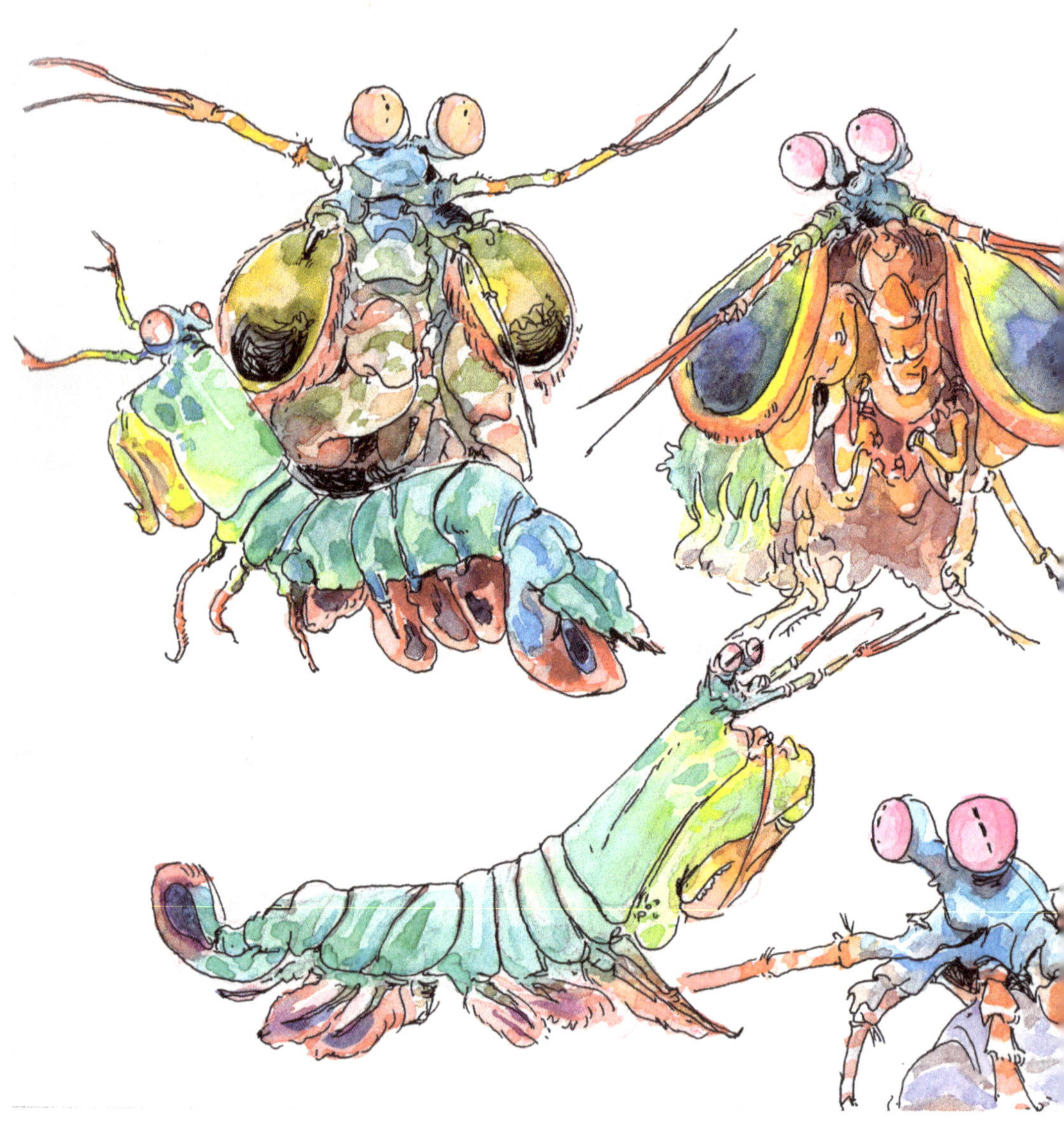

MANTIS SHRIMP STUDIES

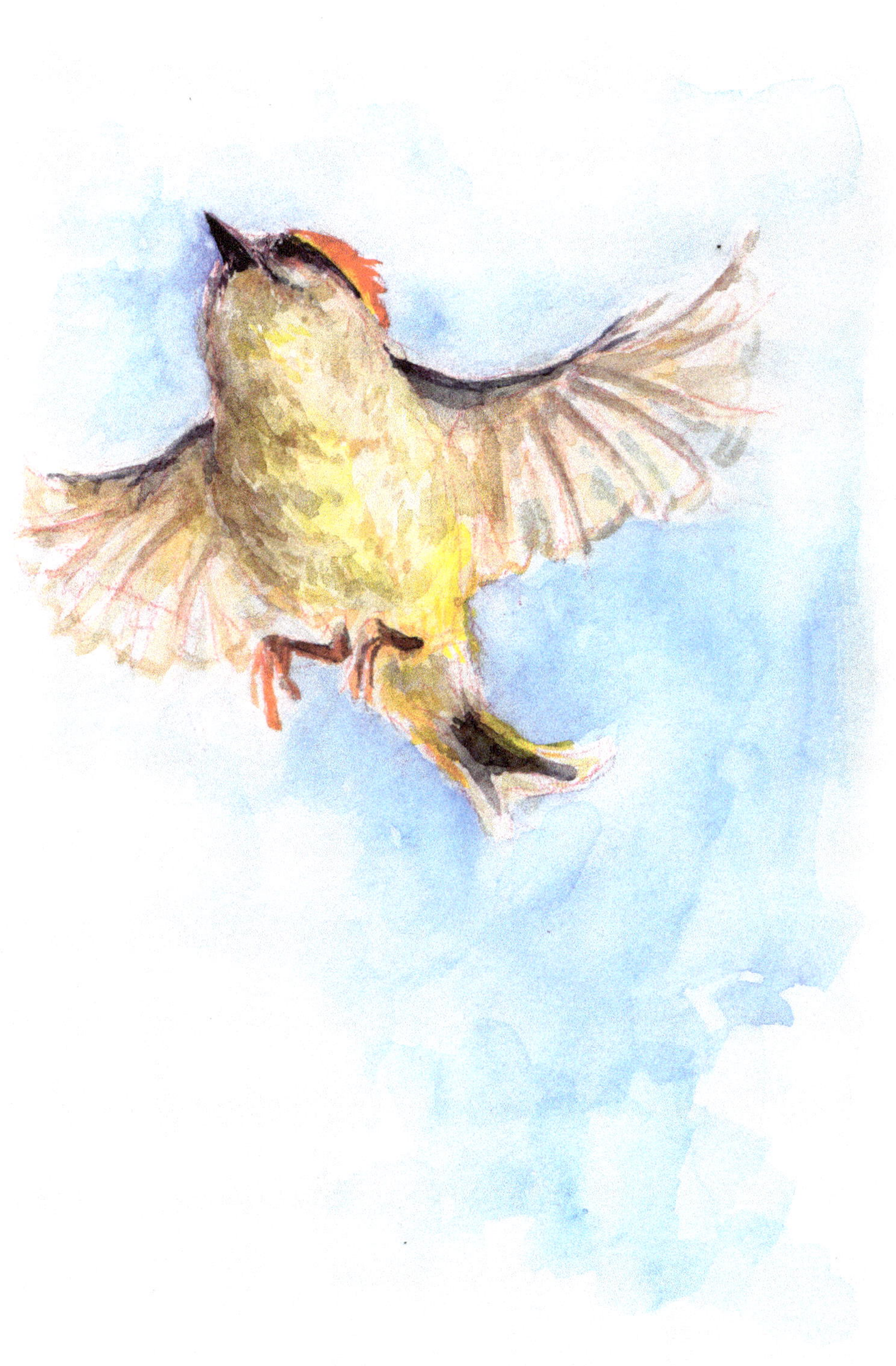

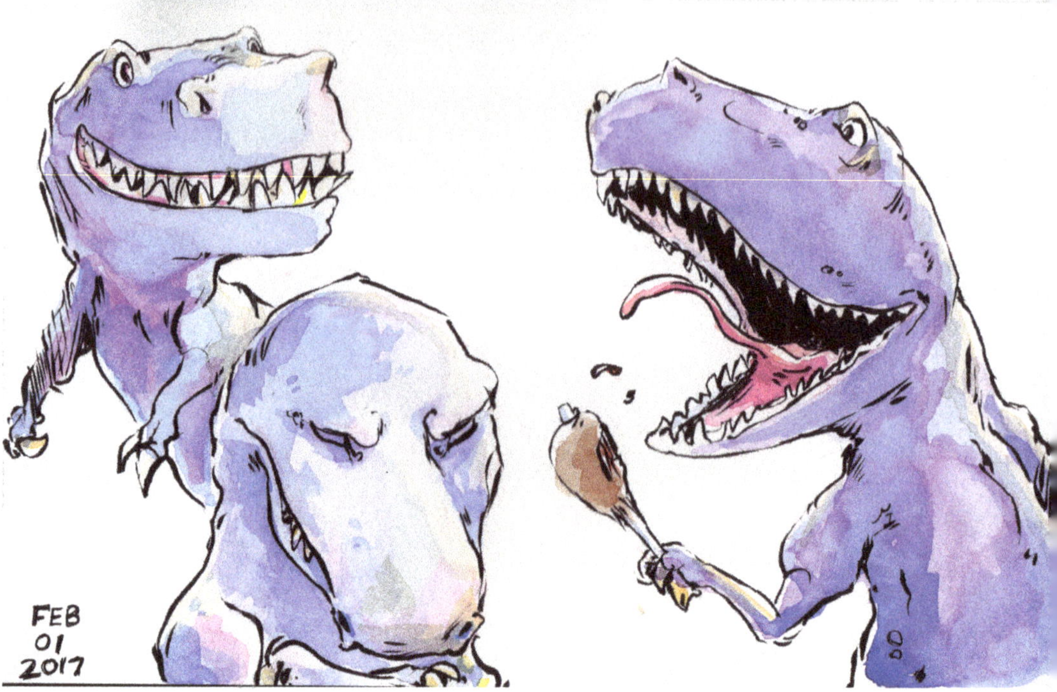

FEB
01
2017

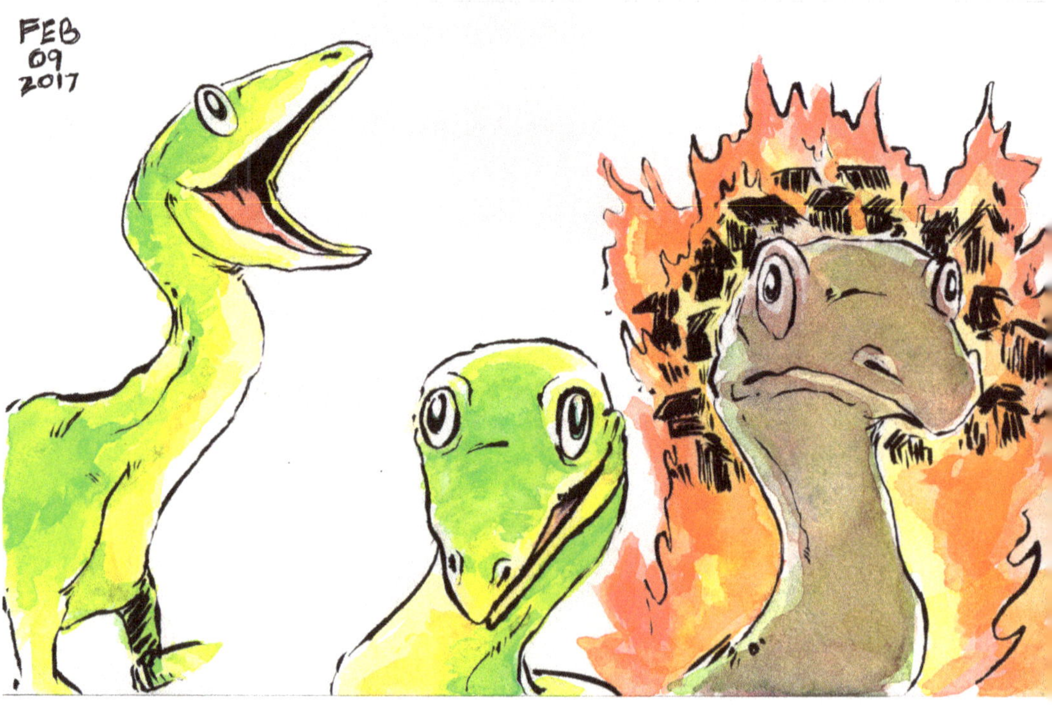

FEB
09
2017

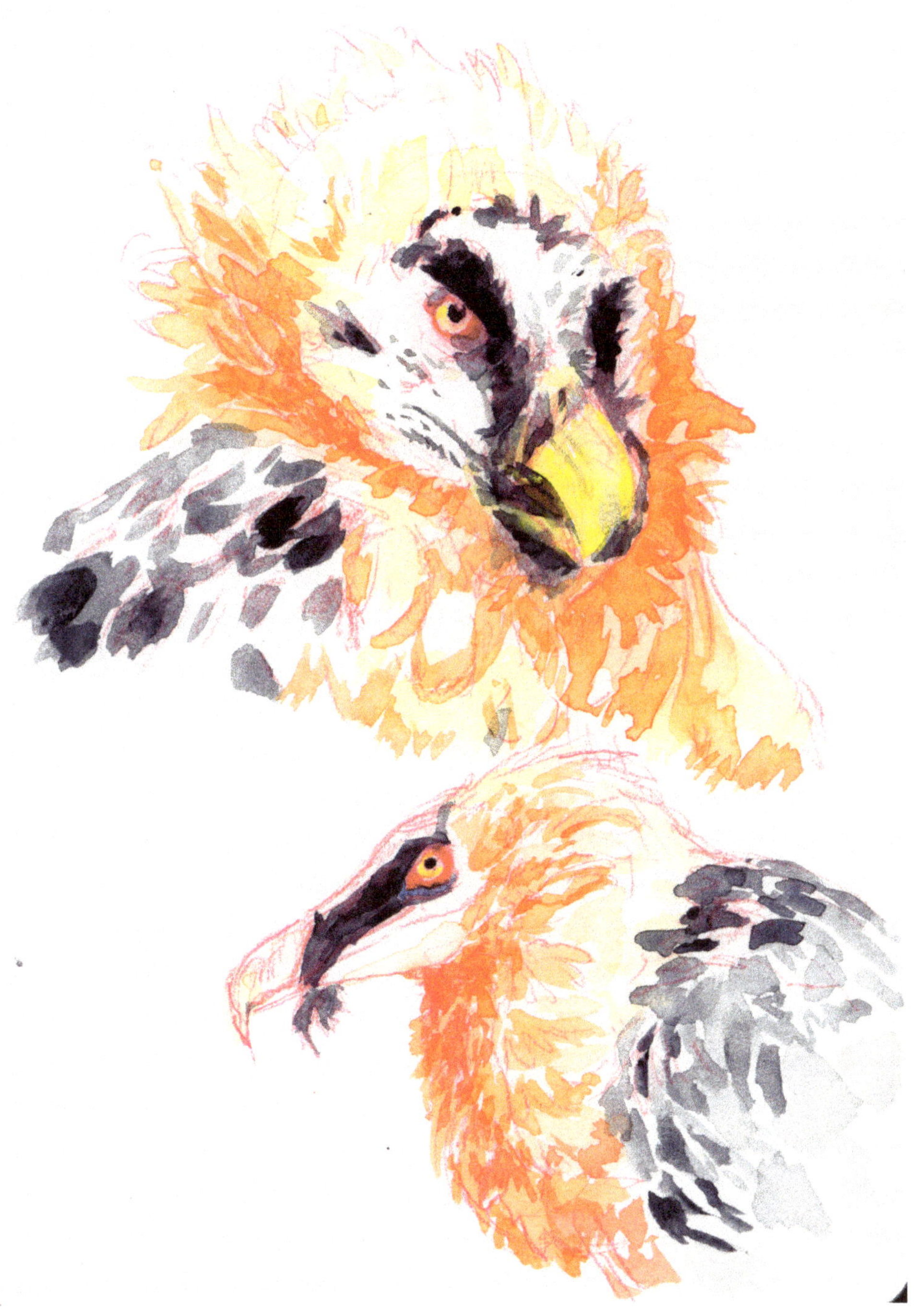

Bearded Vulture
12·22·2016

DRAWING JAM SKETCHES - Costume Room

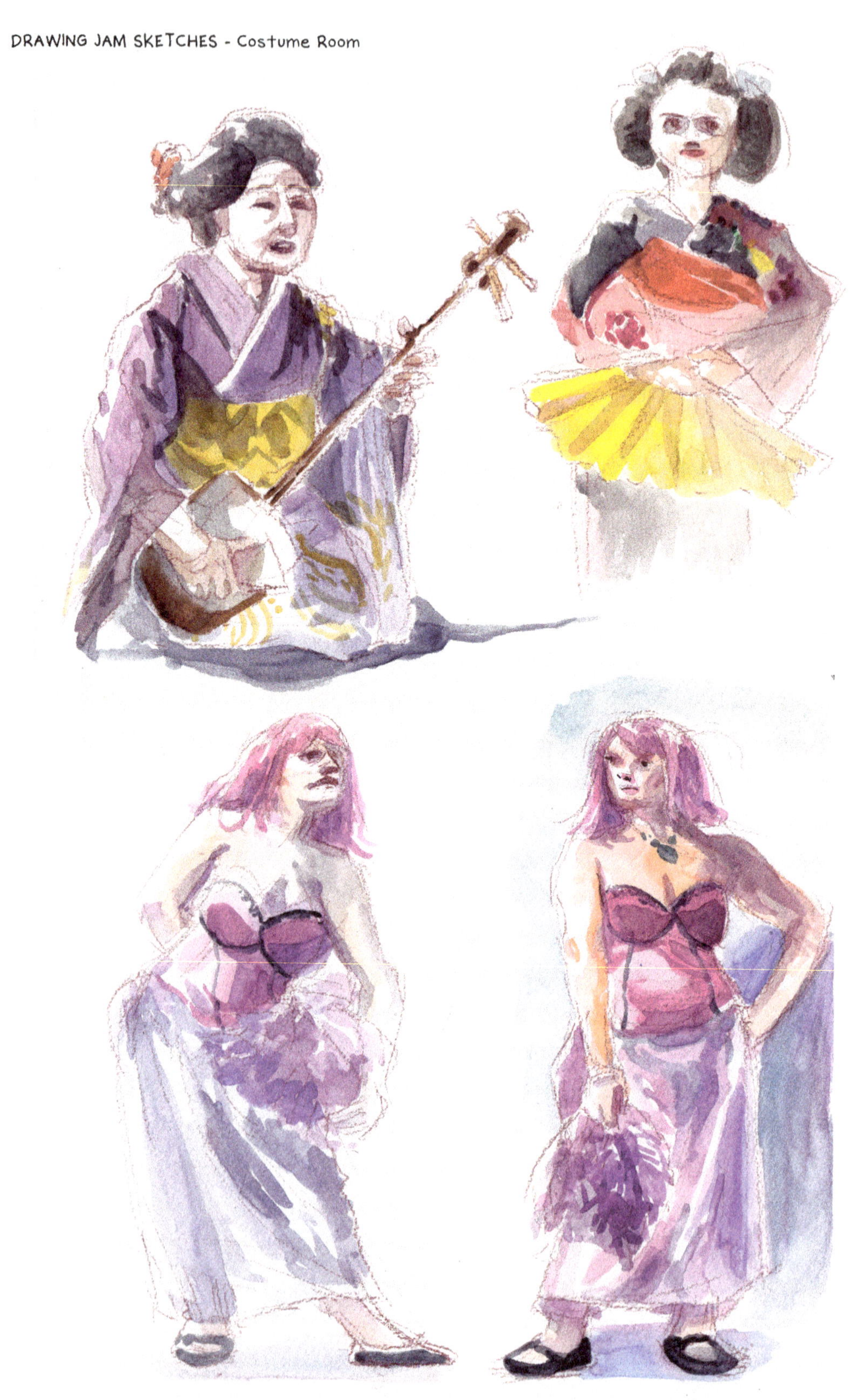

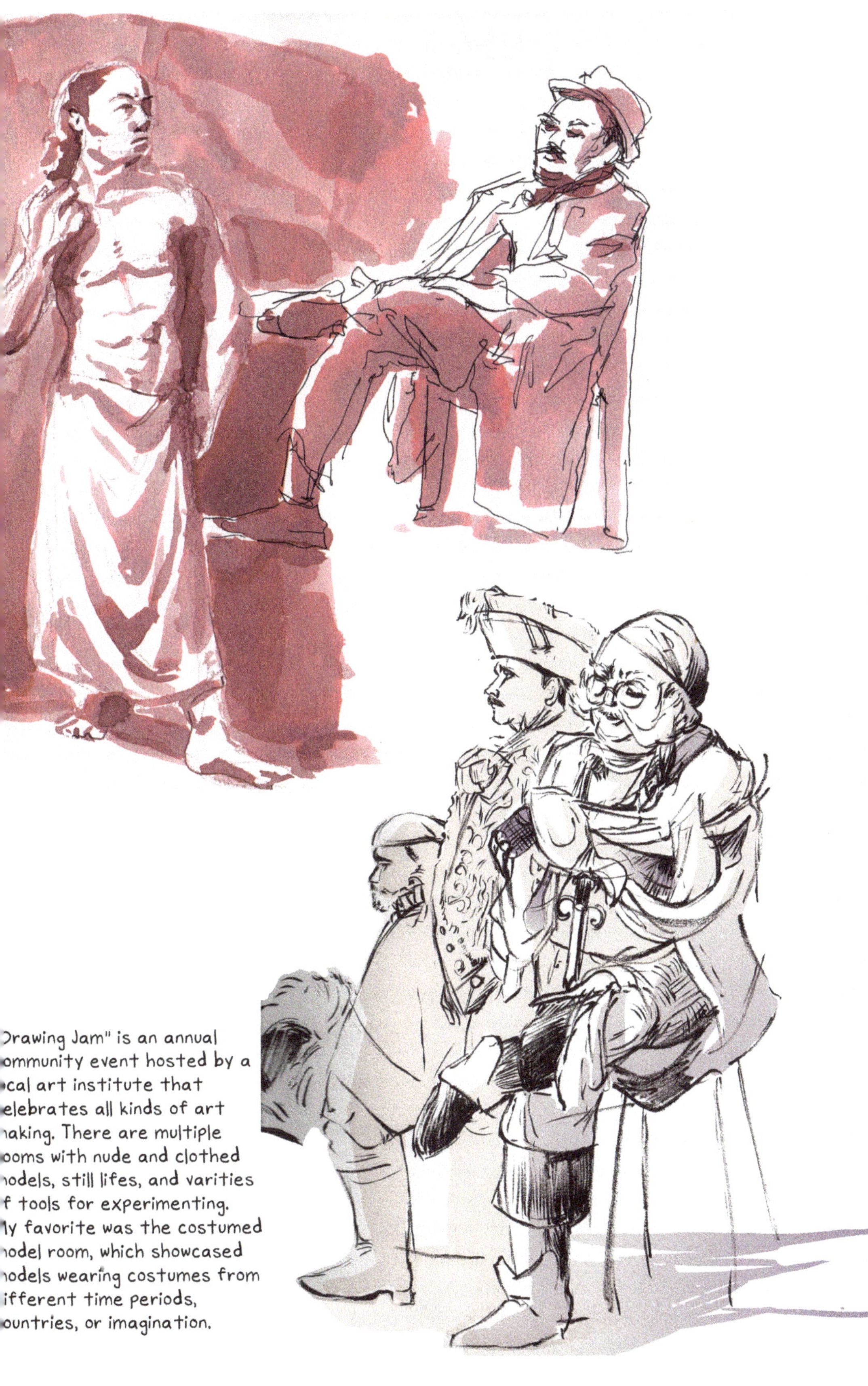

"Drawing Jam" is an annual community event hosted by a local art institute that celebrates all kinds of art making. There are multiple rooms with nude and clothed models, still lifes, and varities of tools for experimenting. My favorite was the costumed model room, which showcased models wearing costumes from different time periods, countries, or imagination.

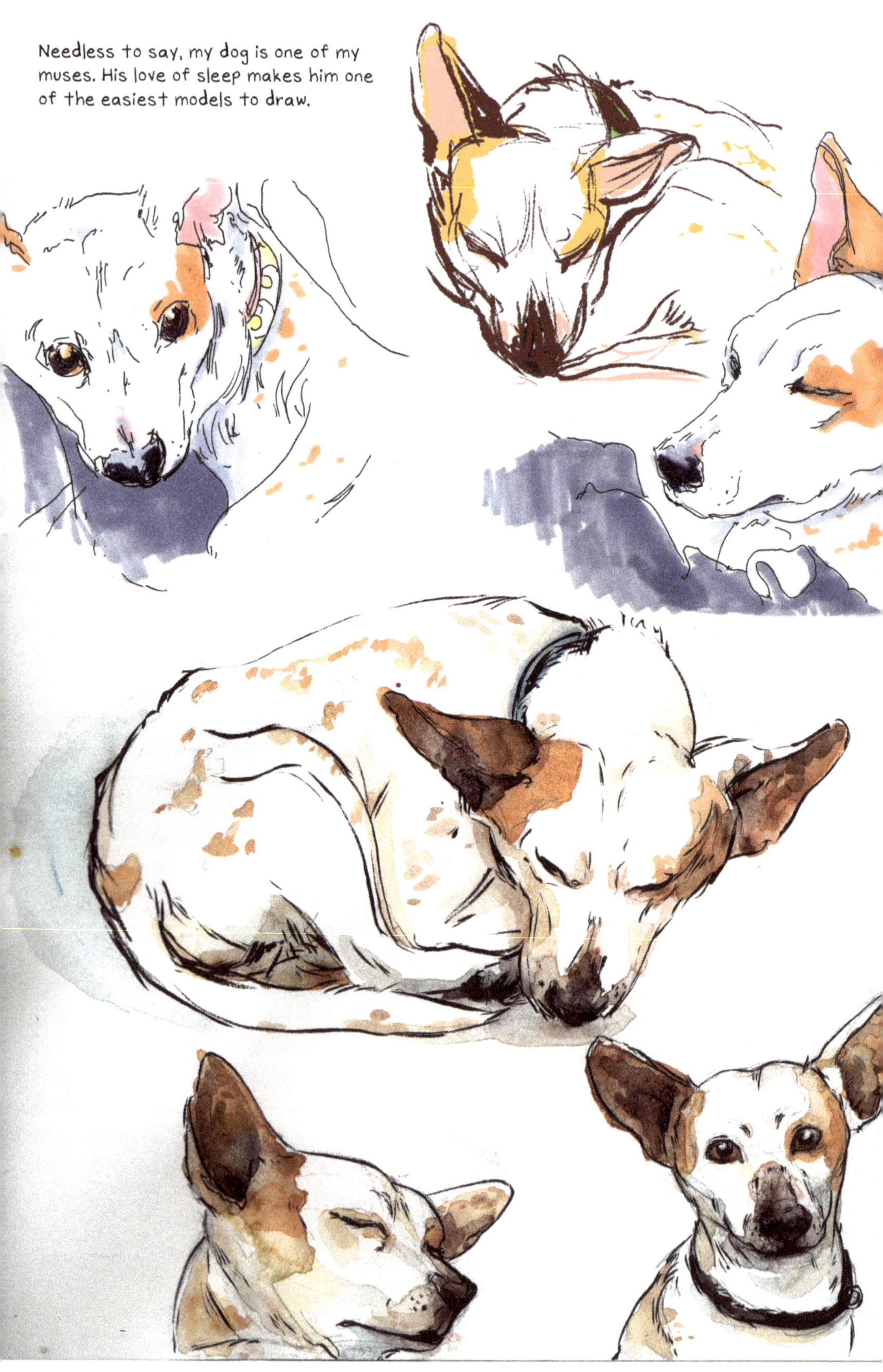

Needless to say, my dog is one of my muses. His love of sleep makes him one of the easiest models to draw.

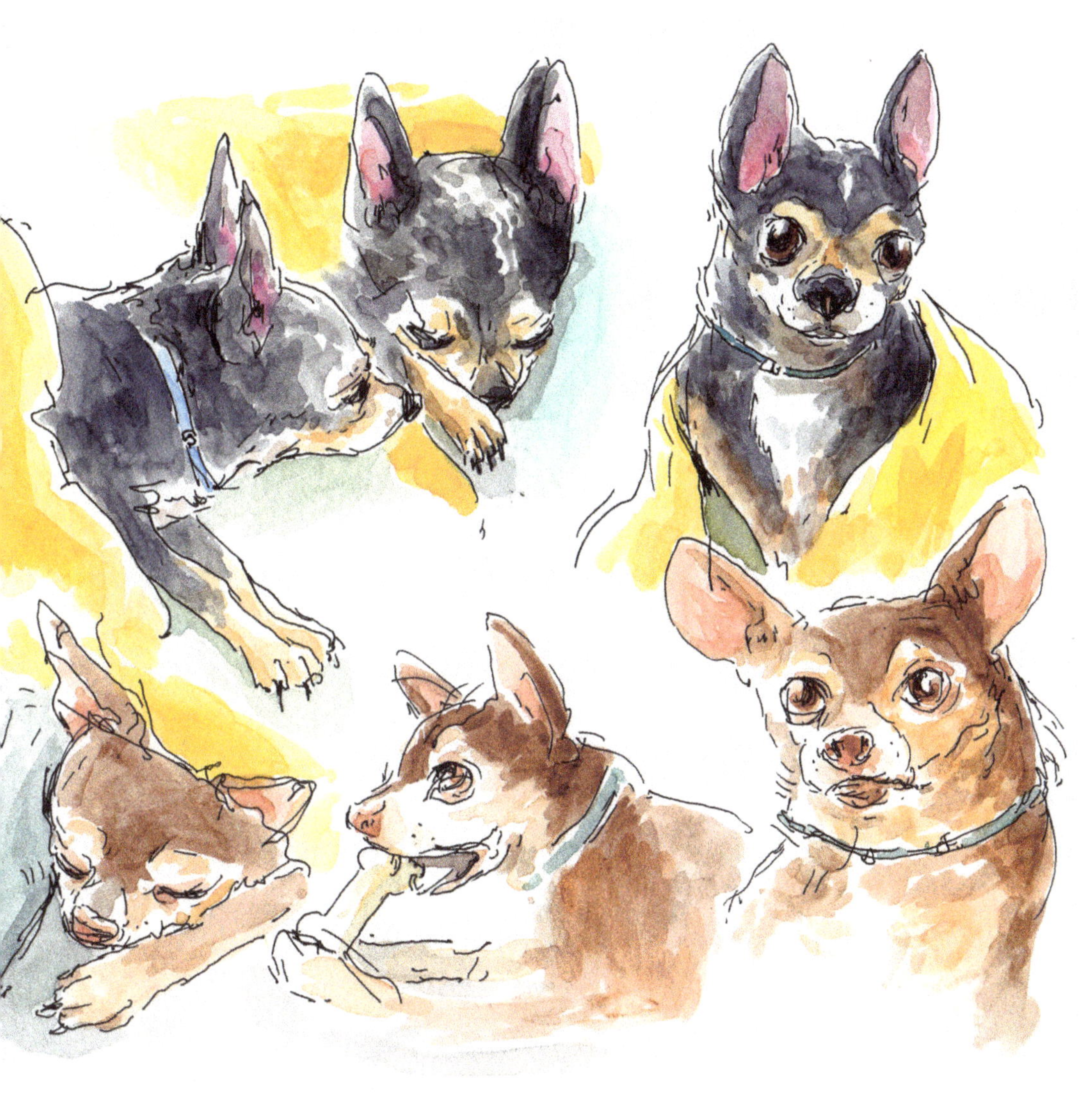

MAMA'S BOYS

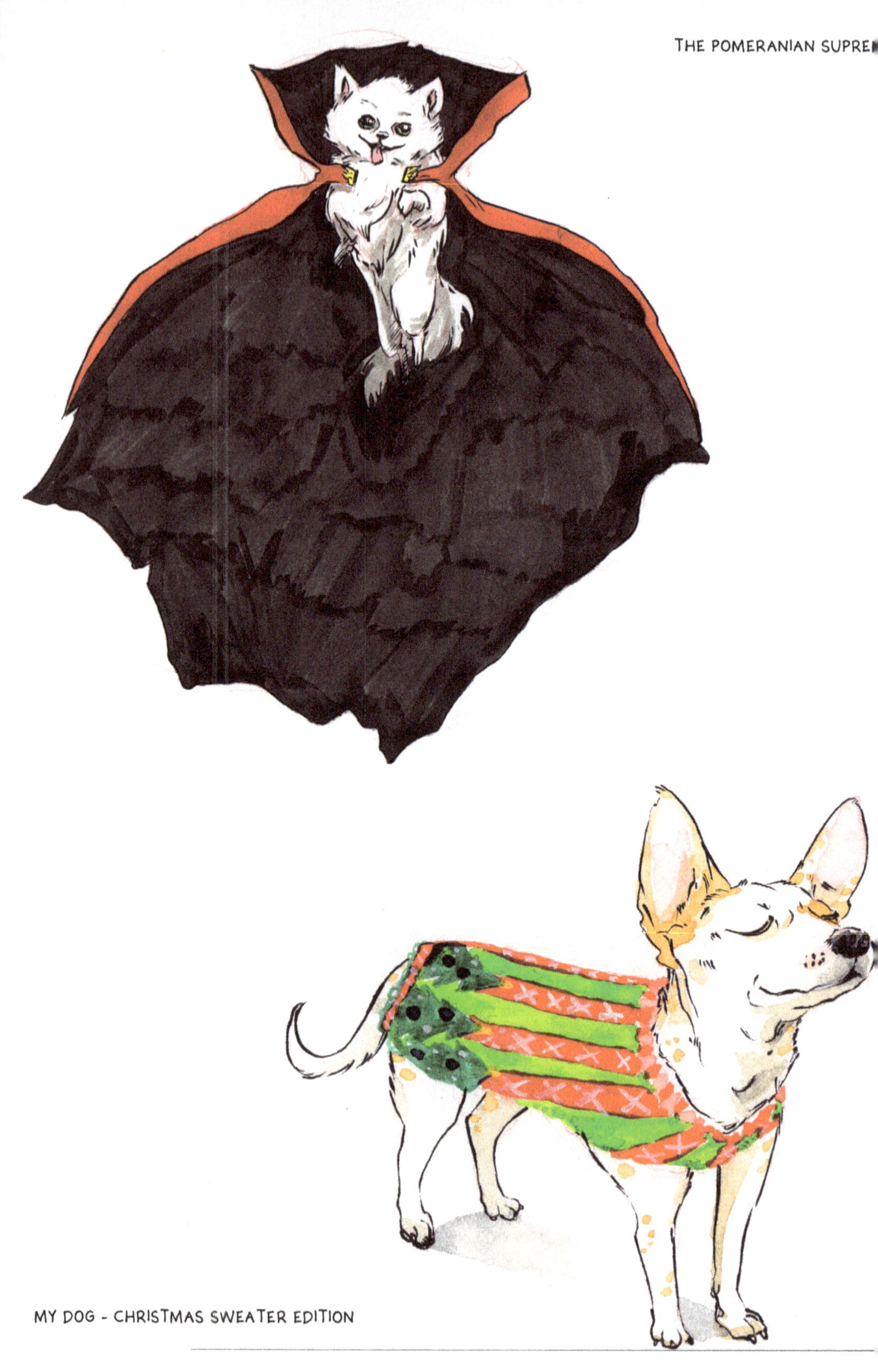

MY DOG - CHRISTMAS SWEATER EDITION

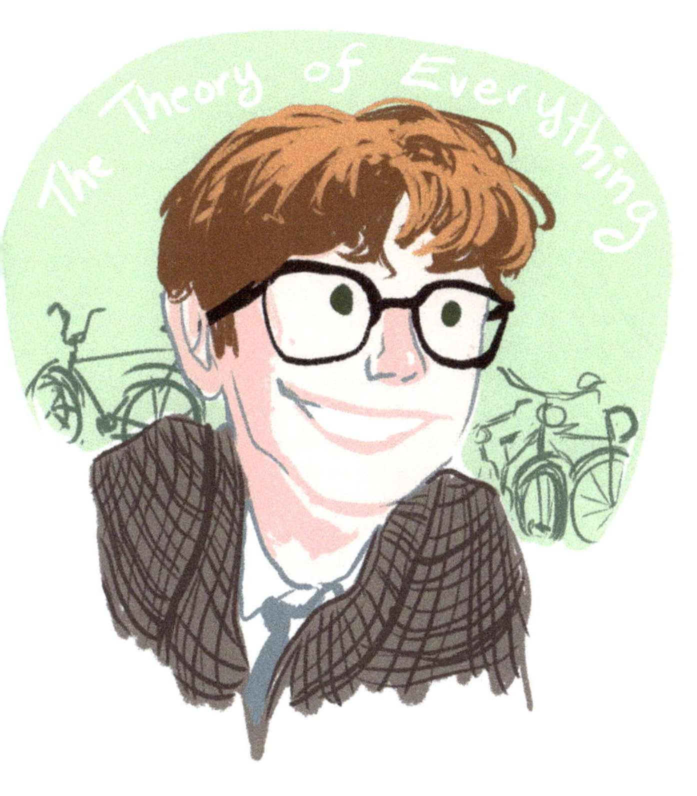
The Theory of Everything

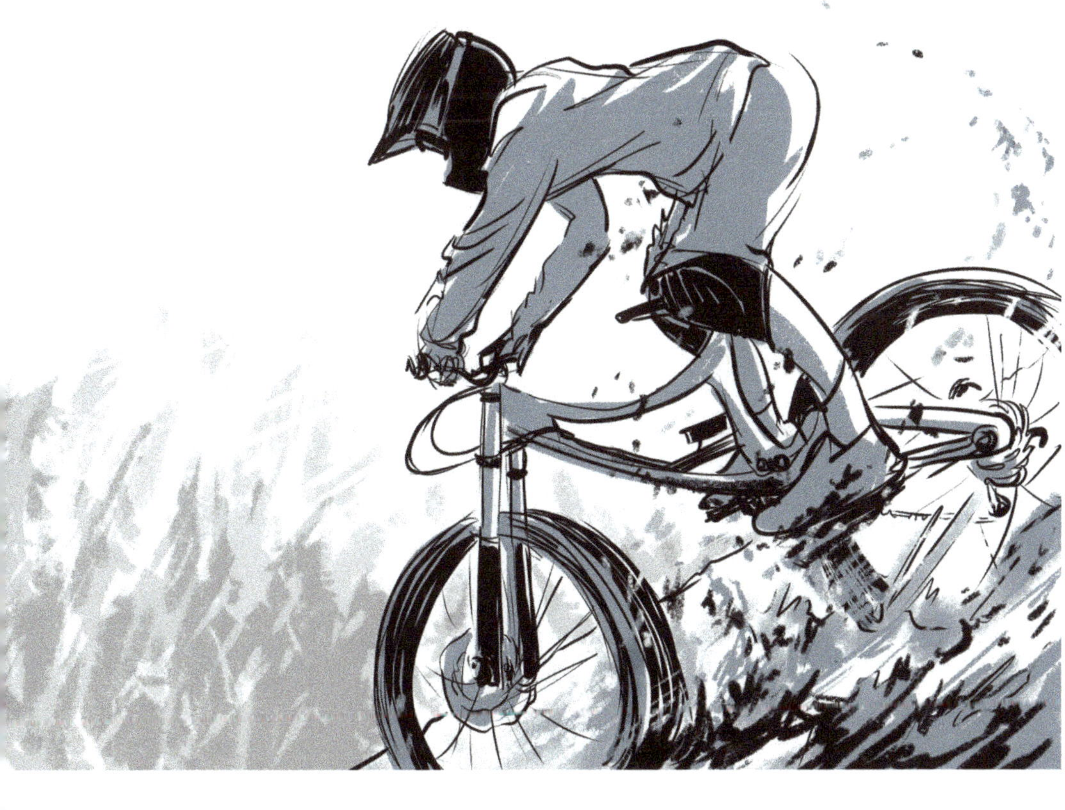

Journal comics are anot[her]
passion of mine. My poor
husband has no choice b[ut]
to be in them.

BELOW: Changing into pajamas is my favorite after-work activi[ty]

Guys Night Out

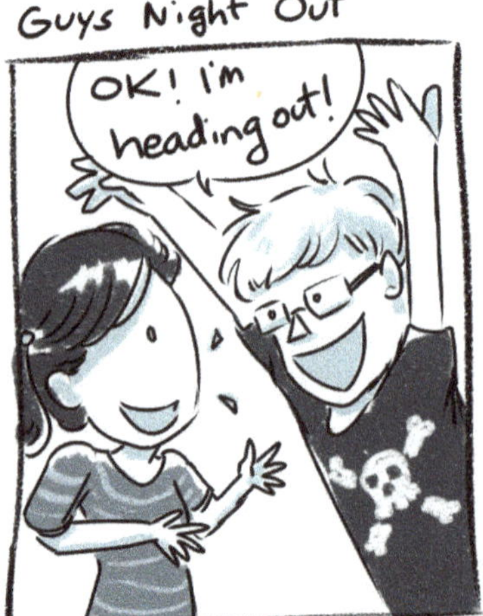

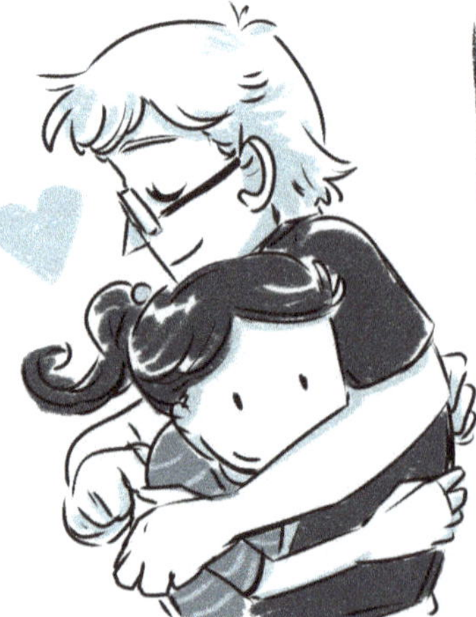

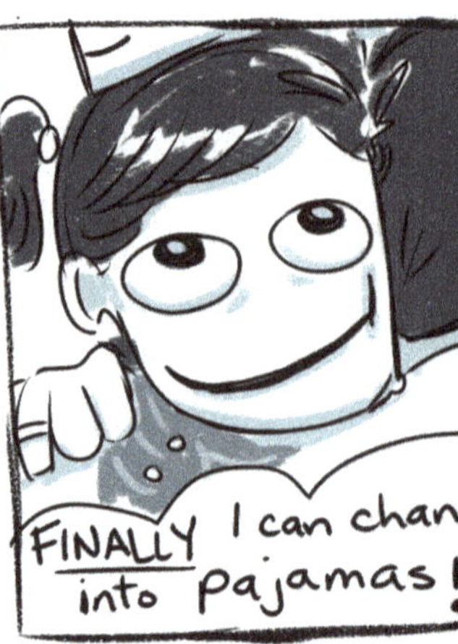

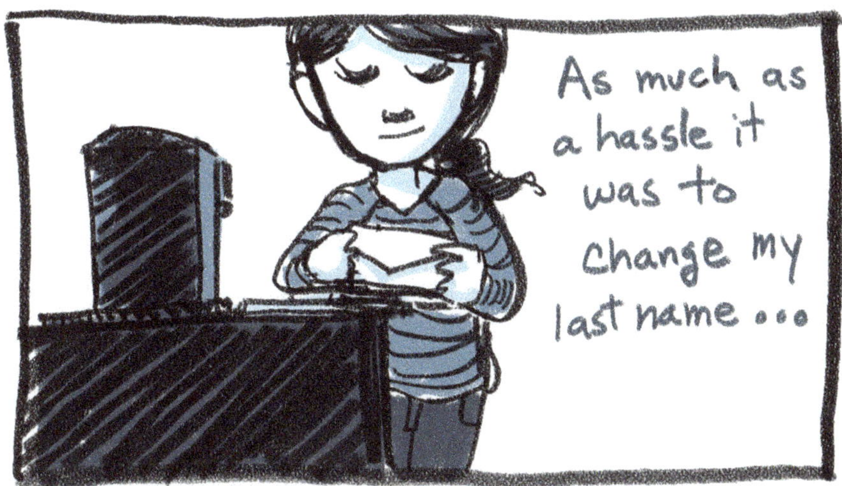
As much as a hassle it was to change my last name...

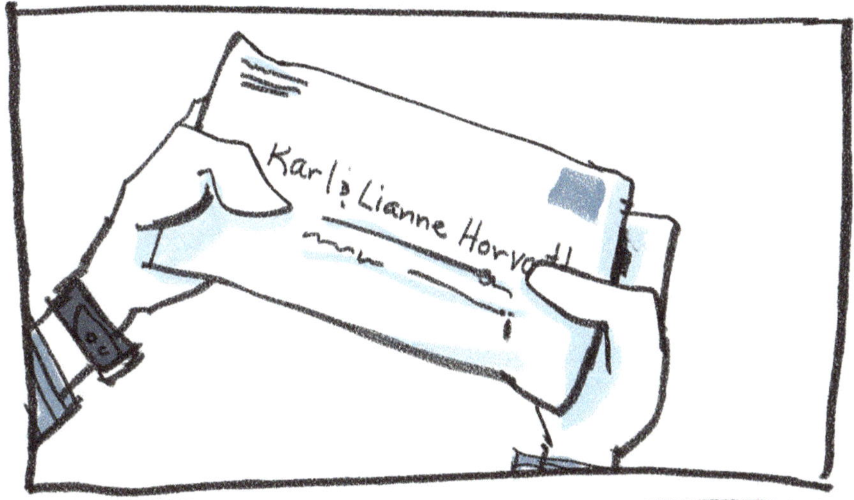
Karl & Lianne Horvo

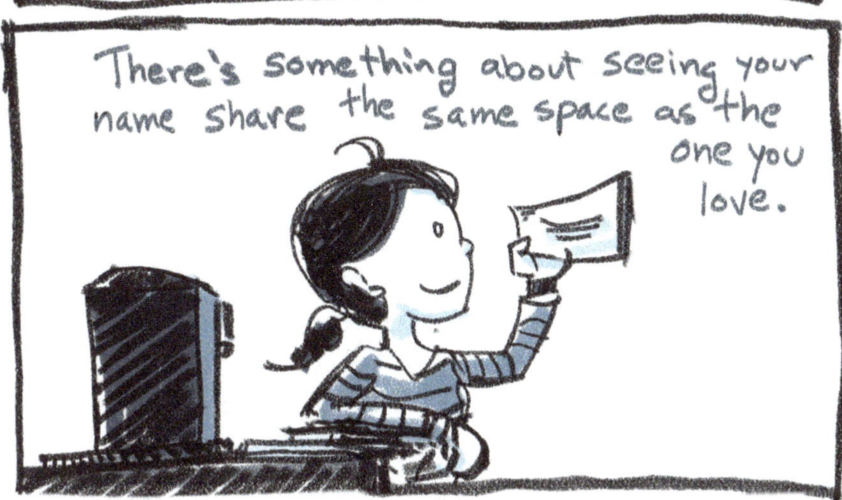
There's something about seeing your name share the same space as the one you love.

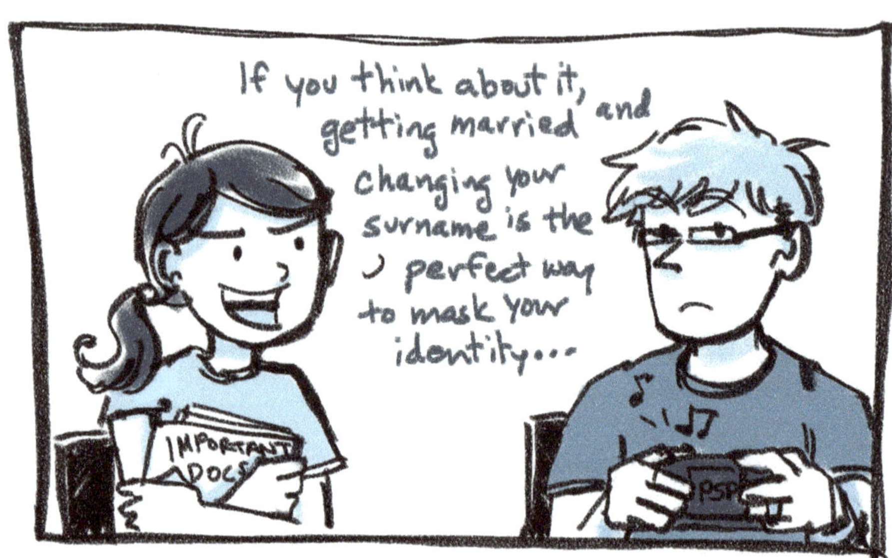

If you think about it, getting married and changing your surname is the perfect way to mask your identity...
IMPORTANT DOCS

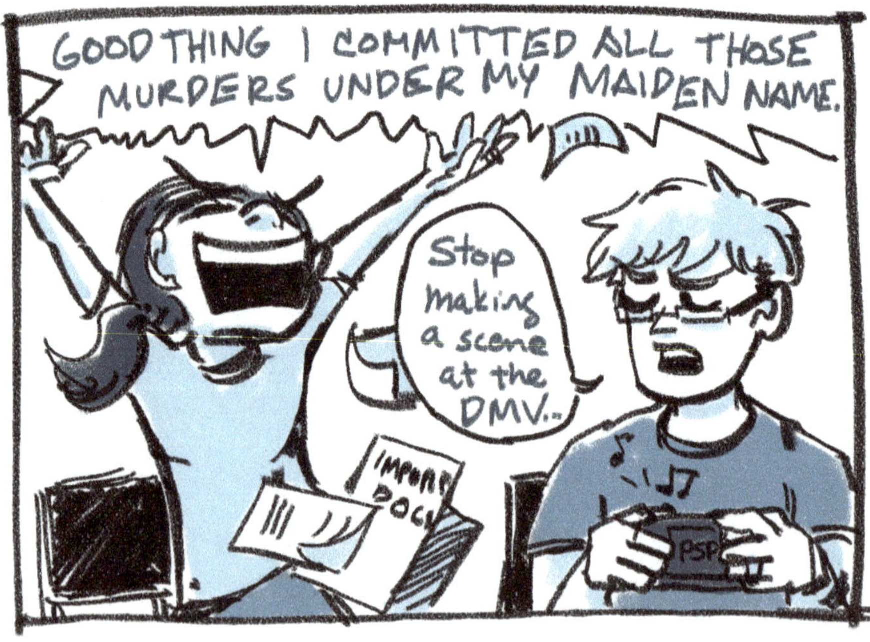

GOOD THING I COMMITTED ALL THOSE MURDERS UNDER MY MAIDEN NAME.
Stop making a scene at the DMV...
IMPORT DOCS

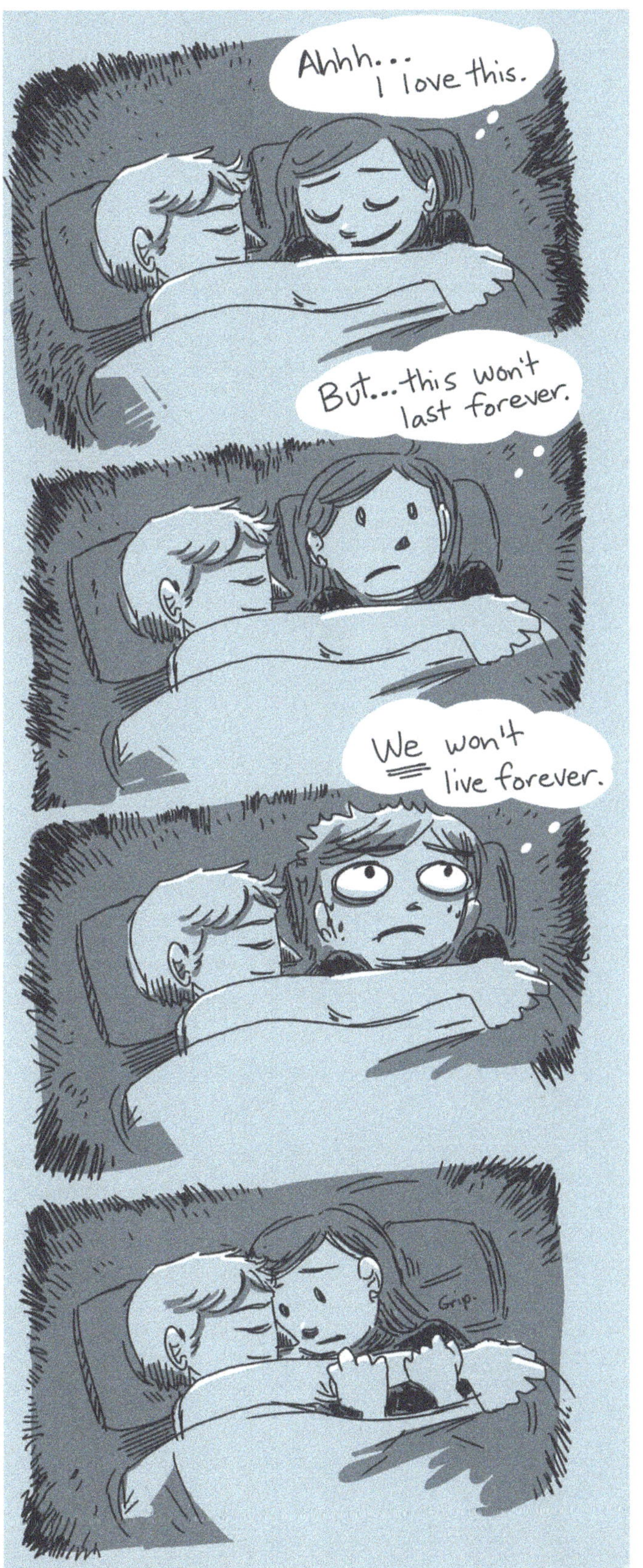

My thoughts get the best of me at 3am.

BUT HOW SAFE ARE YOU, REALLY?

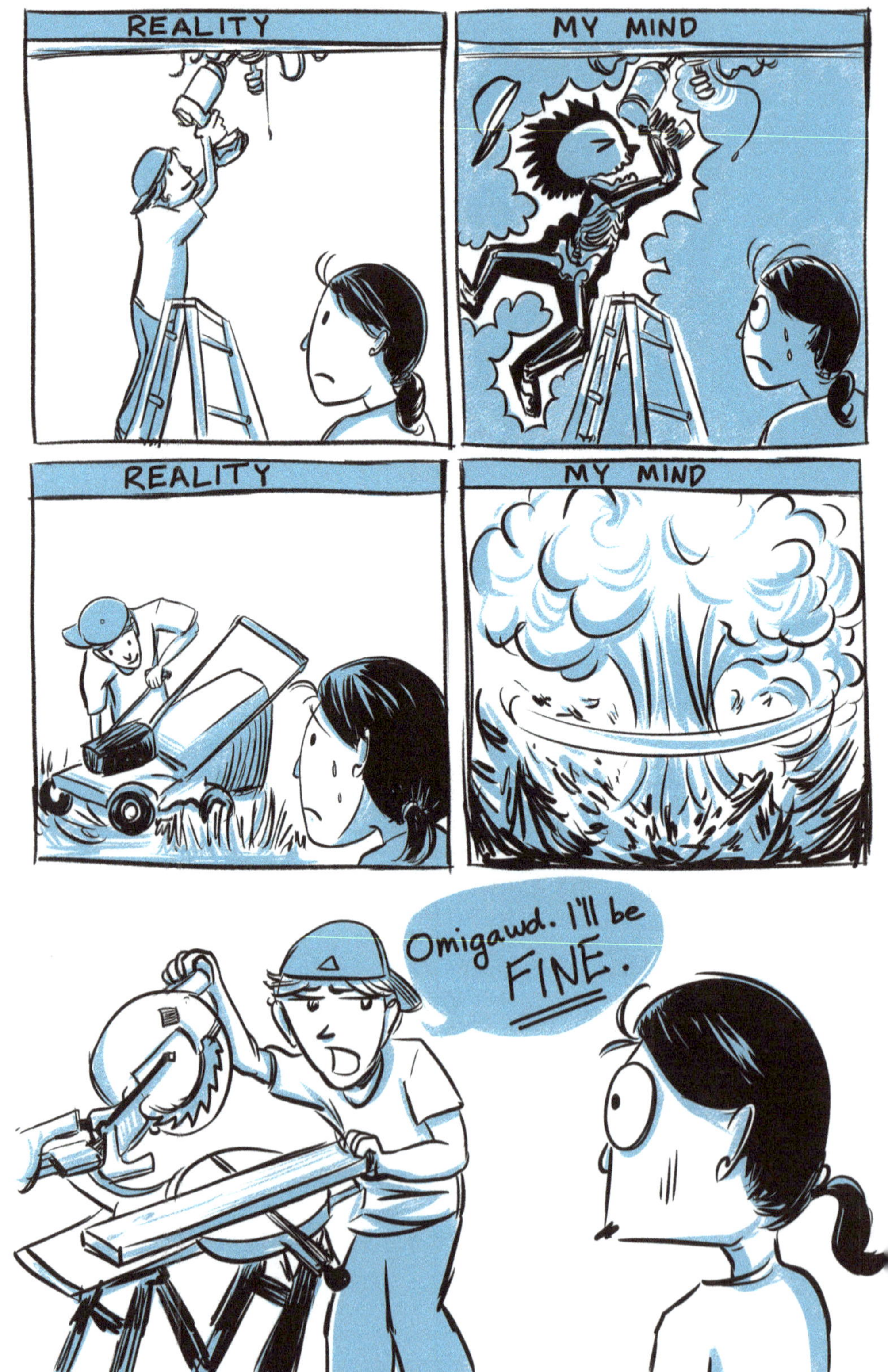
REALITY
MY MIND
REALITY
MY MIND
Omigawd. I'll be FINE.

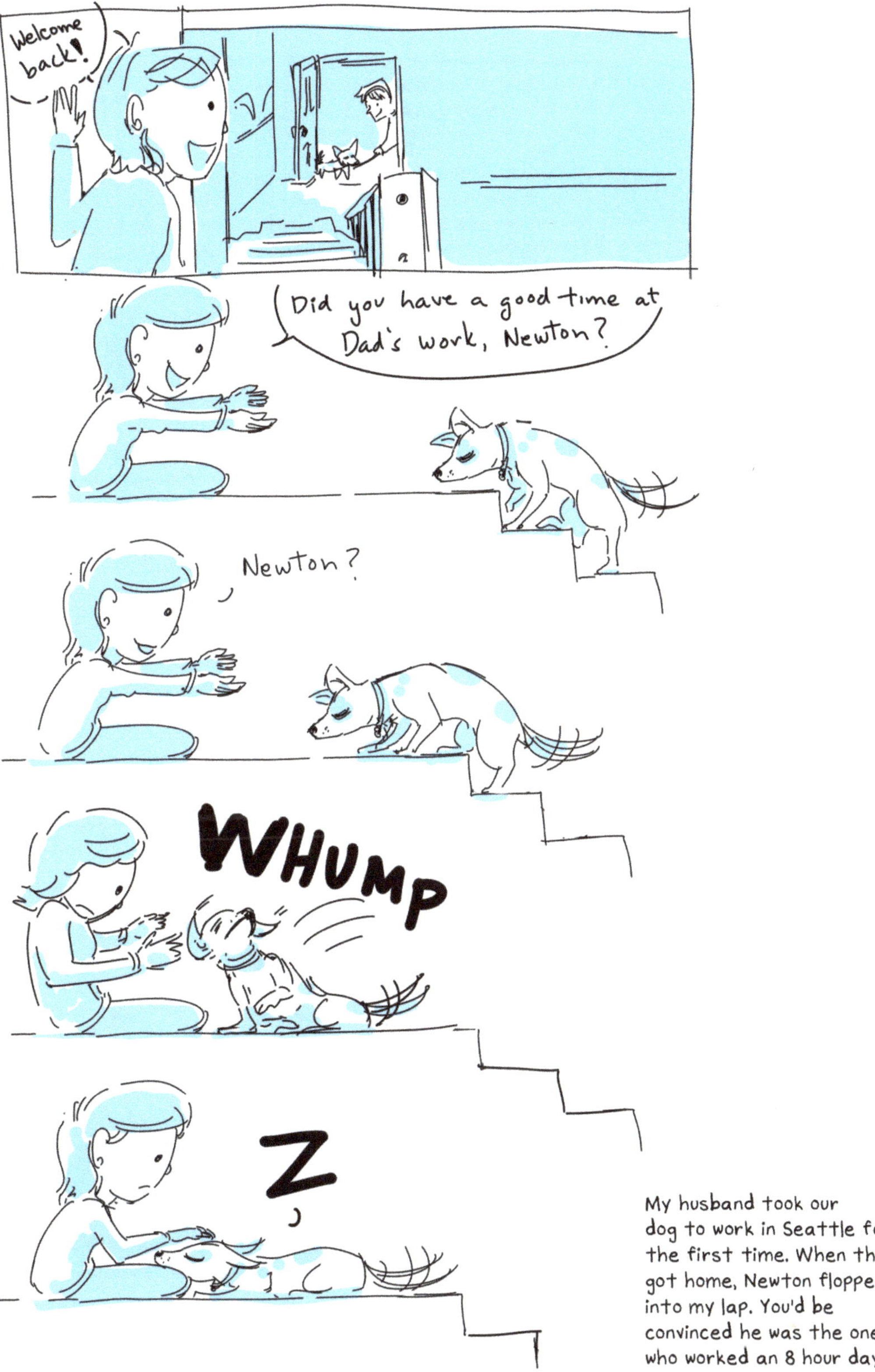

My husband took our dog to work in Seattle for the first time. When they got home, Newton flopped into my lap. You'd be convinced he was the one who worked an 8 hour day!

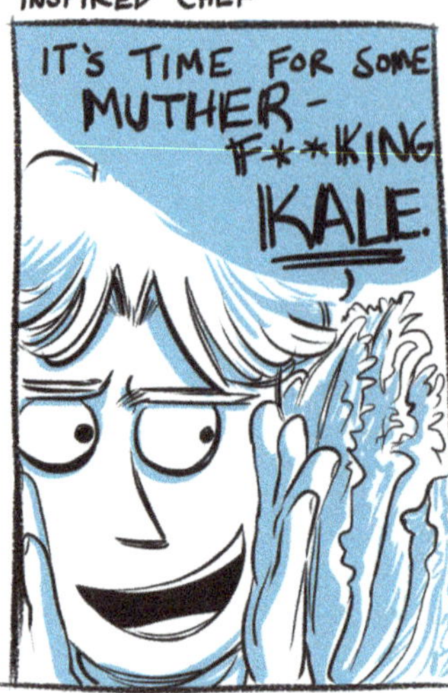

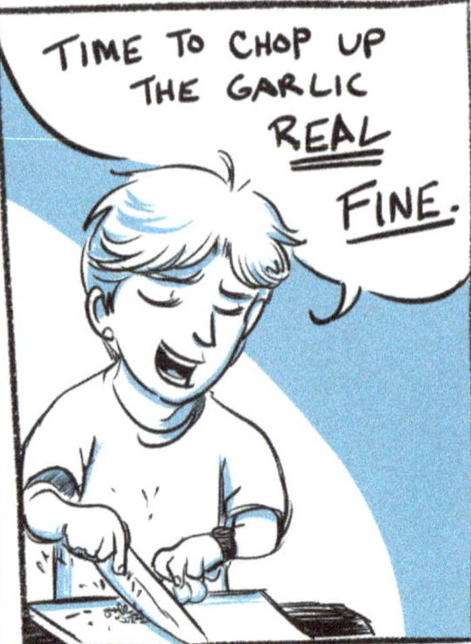

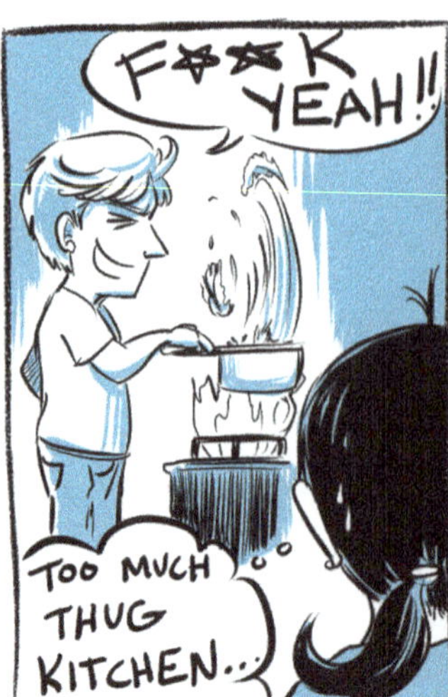

My husband is the better chef between the two of us...but sometimes he draws inspiration from the strangest of places.

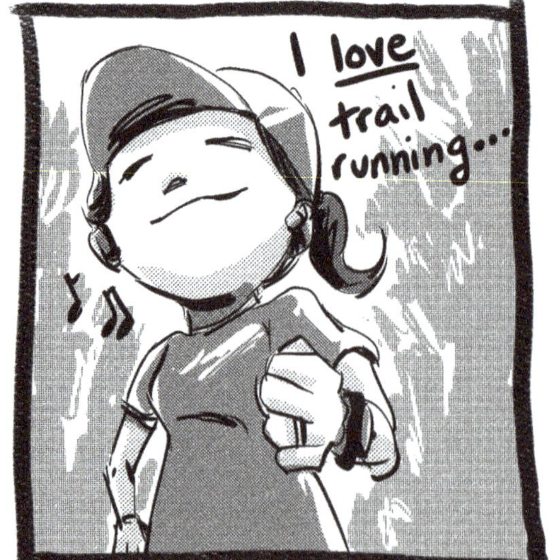

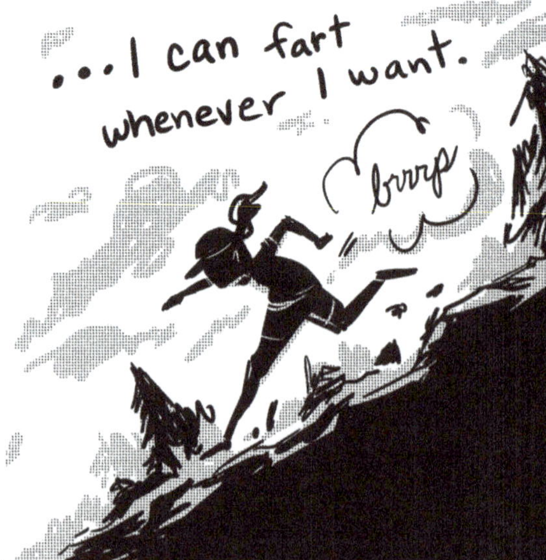

Trail running is great, you guys.

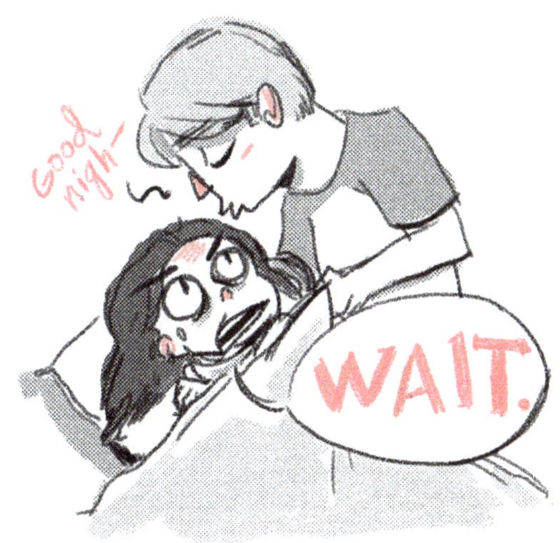

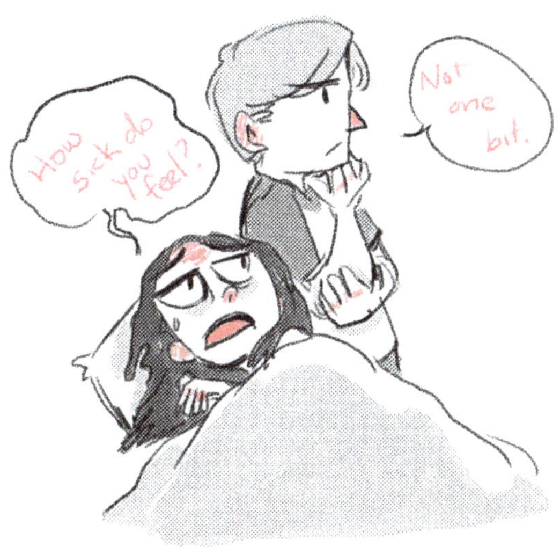

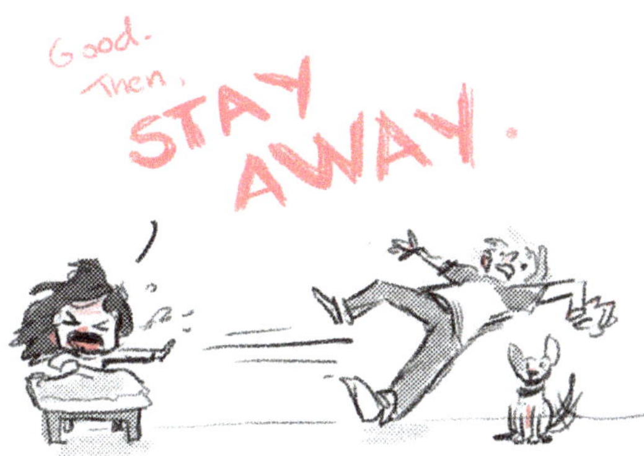

My poor husband was such an excellent caretaker during all this even if I kept pushing him away.

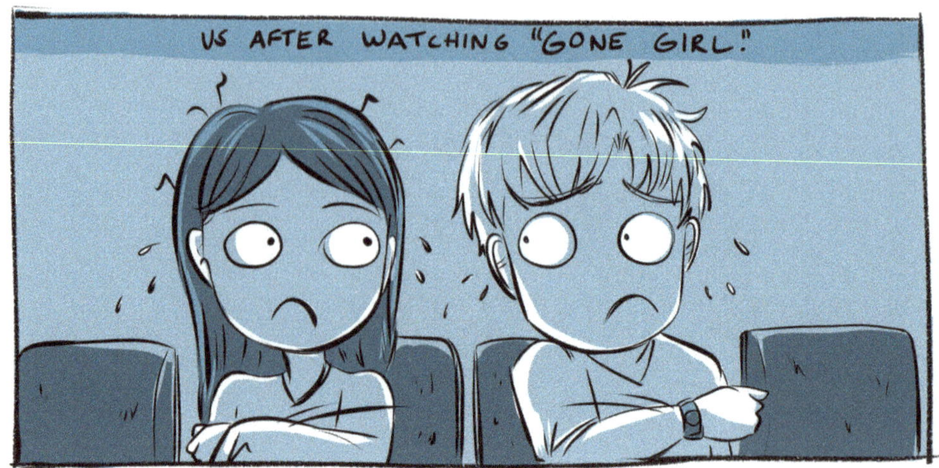

My husband and I caught a matinee showing of "Gone Girl" on a weekday during a time we were both laid off. It might not have been a good idea.

ARTemployed

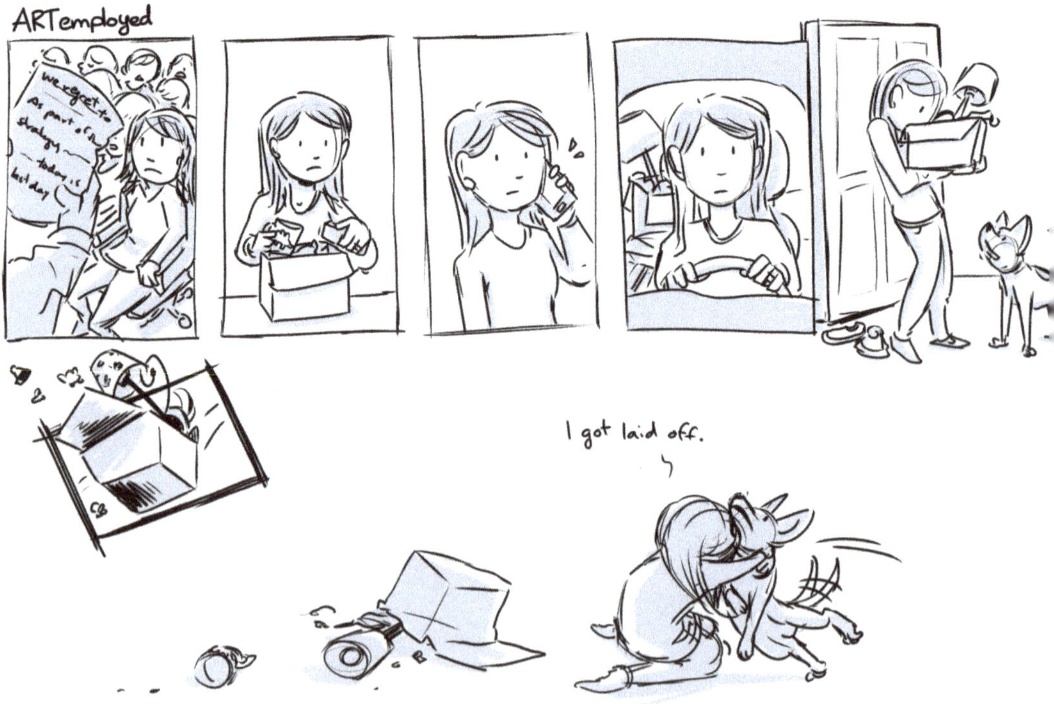

This recounts the 2nd time I've been laid off. I usually handle this life-altering news with a strange calm (probably shock). No matter how you deal with it, my heart goes out to anyone who's experienced this.

For my grandmother's 90th birthday, I
drew the design for the tote bag we gave
away during her party. She loved playing
the piano, which inspired me to learn the
instrument as a child.

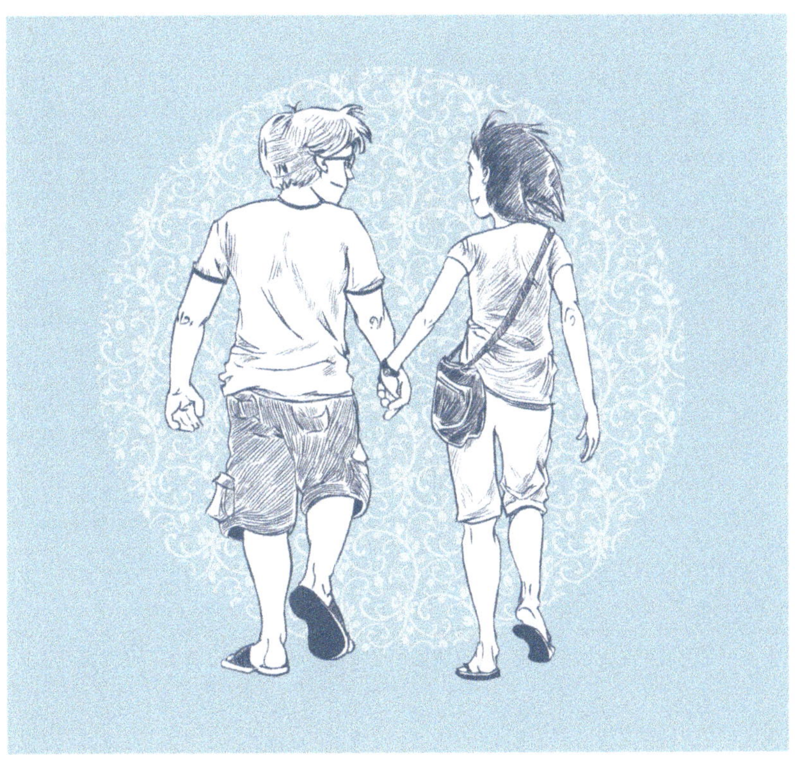

To save on some money, I drew our wedding invitations. This was the graphic I made for it.

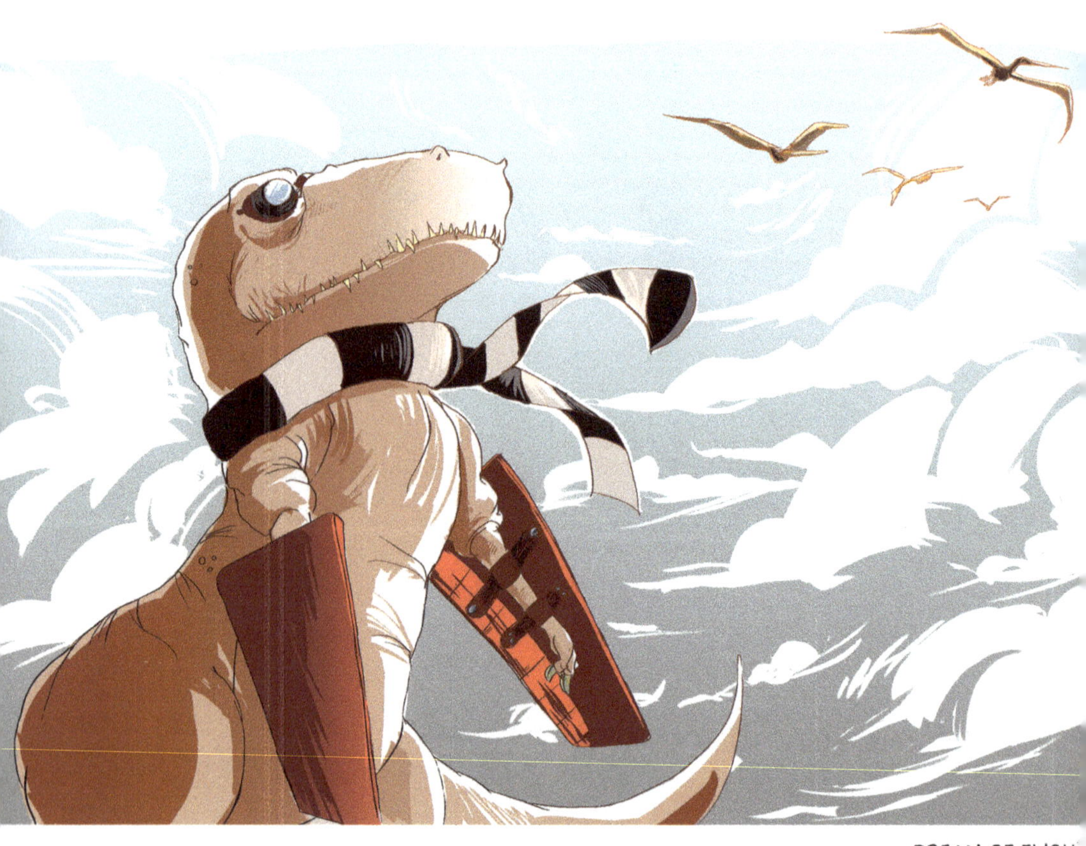

DREAM OF FLIGH

PASSAGE

TRENITALIA
ALLINEA A SINISTRA
ALIGN TO THE LEFT
LA SPEZIA - CENTRALE
BIGLIETTO
TICKET

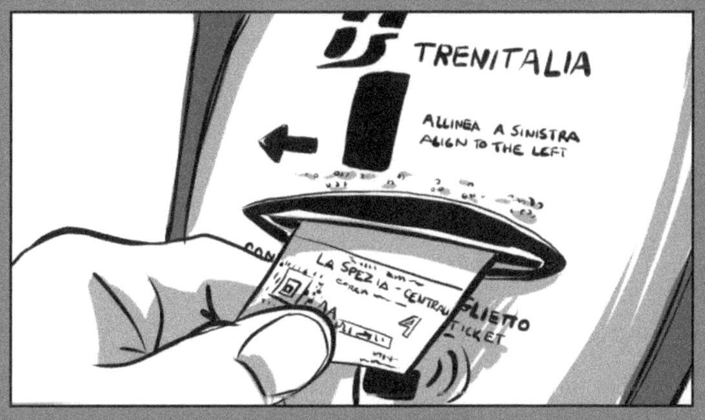

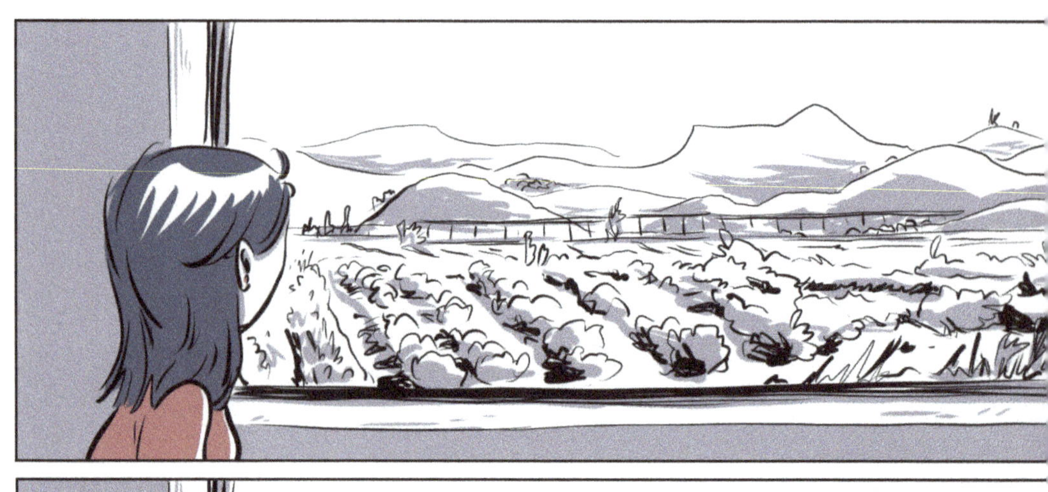

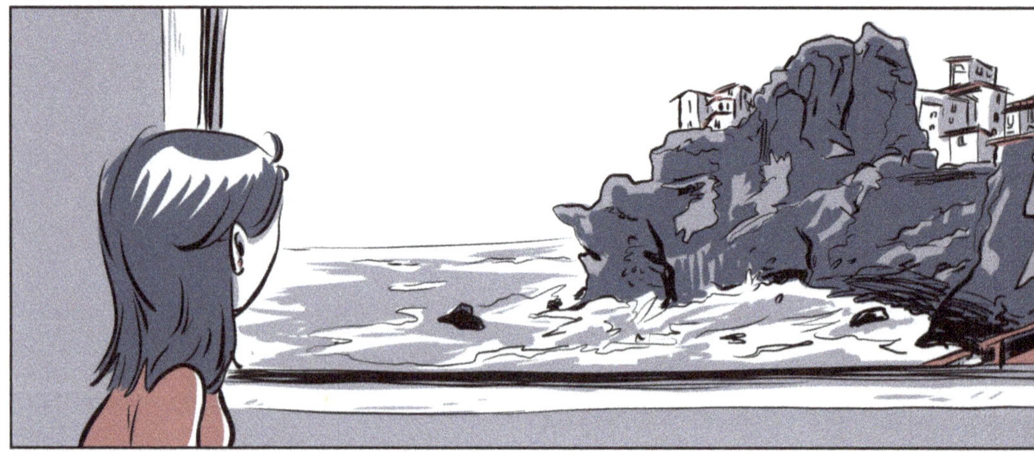

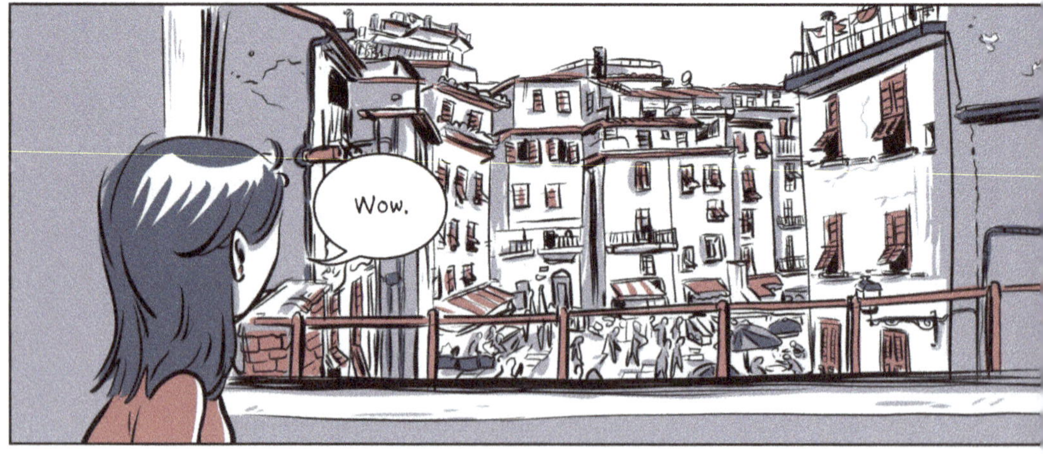

Travel reminds me how small I am in such a big world

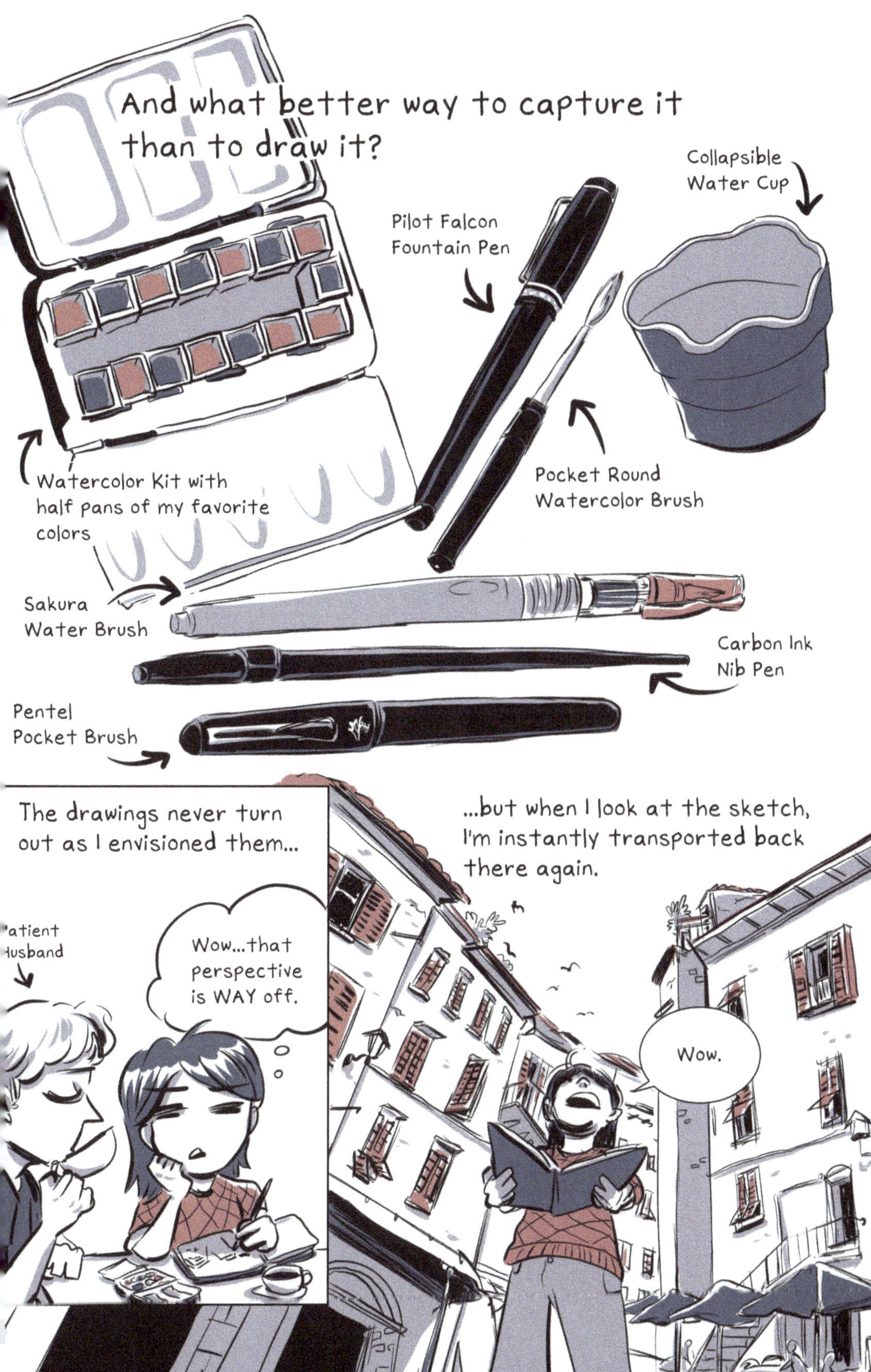

And what better way to capture it than to draw it?
Collapsible Water Cup
Pilot Falcon Fountain Pen
Pocket Round Watercolor Brush
Watercolor Kit with half pans of my favorite colors
Sakura Water Brush
Carbon Ink Nib Pen
Pentel Pocket Brush
The drawings never turn out as I envisioned them...
...but when I look at the sketch, I'm instantly transported back there again.
Patient Husband
Wow...that perspective is WAY off.
Wow.

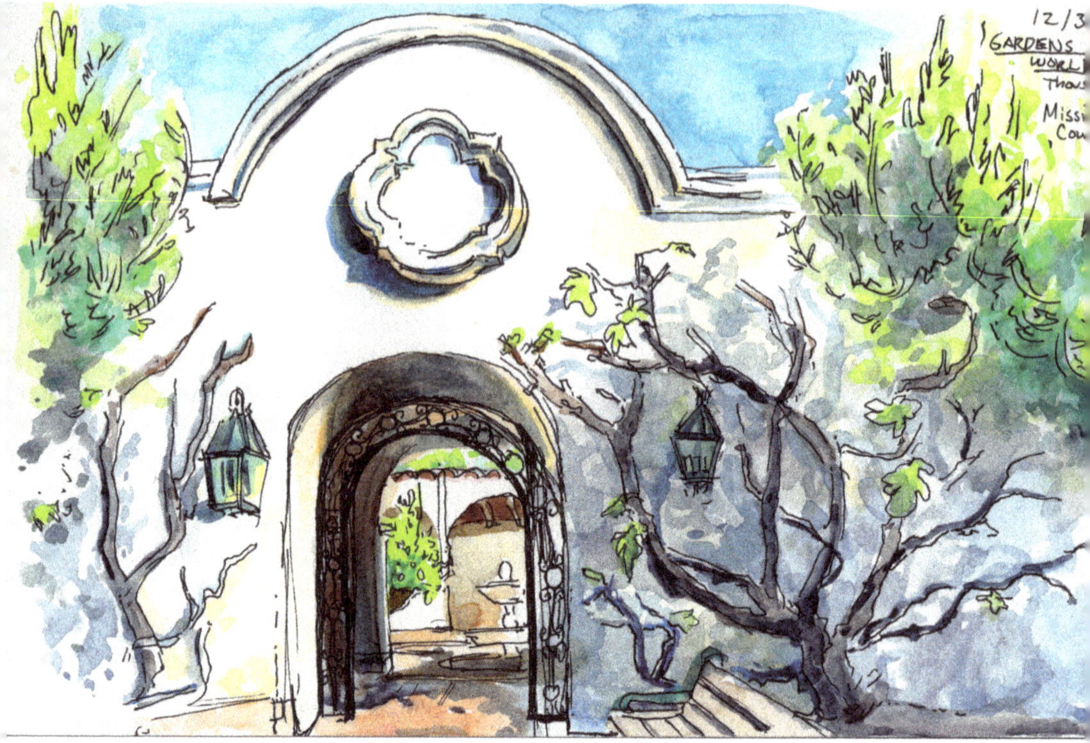

GARDENS OF THE WORLD - Thousand Oaks, CA

Travel sketching is a great mnemonic tool for remembering the sights, sounds, and feeling o
an area. It's a timestamp of your experiences.

DIAMOND HEAD - Honolulu,

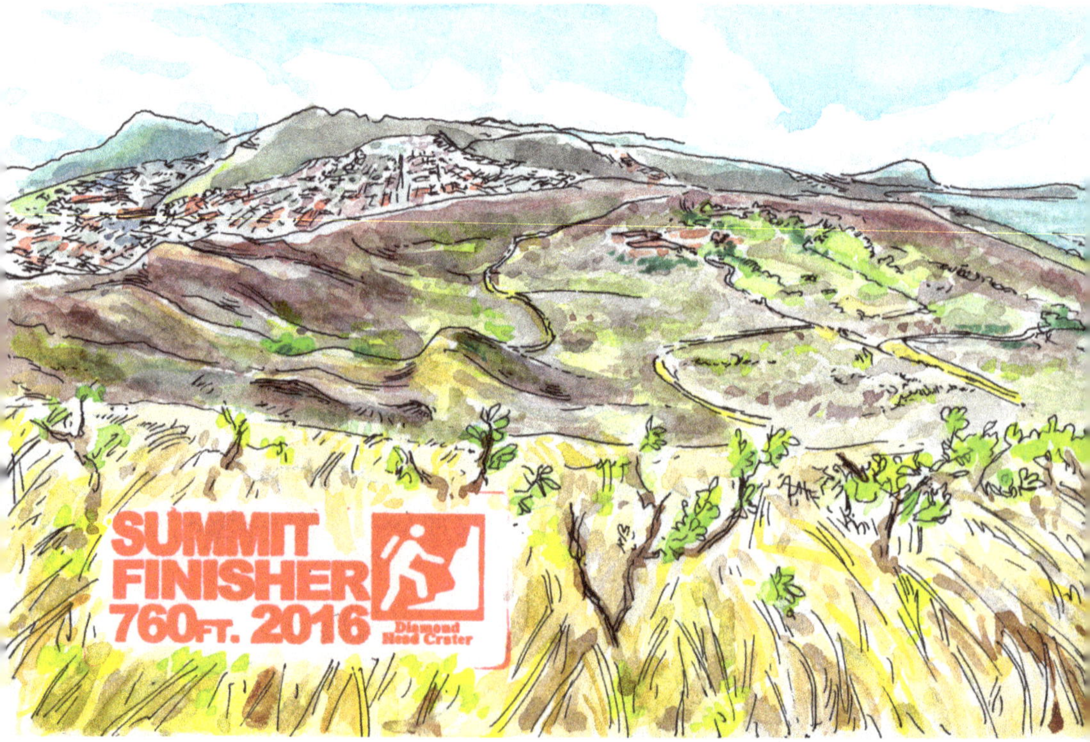

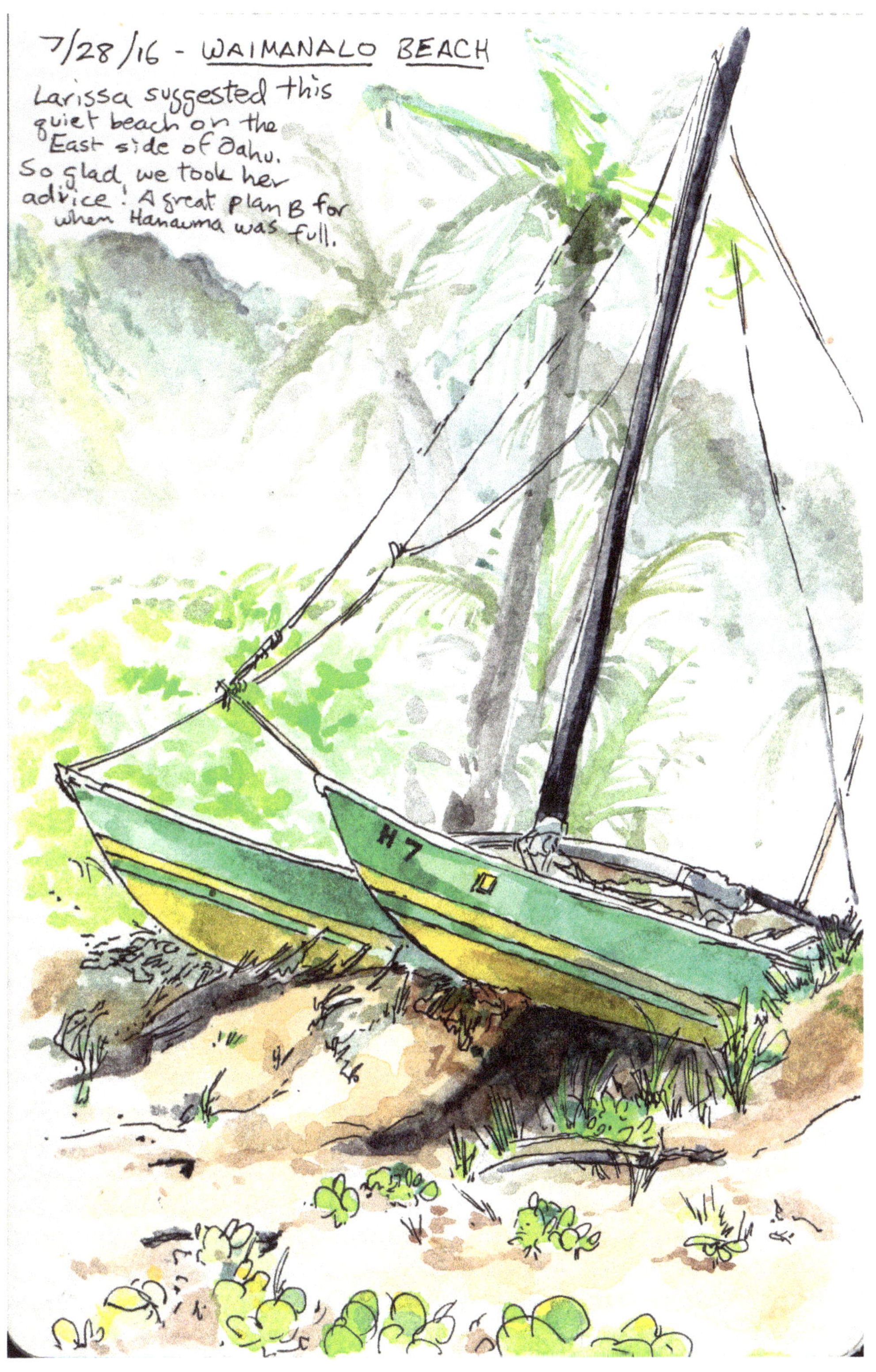
7/28/16 - WAIMANALO BEACH
Larissa suggested this
quiet beach on the
East side of Oahu.
So glad we took her
advice! A great plan B for
when Hanauma was full.
H 7

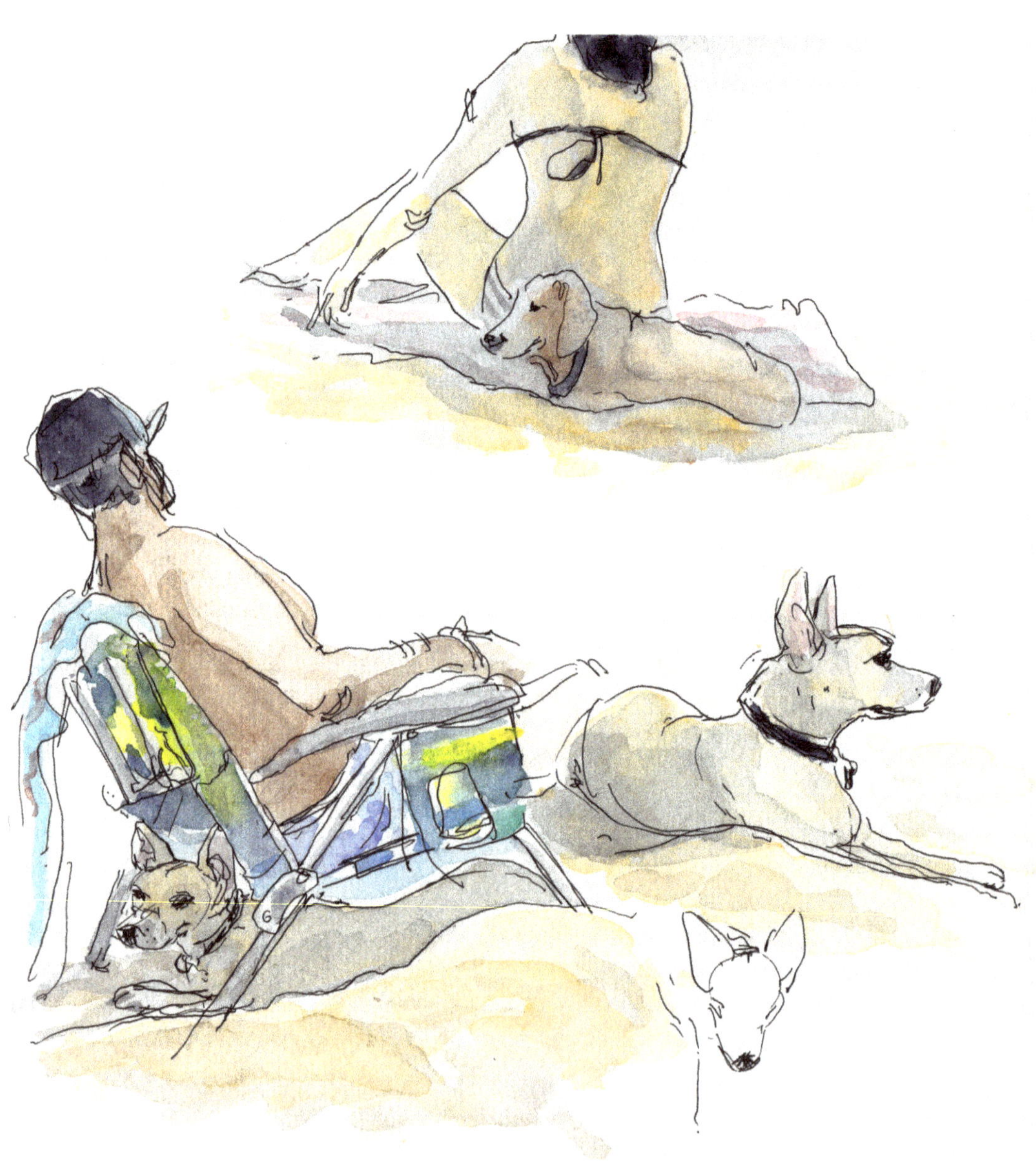

THE DOGS OF KAIMANA - Honolulu,

HT:
awn while waiting
r breakfast in
rt Townsend, WA.
ere were lots of
at boats docked
 the harbor.

LOW:
e of the iconic
ashington State
rries when my
sband, dog, and I
re traveling to
ctoria, B.C.

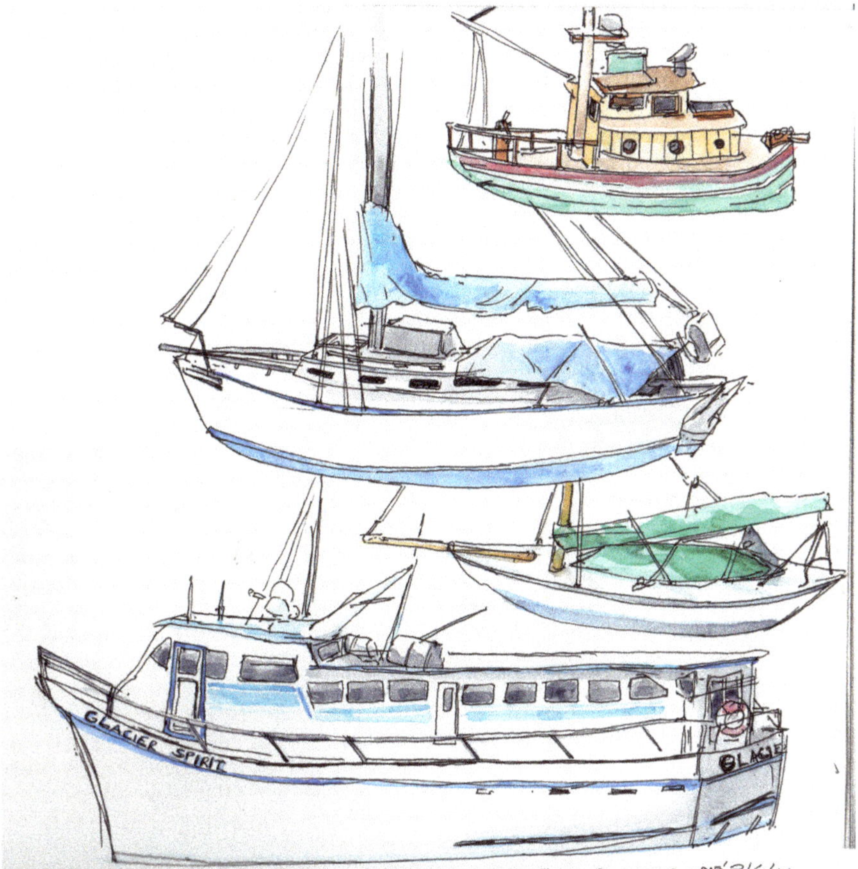

VIEW FROM POINT HARBOR CAFÉ 3/6/16

WASHINGTON STATE FERRY
DOCKED IN ANACORTES
5/23/15

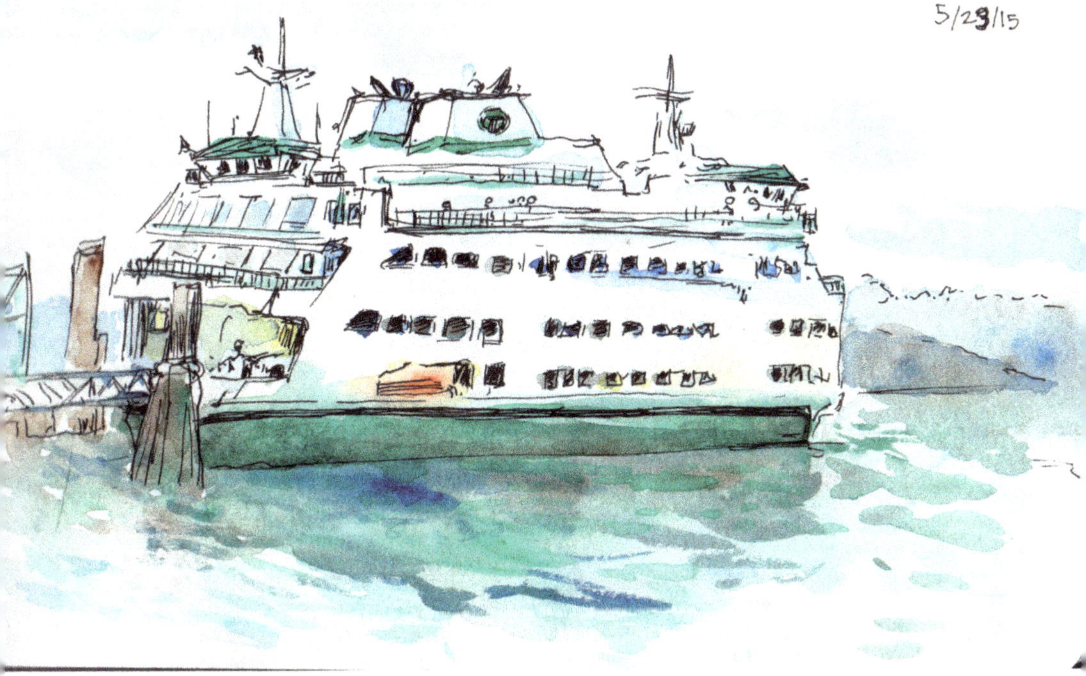

1070 JOAN CRESCENT
(Next door to
CRAIGDORRACH
CASTLE)
5/24/15

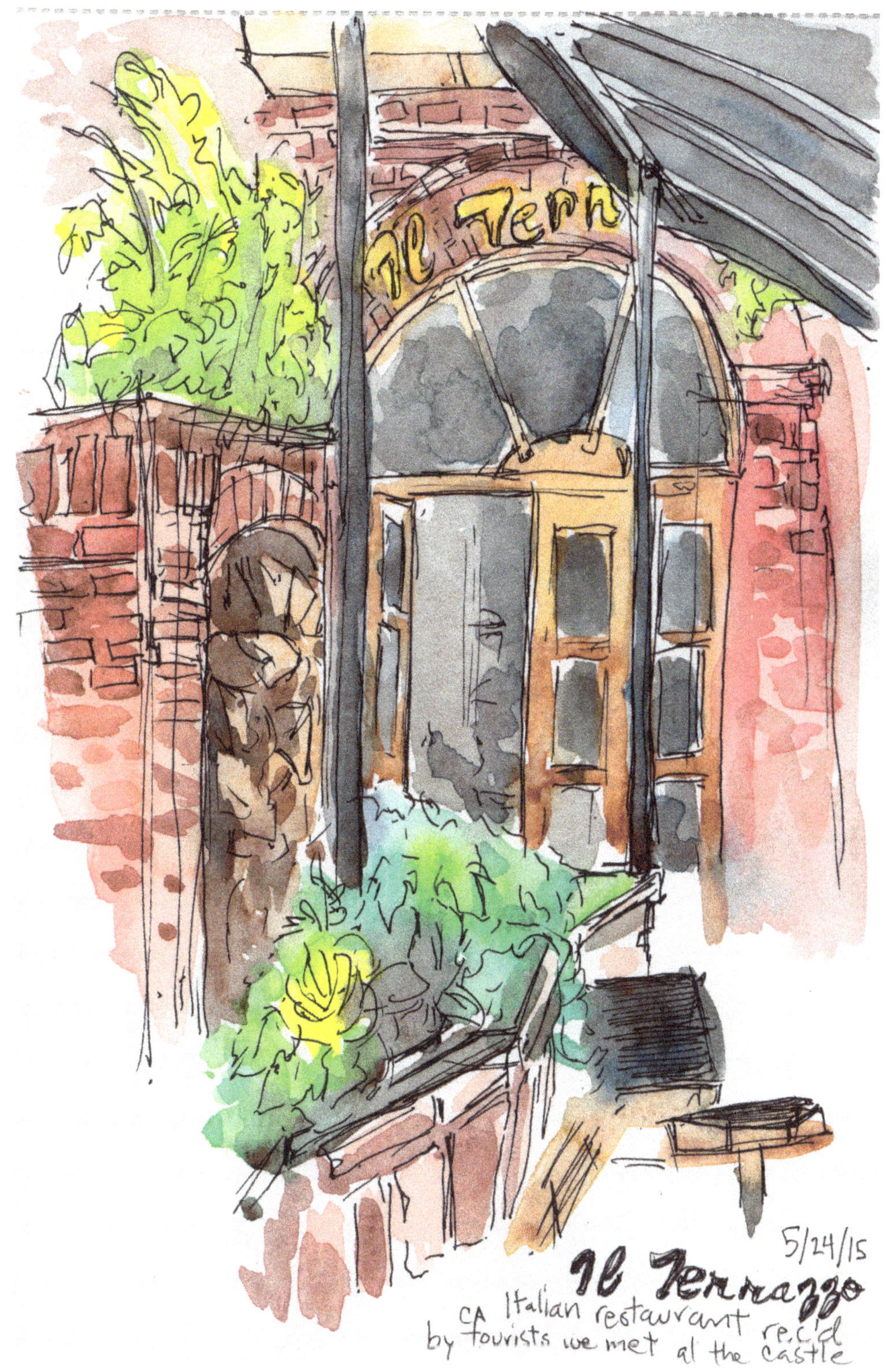
Il Terr
5/24/15
Il Terrazzo
an Italian restaurant rec'd
by tourists we met at the castle

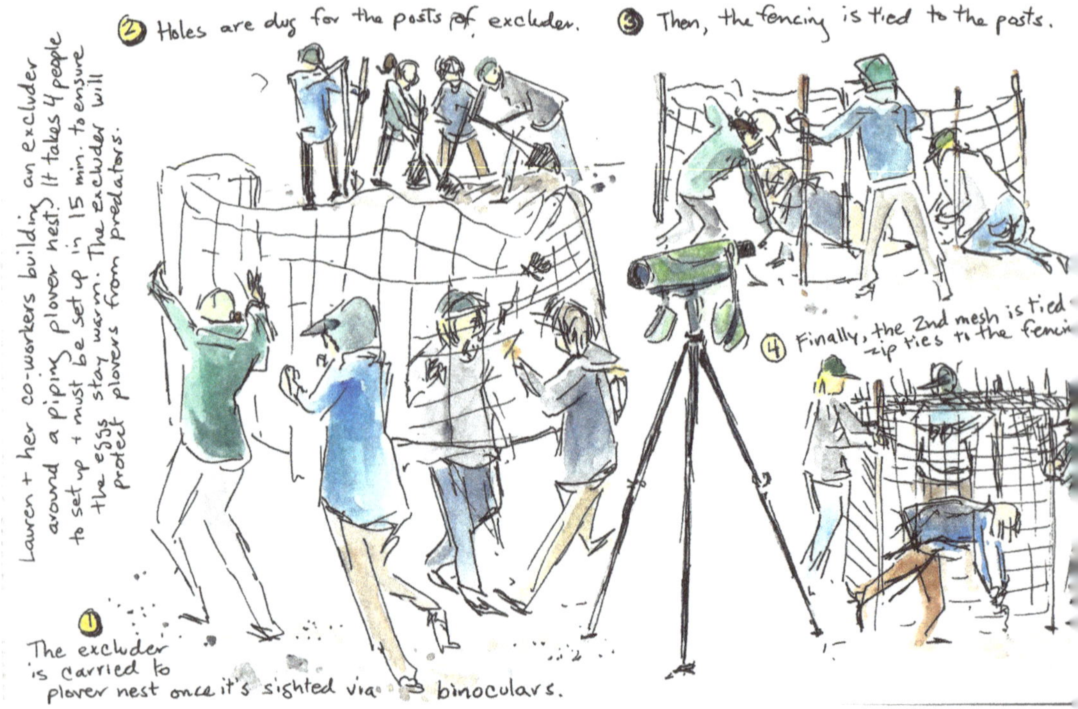

BARNEGAT LIGHTHOUSE STATE PARK - Long Beach Island,

ABOVE: My youngest sister, Lauren, and other wildlife biologists building an excluder for piping plovers. I used sketching as a way to capture the process.

SANTA BARBARA ZOO - Santa Barbara,

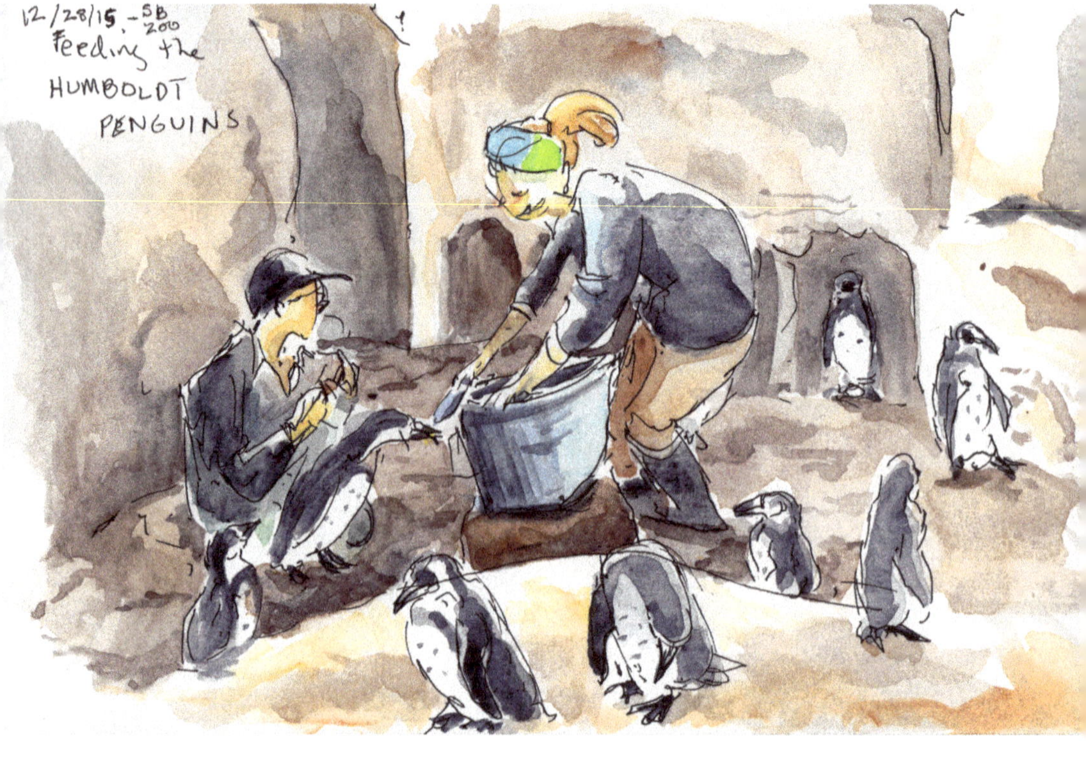

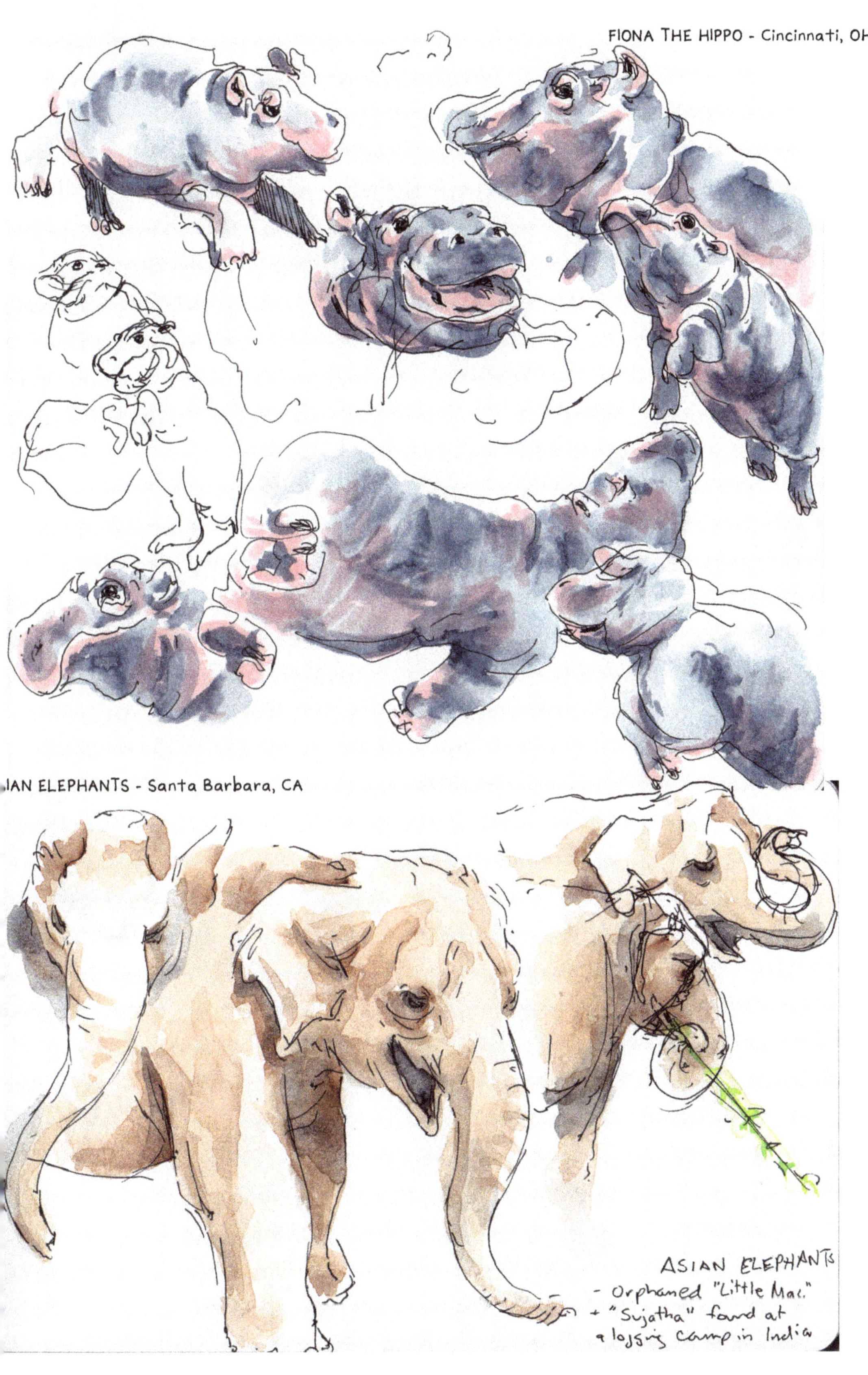

FIONA THE HIPPO - Cincinnati, OH
IAN ELEPHANTS - Santa Barbara, CA
ASIAN ELEPHANTS
- orphaned "Little Mac"
+ "Sujatha" found at
a logging camp in India

RED COW

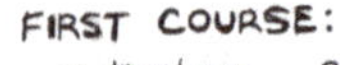

FIRST COURSE:

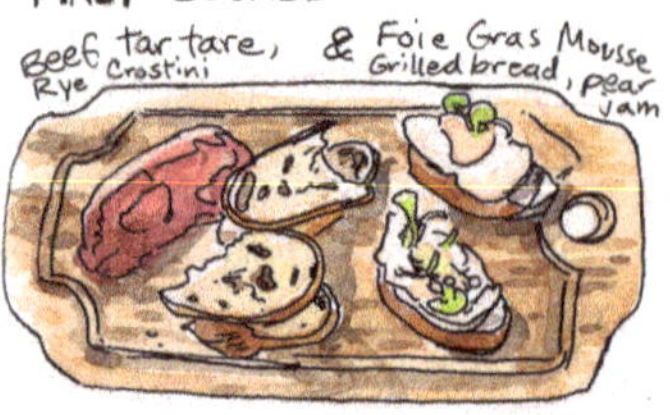

Beef tartare, Rye Crostini & Foie Gras Mousse Grilled bread, pear jam

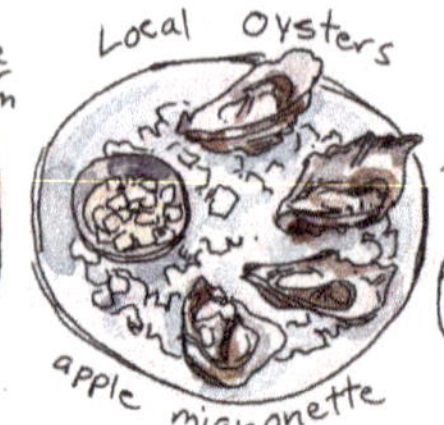

Local Oysters

apple mignonette

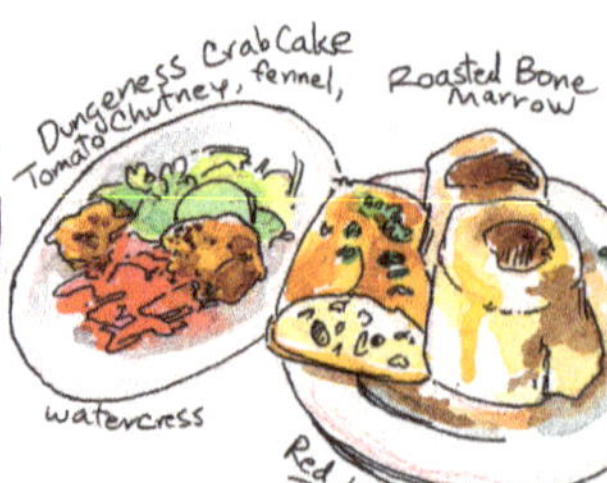

Dungeness Crab Cake Tomato Chutney, fennel, watercress

Roasted Bone Marrow

Red Wine Reduction Toasted Baguette

RIGHT:
I love drawing what I eat. I'll usually take a picture of each course and do the final drawing at home to be respectful to the company I keep at dinner.

SECOND COURSE:
Steamed mussels

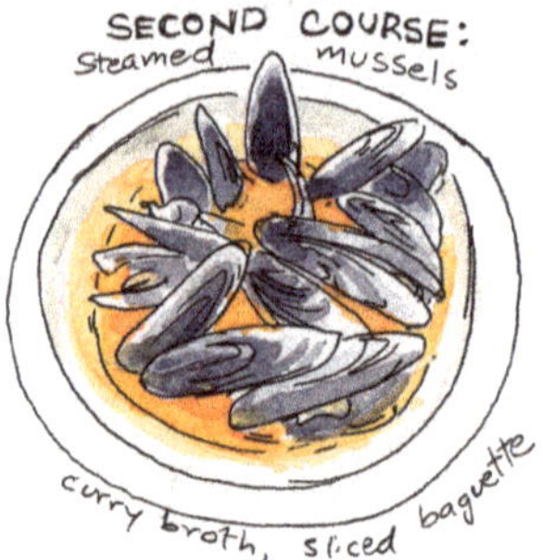

curry broth, sliced baguette

MAIN COURSE:
6oz Wagyu Top Sirloin crispy marble Potatoes, mushrooms, charred cauliflower, truffle butter

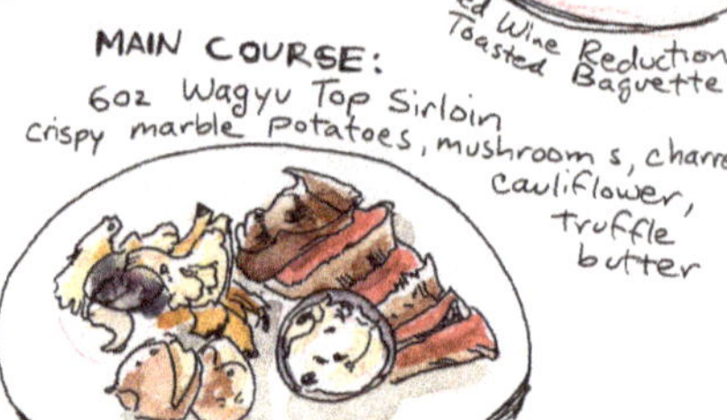

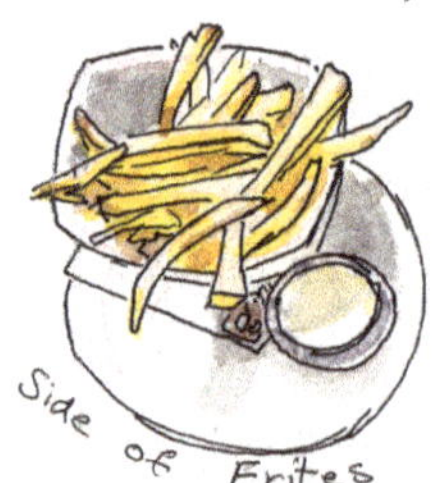

Side of Frites

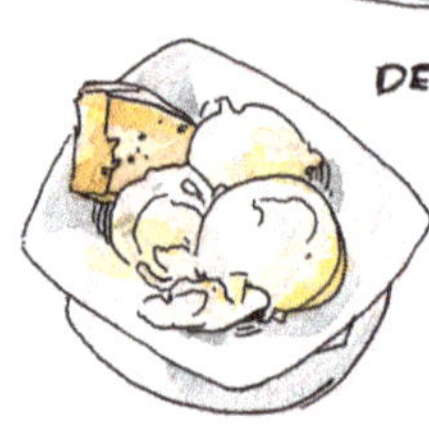

DESSERT:

Spiced Pear Sorbet & Pink peppercorn short bread cookie

VALENTINE'S DAY 2017

THE CENTER FOR WOODEN BOATS - Seattle, WA

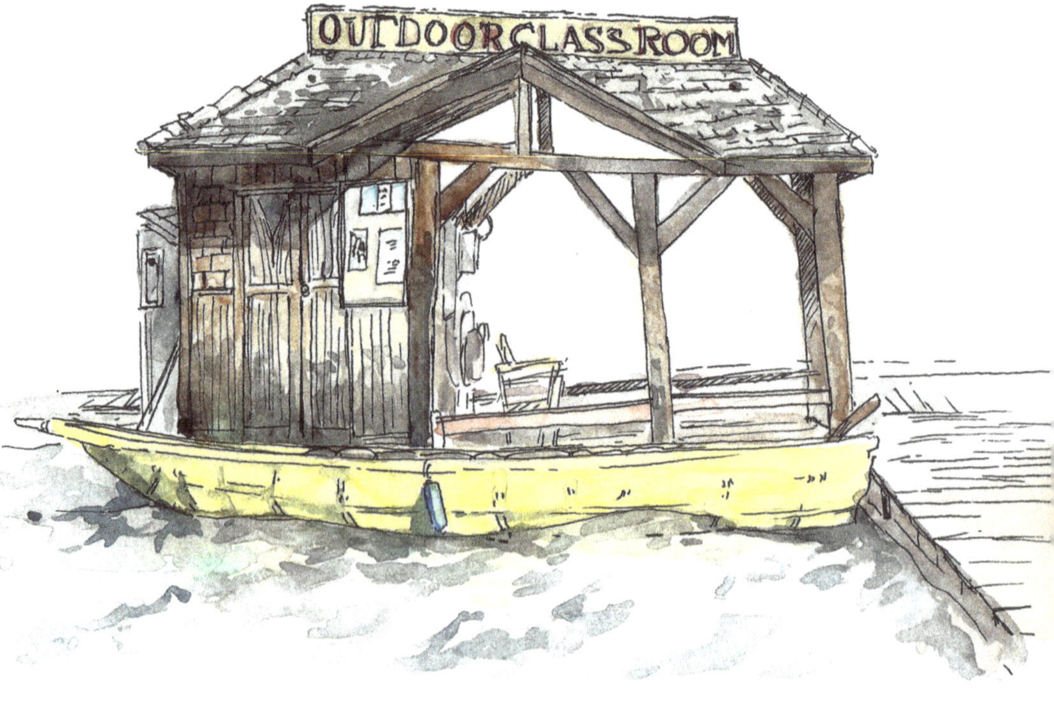

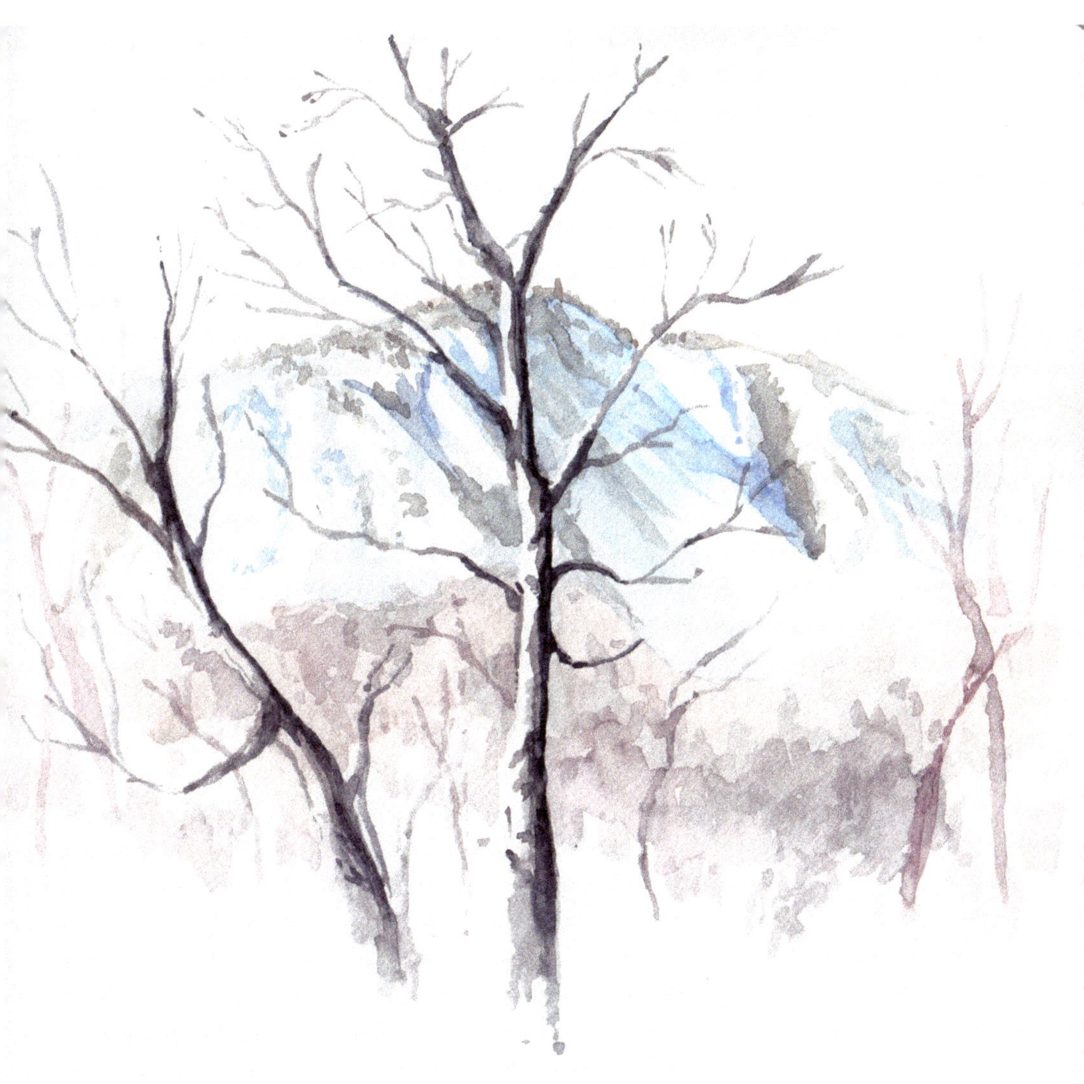

BIRCHFIELD MANOR - Yakima, WA
Drawn while celebrating my 5th year wedding anniversary. Our bed and breakfast had a stunning view of the Cascade mountain range.

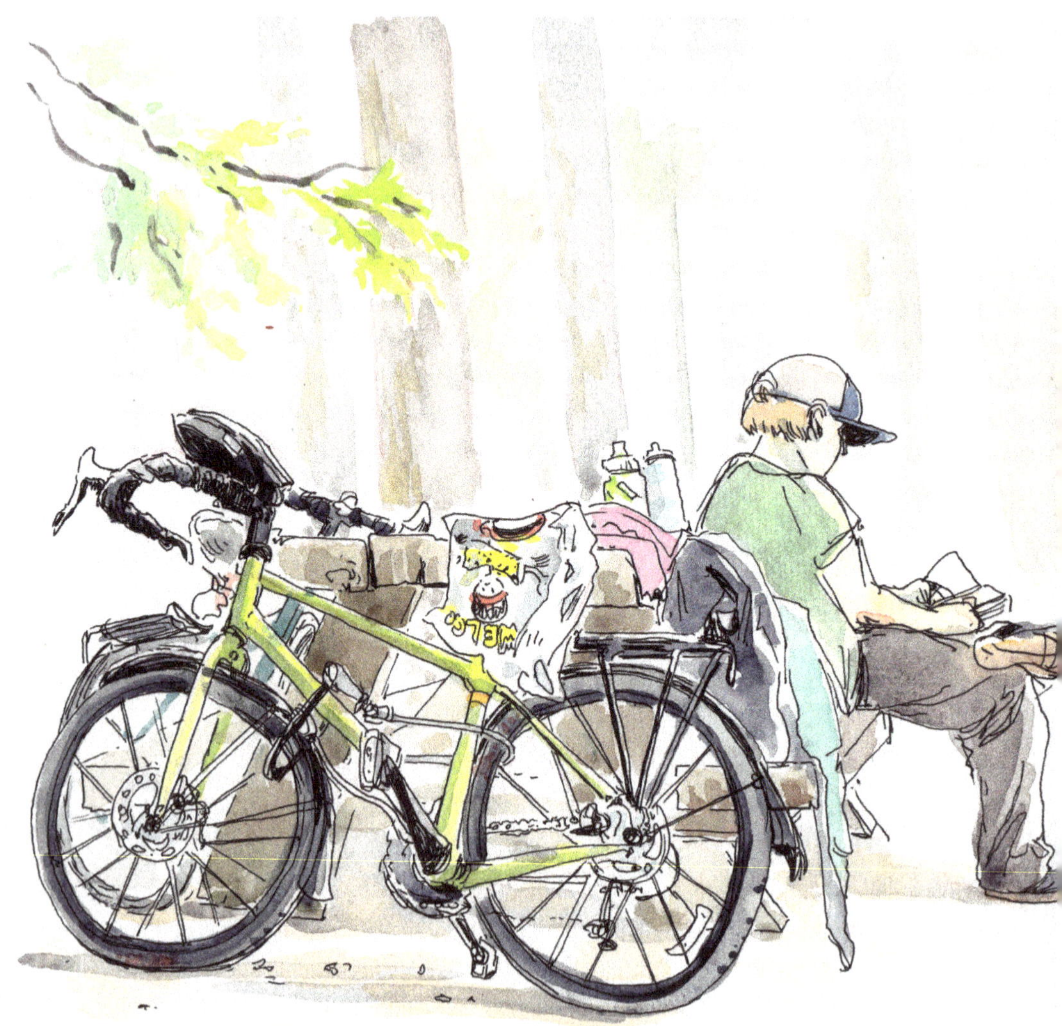

Thanks to all the well-maintained campsites and biking infrastructure in the Pacific Northwest my husband and I have taken to bike camping. We even carry the dog with us! After a handful o trips, I realized that bike camping and sketching go great together. This was drawn during our bike camping trip to Middle Fork Campground.

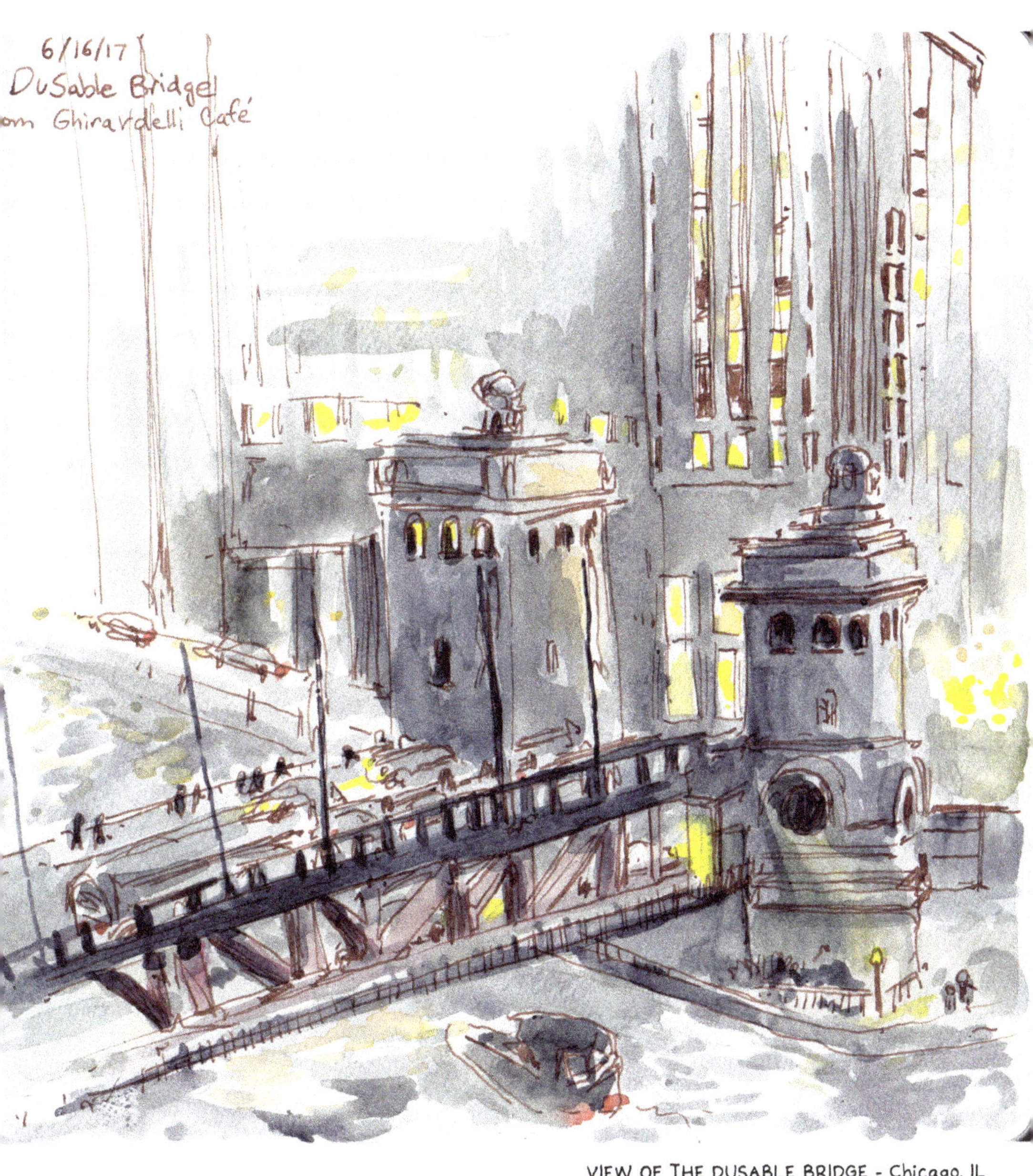

VIEW OF THE DUSABLE BRIDGE - Chicago, IL

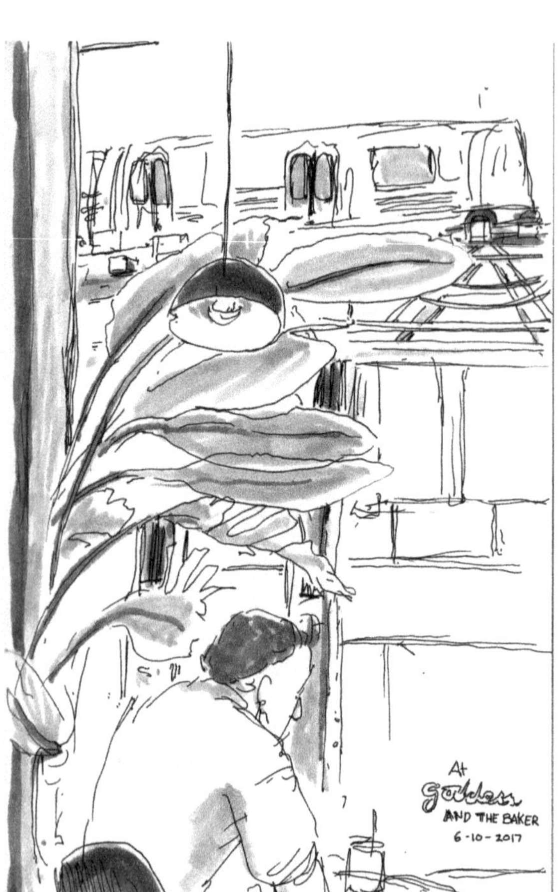

URBAN SKETCHES - Chicago, IL

Urban sketching can feel a bit insular when traveling with others who aren't there to sketch. In those cases, work small, take notes, snap reference photos, or use a limited palette (in these examples, warm grays) so you can still capture what you desire while being present with those you're traveling with.

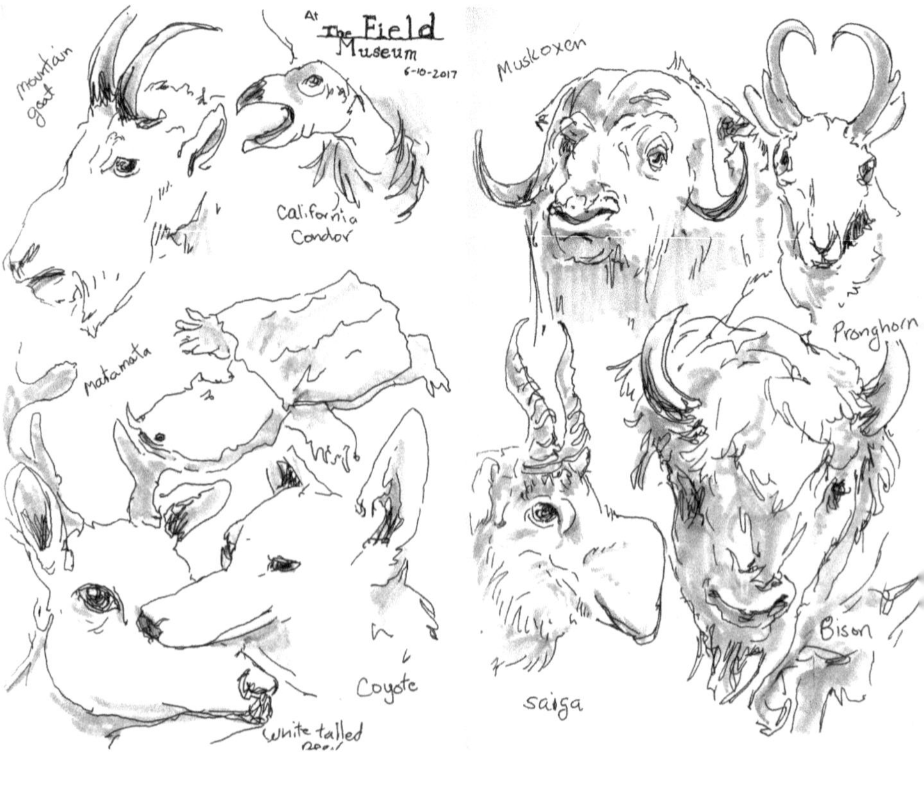

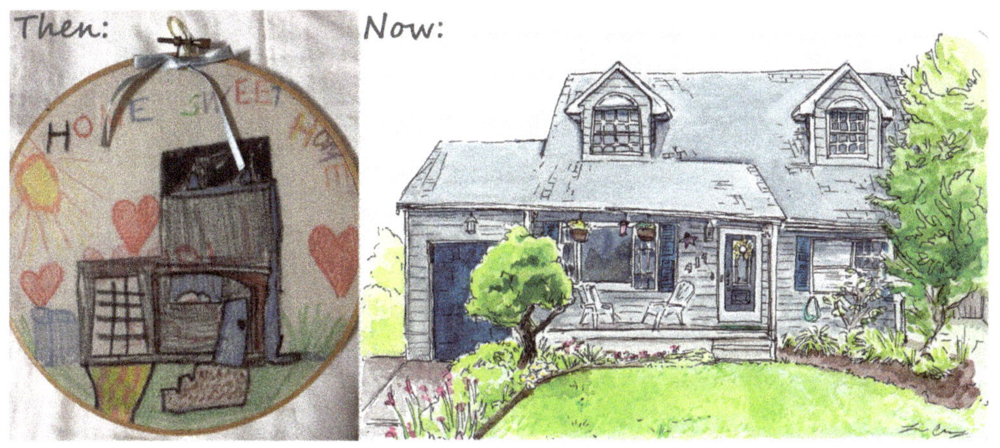

FAMILY HOME - Bayville, NJ
It's always fun to compare sketches over time. Try re-drawing an object you drew 1 year,
5 years, or even 20 years ago.

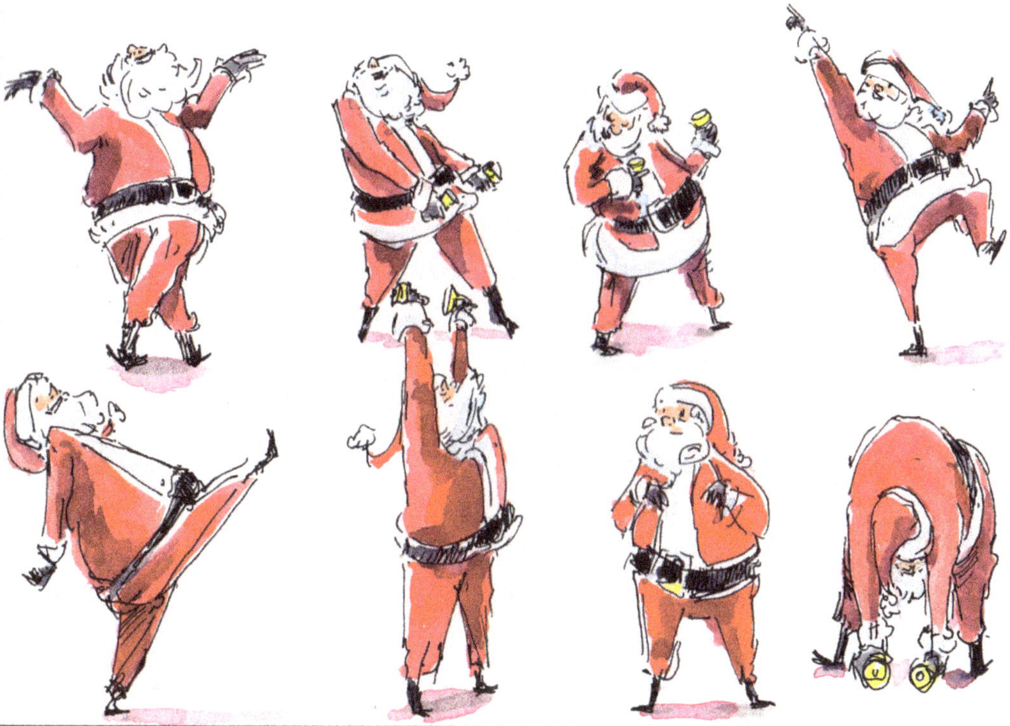

RADIO CITY CHRISTMAS SHOW - New York, NY

These Santas from the Radio City Christmas Show
were first captured as gesture drawings with my
phone and stylus and then extrapolated to
watercolor and ink drawings.

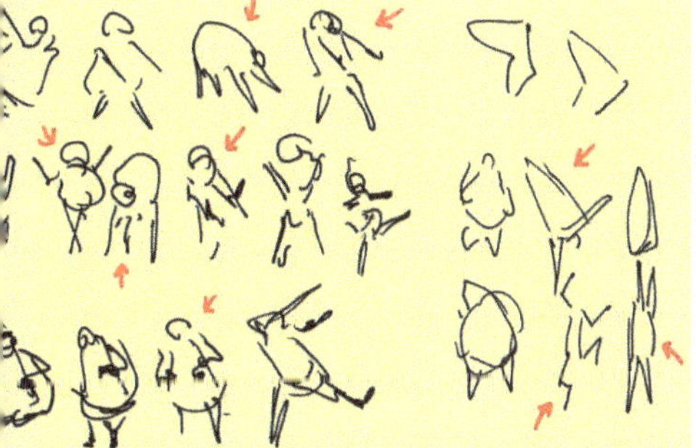

PONTE VECCHIO VIEW

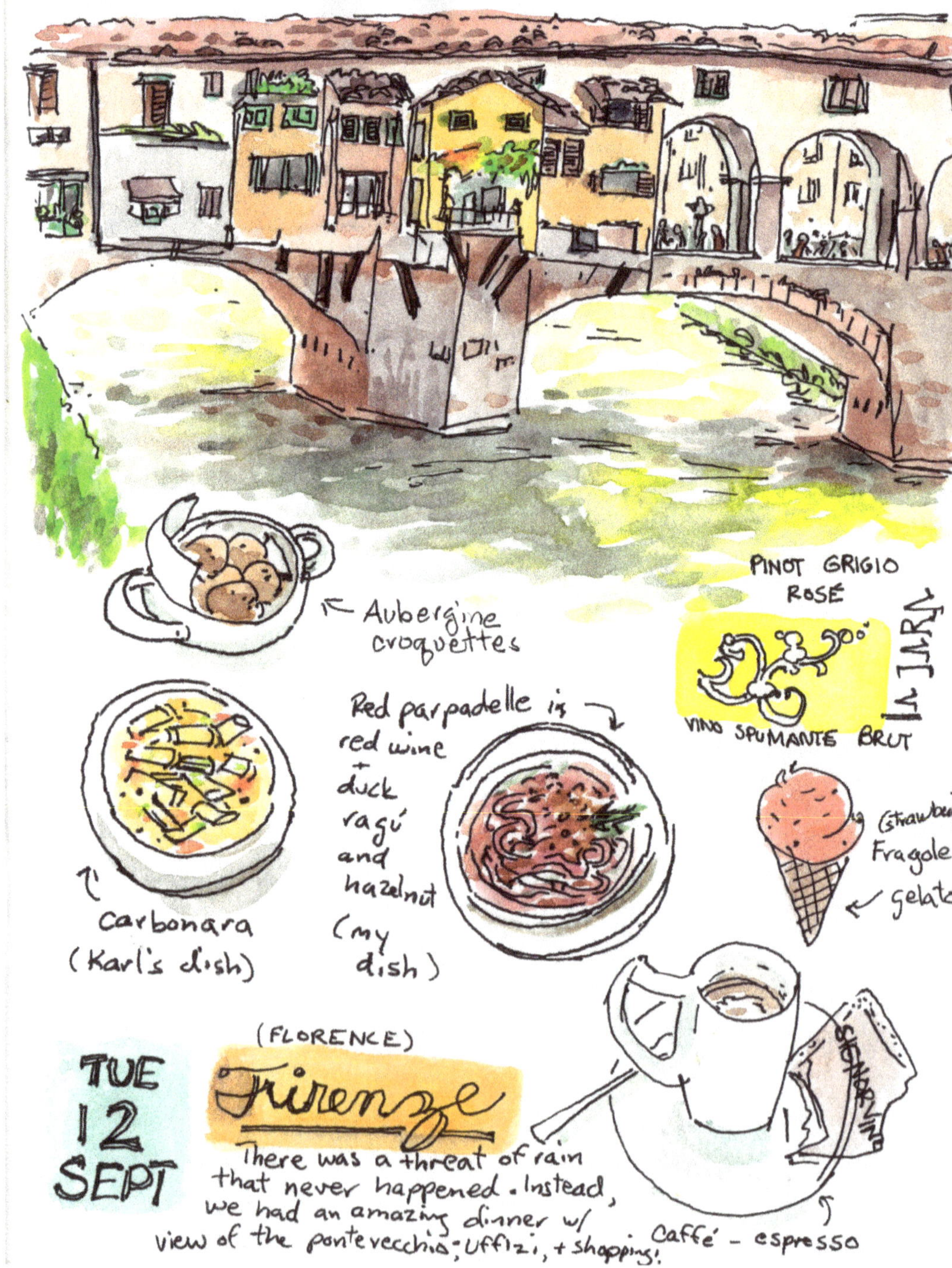

Villa Sassella

It was a rest day after all the celebrating the night before. We spent the day doing laundry (drying operates on Italian time) + lazing about the villa. Karl + I did a short walk around the villa + then I spent time attempting to paint the exterior.

OUR ROOM:
very spacious w/ ensuite bathroom! I loved the vaulted ceiling.

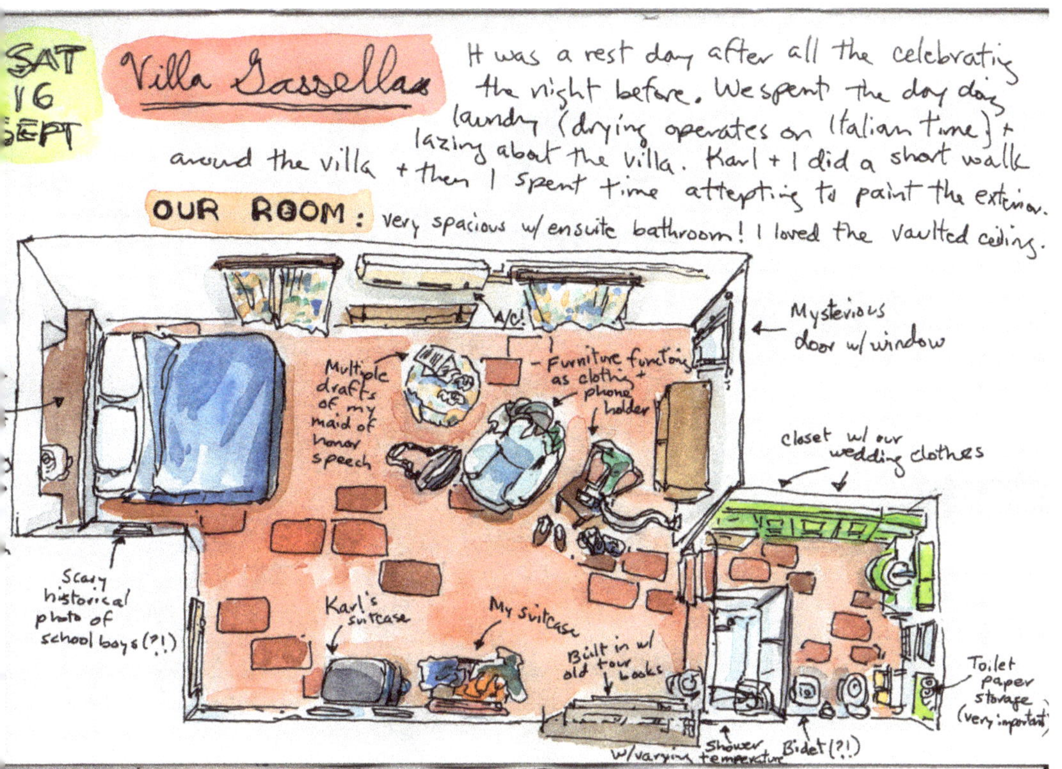

OUR ROOM AT VILLA SASSELLA - Compignano, Italy

ITALY & FRANCE TRAVEL JOURNAL - FALL 2017

In Fall 2017, my husband and I attended my best friend's wedding in Italy. I gave myself the challenge of drawing every day during our trip. I didn't always keep up with my pages, but I made sure to take notes and record as much as I could so I can finsh my drawings when I returned back to the States.

Our Europe trip started in Compignano, in the Tuscan region of Italy. Afterwards, we took the train to the Cinque Terre, and then flew to Paris, France.

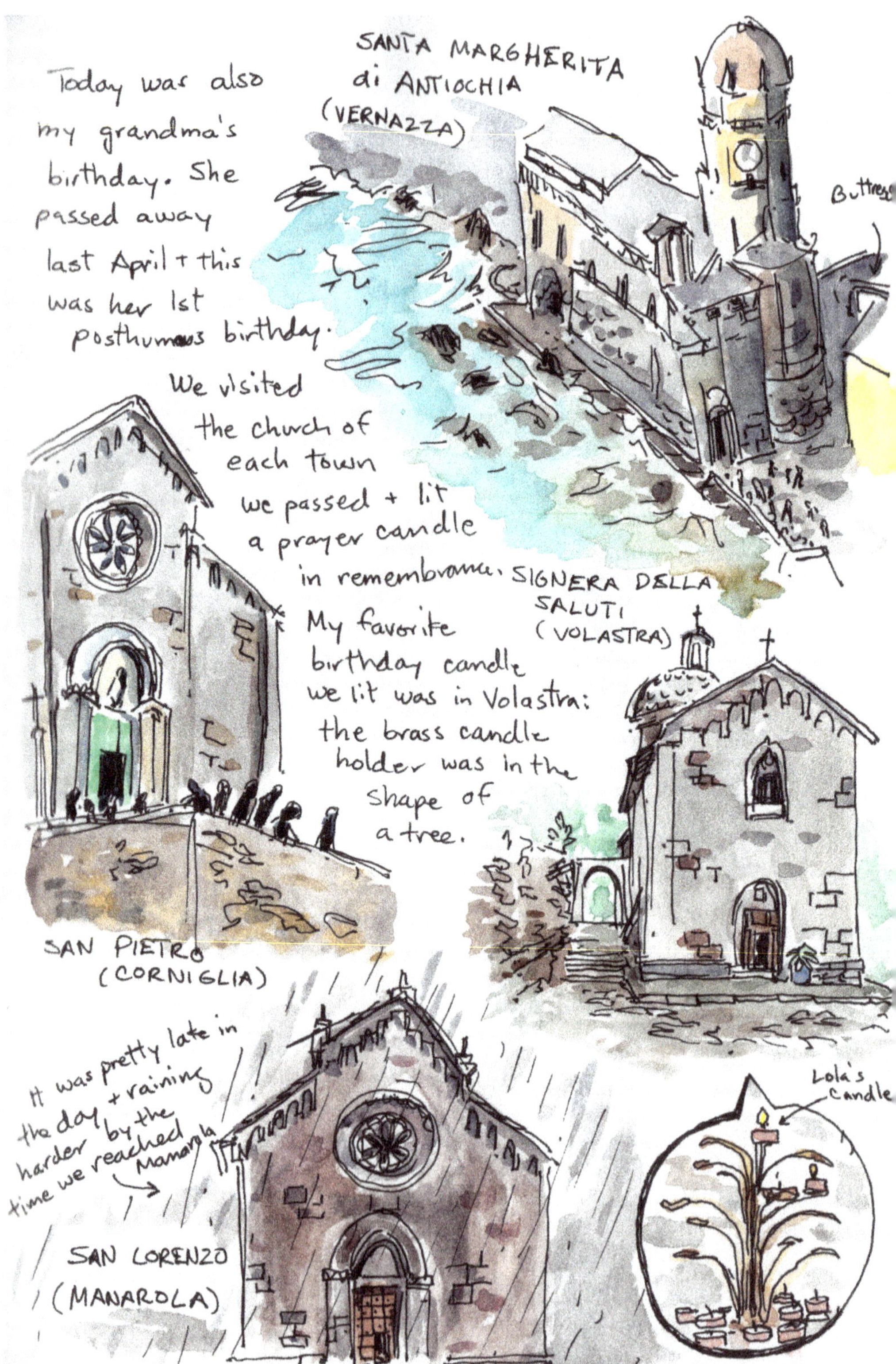
Today was also
my grandma's
birthday. She
passed away
last April + this
was her 1st
posthumous birthday.

We visited
the church of
each town
we passed + lit
a prayer candle
in remembrance.
My favorite
birthday candle
we lit was in Volastra:
the brass candle
holder was in the
shape of
a tree.

SANTA MARGHERITA
di ANTIOCHIA
(VERNAZZA)

Buttress

SIGNERA DELLA
SALUTI
(VOLASTRA)

SAN PIETRO
(CORNIGLIA)

It was pretty late in
the day + raining
harder by the
time we reached
Manarola

SAN LORENZO
(MANAROLA)

Lola's
candle

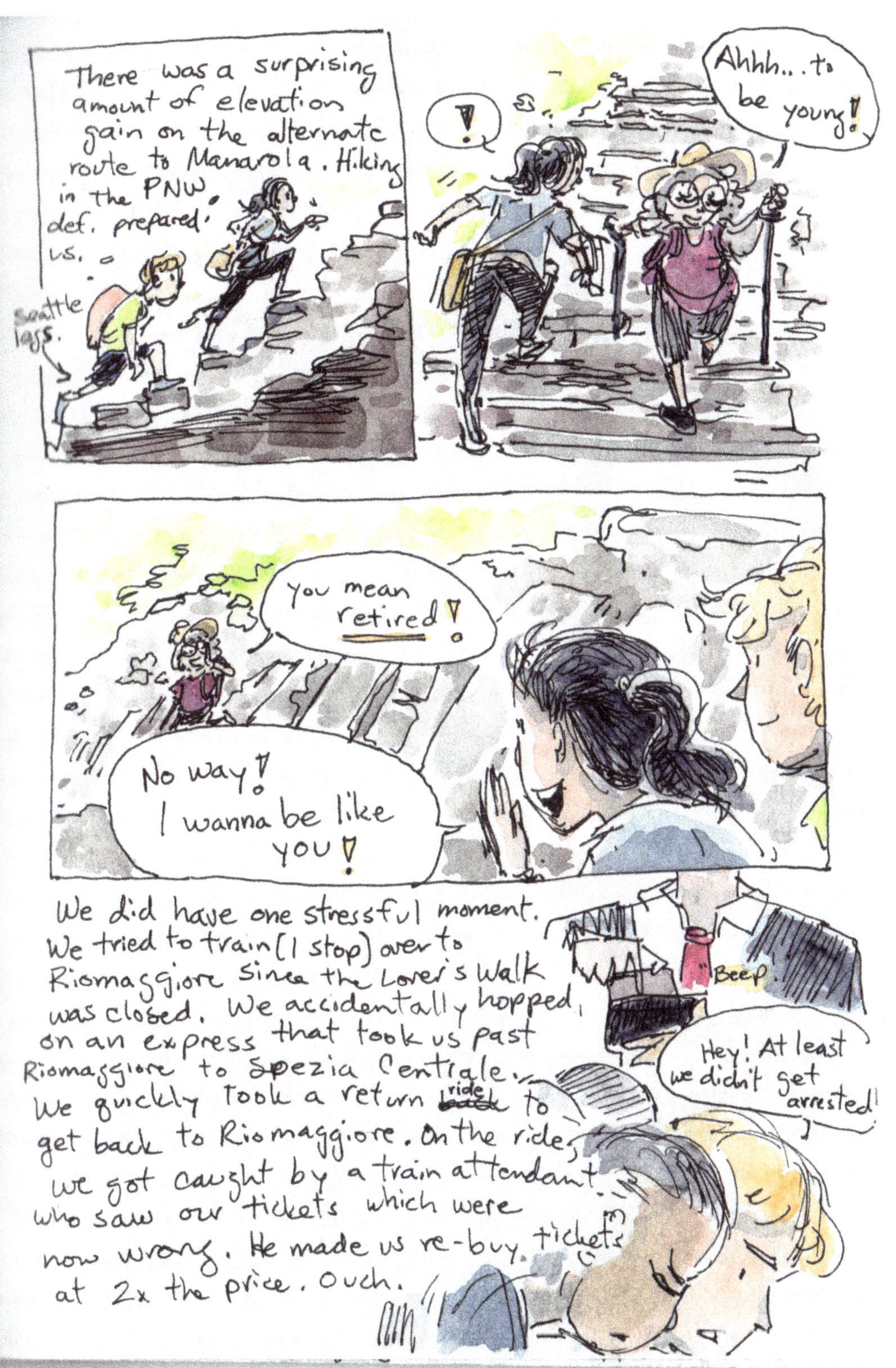
There was a surprising amount of elevation gain on the alternate route to Manarola. Hiking in the PNW. def. prepared us.
Seattle lass.
!
Ahhh...to be young!
You mean retired!
No way! I wanna be like YOU!
We did have one stressful moment. We tried to train (1 stop) over to Riomaggiore since the Lover's walk was closed. We accidentally hopped on an express that took us past Riomaggiore to Spezia Centrale. We quickly took a return ride to get back to Riomaggiore. On the ride, we got caught by a train attendant who saw our tickets which were now wrong. He made us re-buy tickets at 2x the price. Ouch.
Beep
Hey! At least we didn't get arrested!

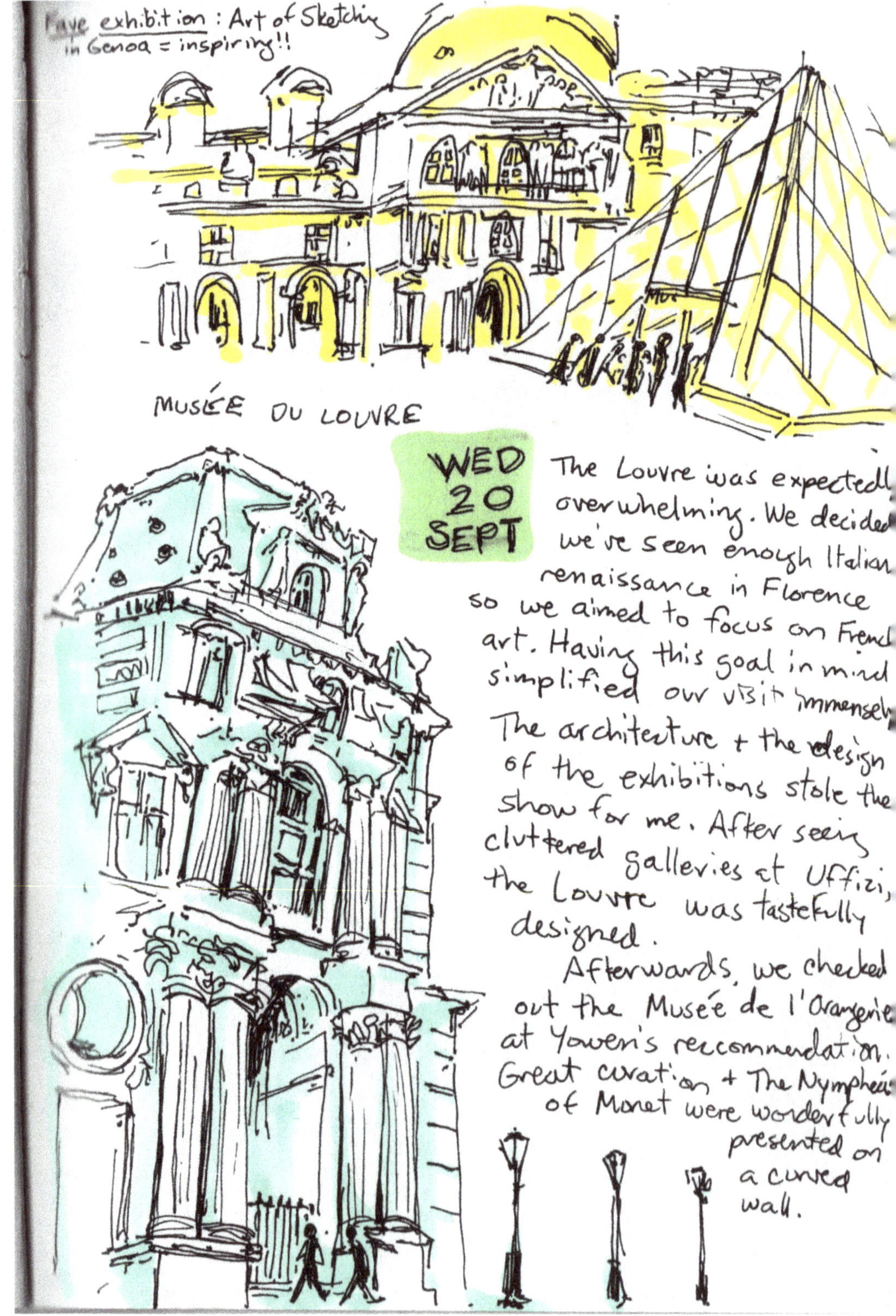

The Louvre was expectedly overwhelming. We decided we've seen enough Italian renaissance in Florence so we aimed to focus on French art. Having this goal in mind simplified our visit immensely.

The architecture + the design of the exhibitions stole the show for me. After seeing cluttered galleries at Uffizi, the Louvre was tastefully designed.

Afterwards, we checked out the Musée de l'Orangerie at Yowen's recommendation. Great curation + The Nymphéas of Monet were wonderfully presented on a curved wall.

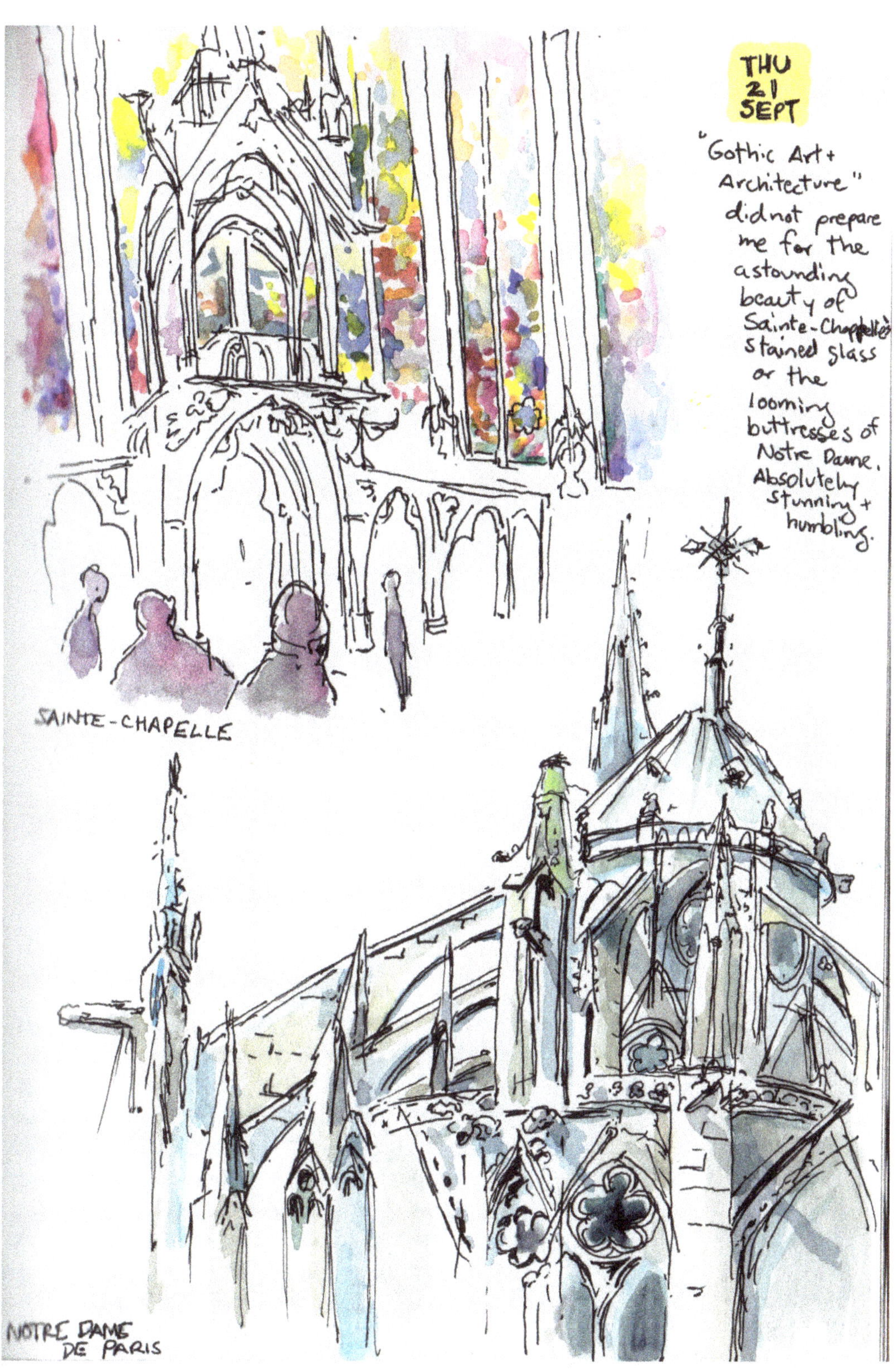
THU
21
SEPT

"Gothic Art +
Architecture"
did not prepare
me for the
astounding
beauty of
Sainte-Chapelle's
stained glass
or the
looming
buttresses of
Notre Dame.
Absolutely
stunning +
humbling.

SAINTE-CHAPELLE

NOTRE DAME
DE PARIS

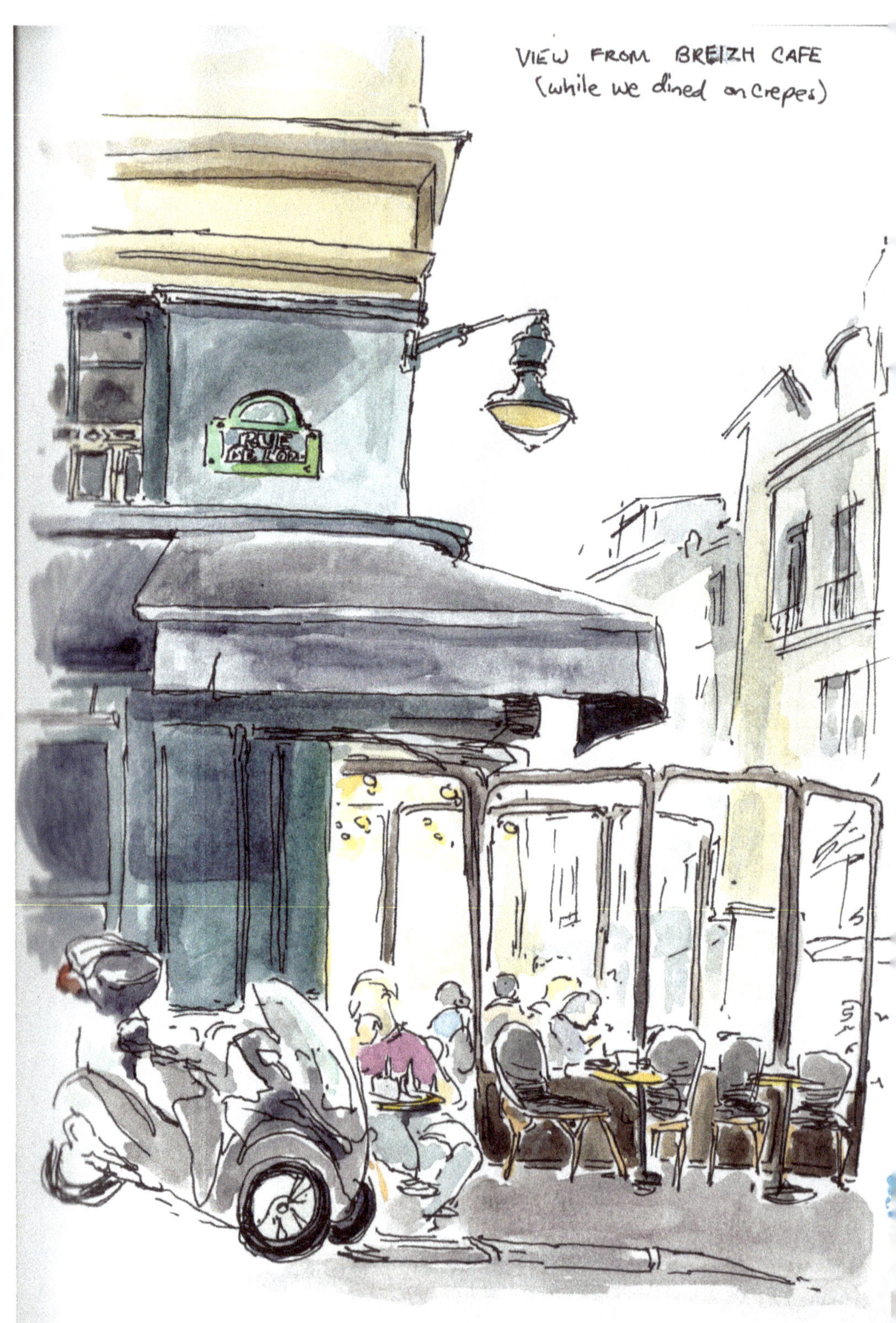

CAFE SKETCH - Paris, France
VIEW FROM BREIZH CAFE
(while we dined on crepes)
RUE DE L'OR

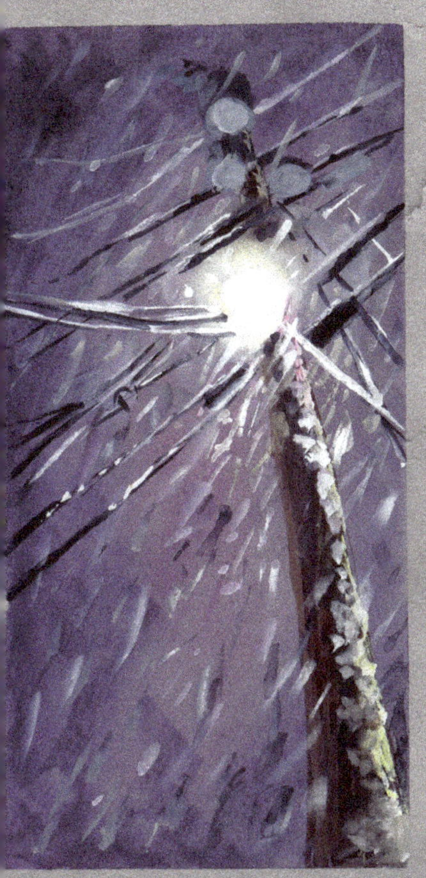

GOUACHE STUDIES - Kirkland, WA

The year we decided to not travel
during the holidays, it snowed on Christmas
Eve. The usual route we walked our dog in our
neighborhood transformed with this blanket of
newly fallen snow.

The purplish hues left such a strong impression
on me that I wanted to try to capture it with
a medium I had a love/hate relationship with:
gouache. Painting with gouache on toned paper
was outside my comfort zone, but I learned
tons trying it.

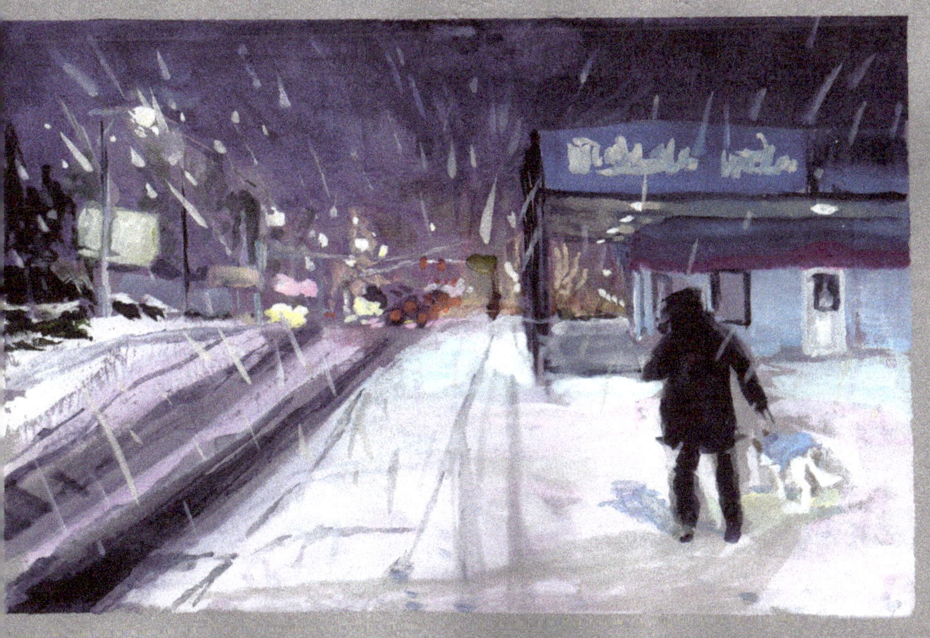

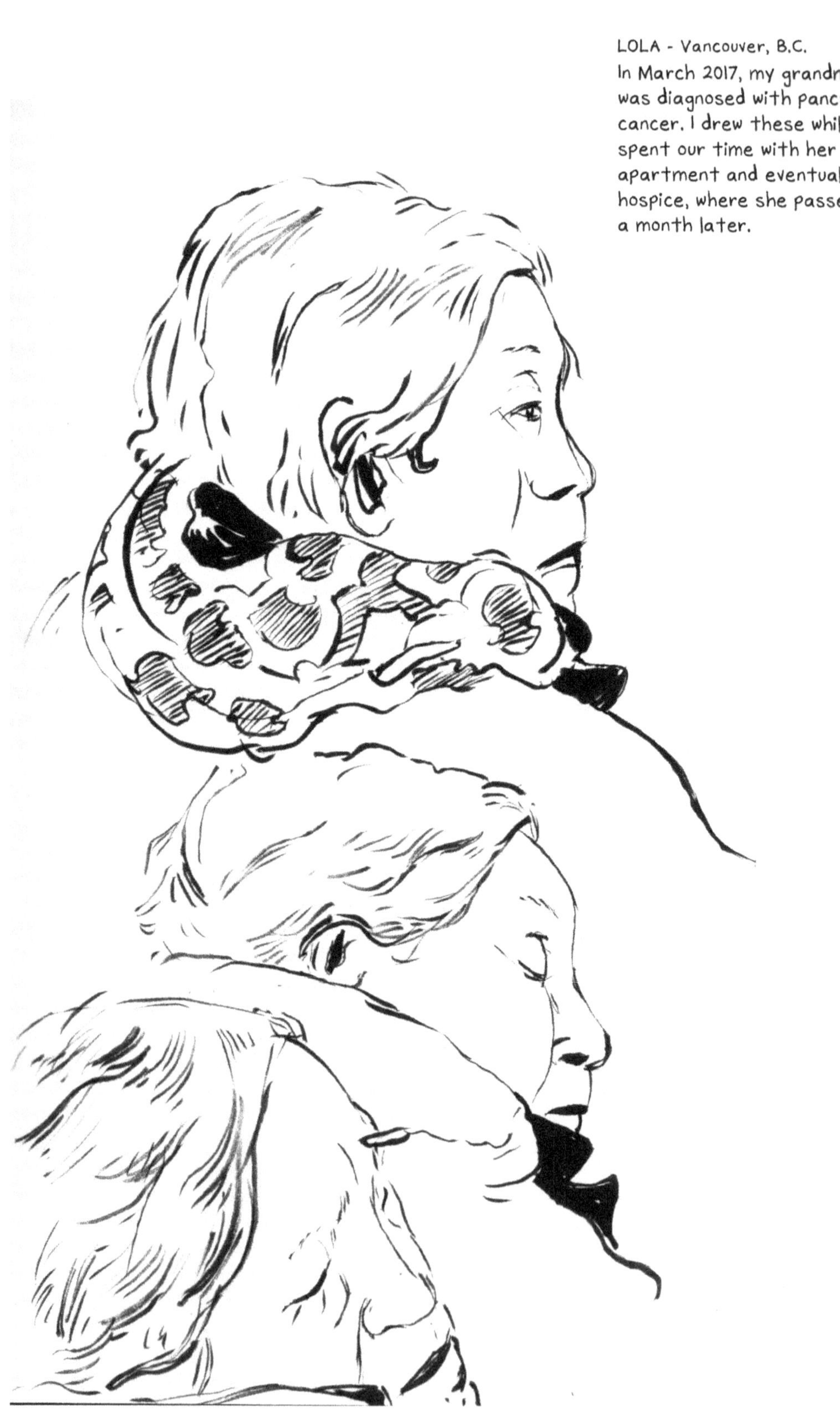
LOLA - Vancouver, B.C.
In March 2017, my grandmother
was diagnosed with pancreatic
cancer. I drew these while we
spent our time with her at her
apartment and eventually, the
hospice, where she passed away
a month later.

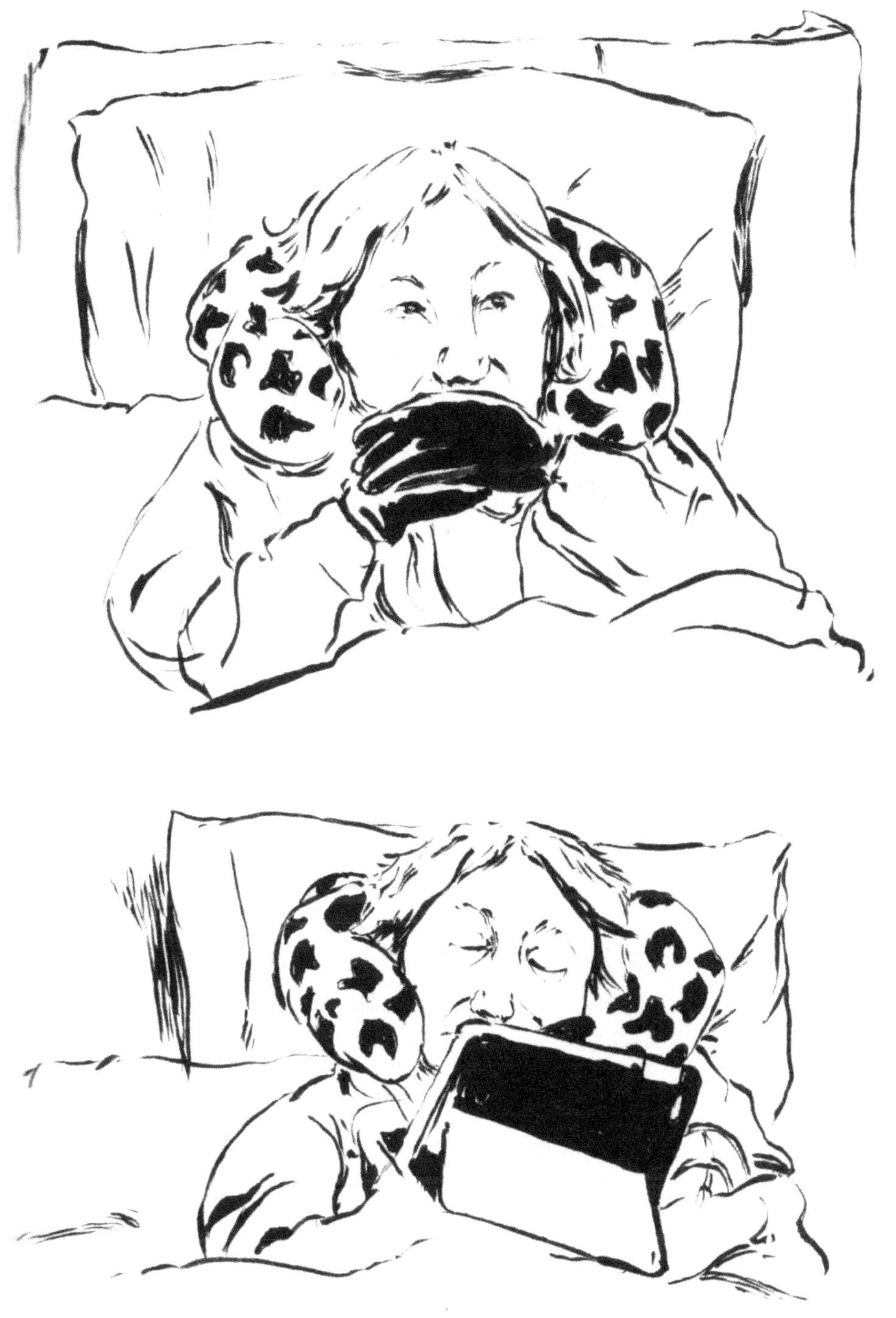

The drawings aren't perfect, but they are my way of trying to preserve the qualities I loved and saw in her: her independent spirit and tranquility. It made these drawings the most invaluable and precious to me out of my entire sketchbook.

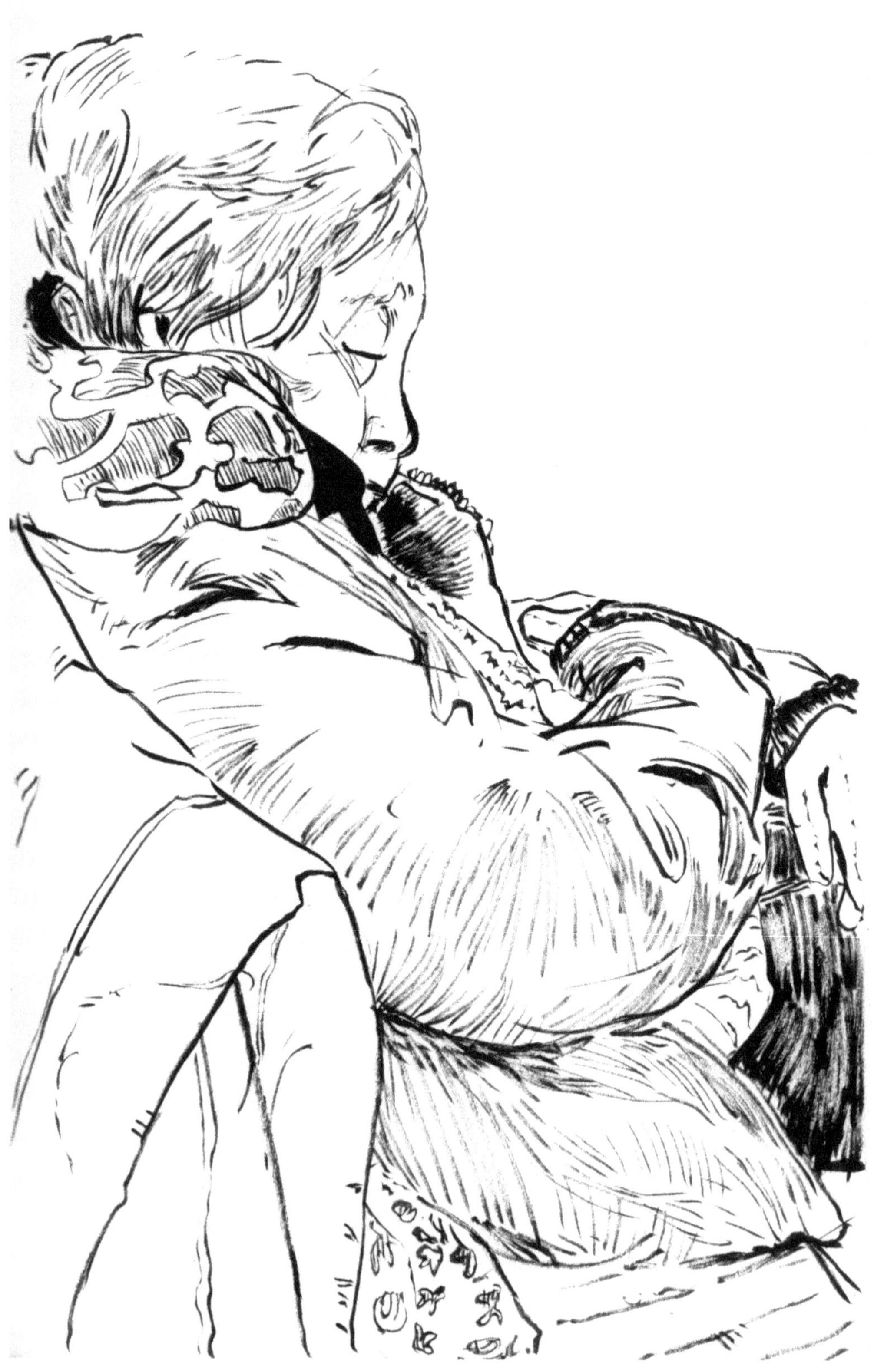

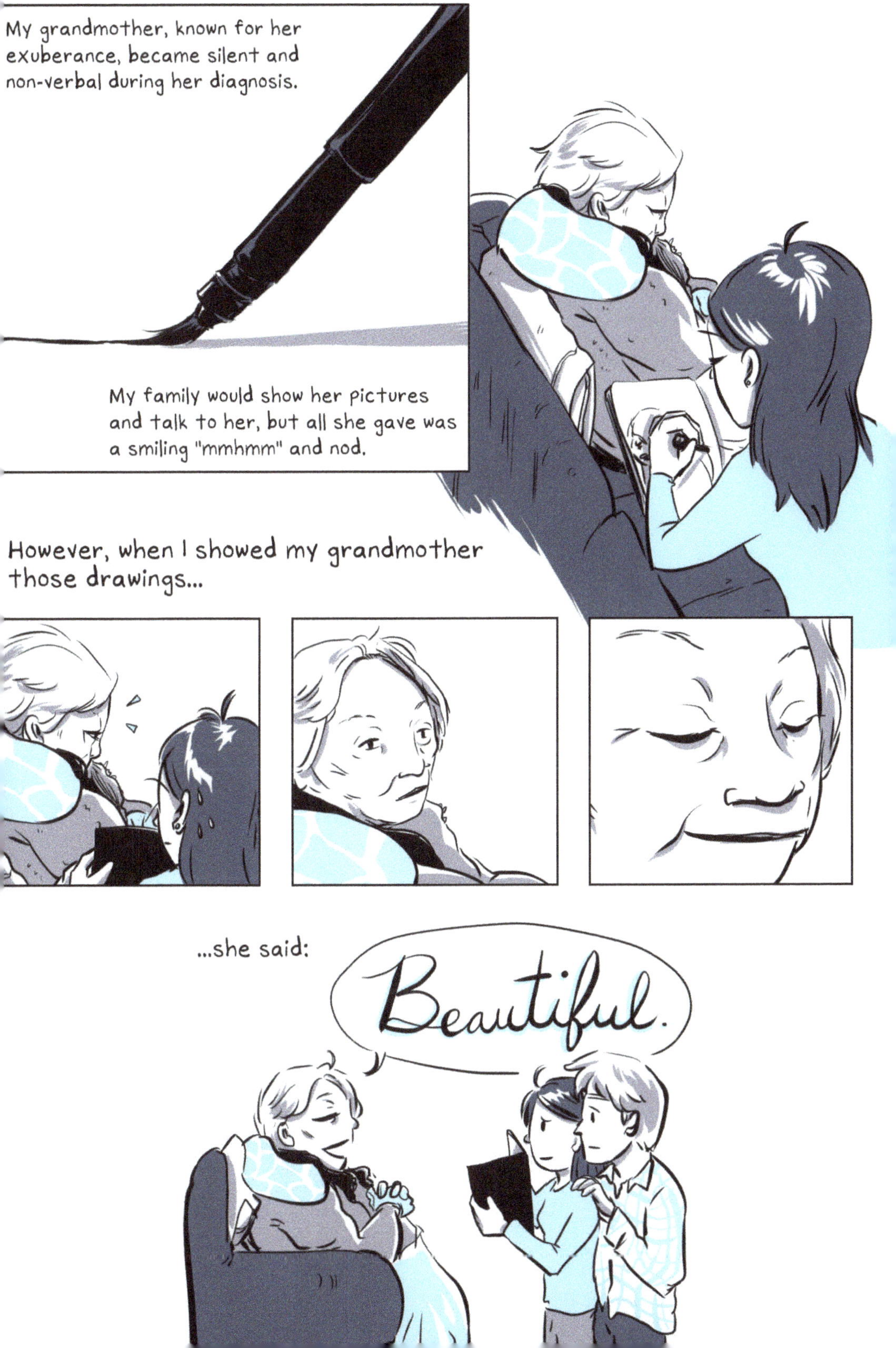

My grandmother, known for her exuberance, became silent and non-verbal during her diagnosis.

My family would show her pictures and talk to her, but all she gave was a smiling "mmhmm" and nod.

However, when I showed my grandmother those drawings...

...she said:

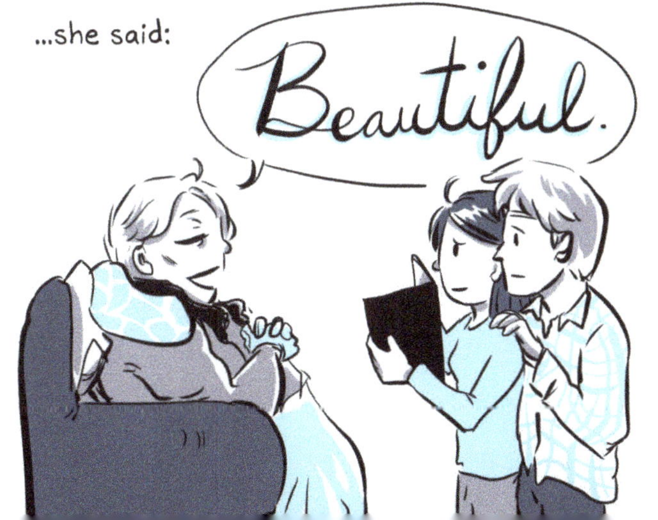

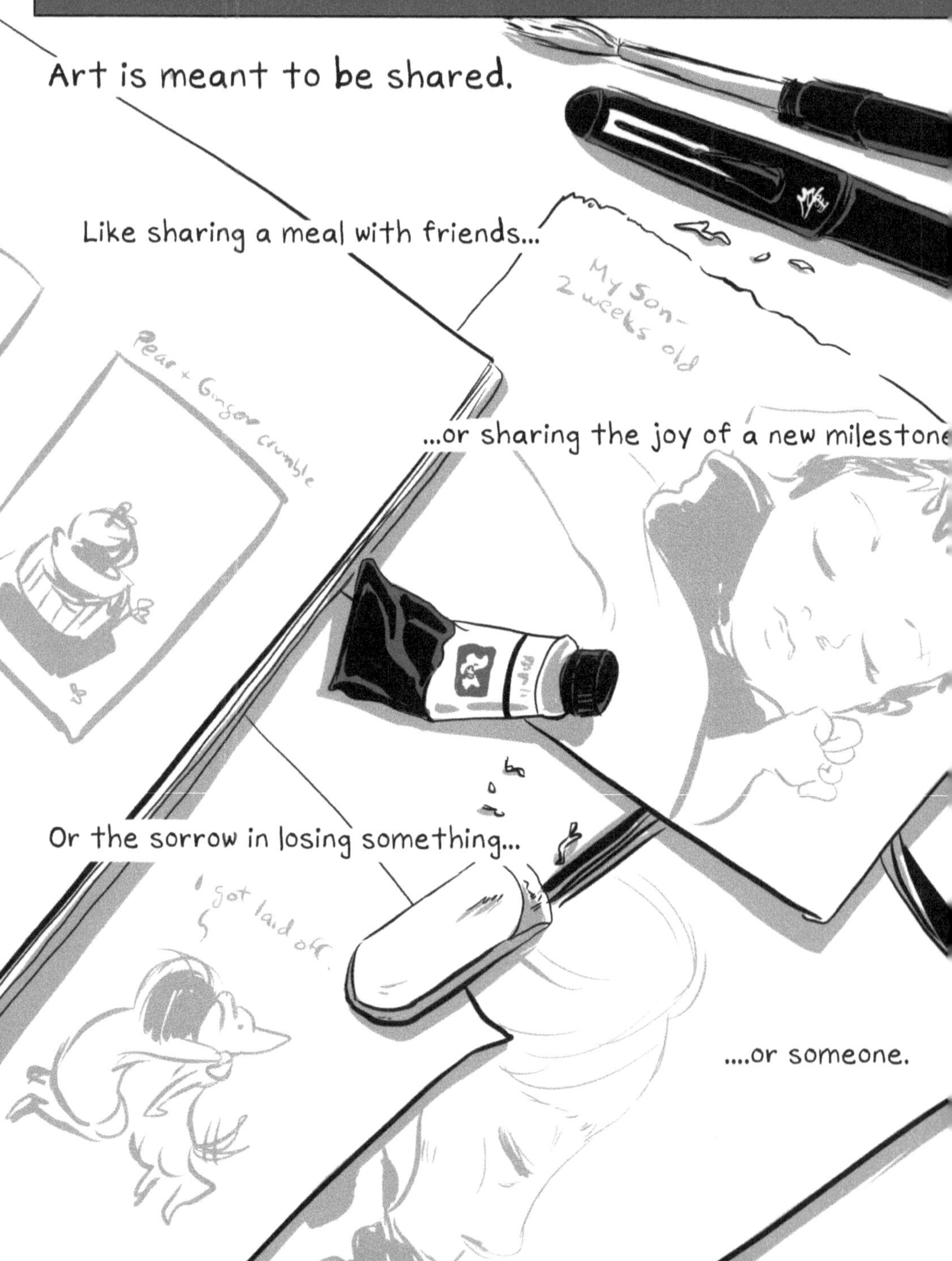

It made me regret never showing her any of my other sketches all these years.
Art is meant to be shared.
Like sharing a meal with friends...
Pear + Ginger Crumble
My Son-
2 weeks old
...or sharing the joy of a new milestone
Or the sorrow in losing something...
I got laid off
....or someone.

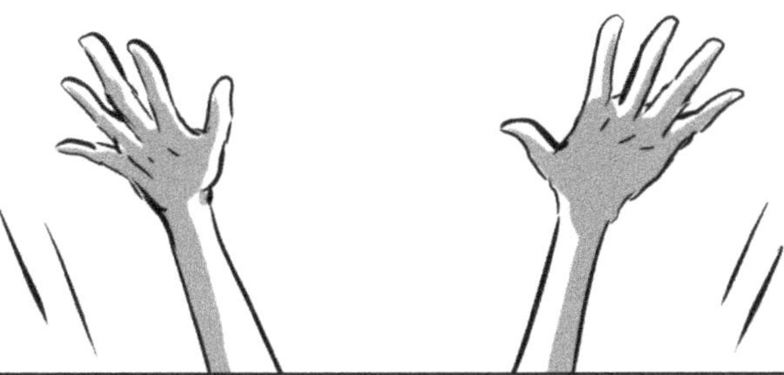

We as people are meant to share our experiences with each other whether it's in a conversation, a book, a meal, or a drawing.

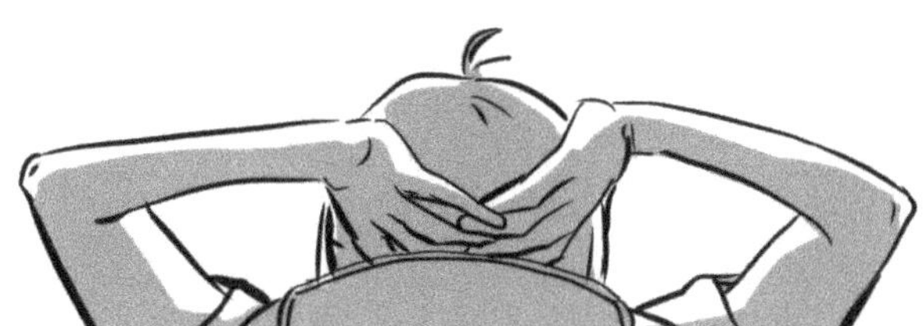

It doesn't matter if it's perfect, as long as it exists...

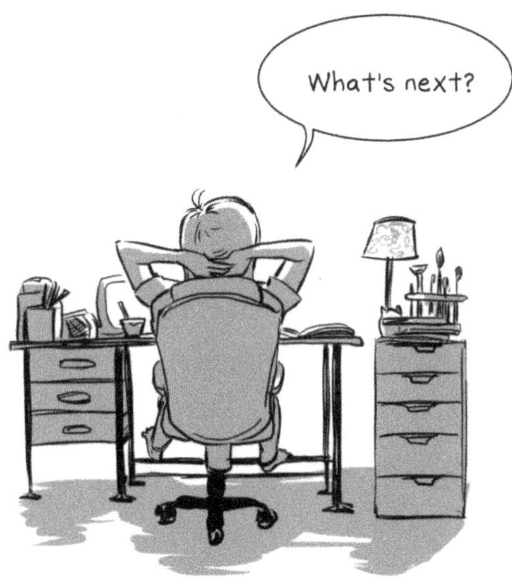

...and that's what makes it all beautiful.

ACKNOWLEDGEMENTS

This book's cover font was created by Syaf Rizal. You can find more of his work at:
https://www.behance.net/khurasan

The kernel of this book was seeded by all the family, friends, and co-workers who asked if I was ever going to compile my drawings into a book. Thank you all for your nudges and encouragement.

I am forever grateful to Samantha, Adam, and the Read Furiously team for their hours spent on helping me complete this item on my bucket list and lending me their patience when my son was born during the production of this book. Thank you, Sam, for taking a chance on me. Never had I imagined these many, many years ago that our friendship would lead us to such a happy collaboration.

Dana, thank you for workshopping the book's and sections' titles with me, as well as ghostwriting my bio. You always have the perfect words.

Thank you Mom, Dad, Larissa, and Lauren for being fans of my work since the early days when they were poorly drawn comics on a refrigerator wall. My original cheerleaders, you are the reason I am where I am now. And Mom, thank you for helping Karl keep the house afloat after Ben's birth while I chipped away on my book during that first hard month.

Benjamin and Newton, my muses, thank you for your neverending cuteness. It makes me want to capture you on paper constantly.

Karl, you are the reason this book exists. You shouldered so much both before and after baby just so I can work on this book. Thank you for taking care of our family and our chores when I couldn't, and thank you for believing in me when I wouldn't. This book is a culmination of all the pockets of time you gifted me so I can create. You have my deepest gratitude and my love always.

A Note to our Furious Readers

From all of us at Read Furiously, we hope you enjoyed our latest title, Pursuit. There are countless narratives in this world and we would like to share as many of them as possible with our Furious Readers.

It is with this in mind that we pledge to donate a portion of these book sales to causes that are special to Read Furiously and its creators. These causes are chosen with the intent to better the lives of others who are struggling to tell their own stories.

Reading is more than a passive activity - it is the opportunity to play an active role within our world. At Read Furiously, its editors and its creators wish to add an active voice to the world we all share because we believe any growth within the company is aimless if we can't also nurture positive change in our local and global communities. The causes we support are culturally and socially-based to encourage a sense of civic responsibility associated with the act of reading. Each cause has been researched thoroughly, discussed openly, and voted upon carefully by our team of Read Furiously editors.

To find out more about who, what, why, and where Read Furiously lends its support, please visit our website at readfuriously.com/charity

Happy reading and giving, Furious Readers!

Read Often, Read Well,
Read Furiously!